Suzanne St Albans was born in Kuala Lumpar, Malaysia in 1921. In 1947 she married Colonel Charles Beauclerk in Vienna, where he was Controller, Information Services, Allied Commission for Austria. He inherited his cousin's title and became the 13th Duke of St Albans in 1964. On his death, she became the Dowager Duchess of St Albans. She now lives in Berkshire where she spends her time doing historical research.

mango
and mimosa

A memoir of early life

Suzanne St Albans

A *Virago* Book

Published by Virago Press 2001
First published by Virago Press 2000

Copyright © Suzanne St Albans 2000

The moral right of the author has been asserted

A CIP catalogue record for this book is available from
the British Library

ISBN 1 86049 894 9

Typeset in Berkeley by M Rules
Printed and bound in Great Britain by
Bookmarque Ltd, Croydon, Surrey

Virago Press
A Division of
Little, Brown and Company (UK)
Brettenham House
Lancaster Place
London WC2E 7EN

*This book is dedicated to
the three most dauntless people
I have ever known –
my father, mother and Marie*

contents

PART ONE

mango and mimosa

1922–30

chapter one

Soon after the First World War, when I was twelve months old, my parents, who shared a nebulous but incurable longing for roots and close contact with the soil, bought an old farmhouse which went with a strip of land on a hillside near the small town of Vence, at the foot of the Alpes Maritimes in Provence, and set about making it into a family home. When it was finished they called it 'Mas Mistral' – after the poet, not the wind.

The ground floor, where the farmer and his donkey had bedded down together, became the dining-room, while a flight of outside stone steps led to the first floor. The cooking was done on a charcoal fire out of doors. Old Provençal tiles covered the roof, and the thick walls and small square windows ensured a cellar-like coolness in the hottest months, while an enormous fireplace, in which half an olive-tree could burn away happily, kept the dining-room warm and cosy in the winter. The iron ring to which the donkey had been tied remained in its place, and is still there to this day.

With a gang of builders, masons, carpenters and plumbers and a fleet of ancient lorries, my father began his building operations. In contrast to the shaky, wobbly constructions he had lived in in Malaya (later, at Assam Java, Papa's Malayan estate, we were forbidden to run on the first-floor landing in case the house should collapse on top of us), this one was to be built, literally, on rock. And he dug until he found it. Huge foundations were excavated and great stones three feet thick were dug out of the mountainside and used for the walls. Papa wanted to make sure *this* house wouldn't wobble. And so preoccupied was he with indestructibility that all architectural charm and grace were forgotten, and the house that rose from the ground was square, plain and unattractive – but infinitely durable.

The new house, the plans for which had been drawn up by my father, was tacked onto the old farm, and doors were pierced through the wall on two floors. How Papa managed to devise anything so complicated defies understanding, and makes description difficult. However much I puzzle over it, and scrutinise the building both from the inside and the outside, I fail to understand how the various levels fit in and join up together. There is no front door, or perhaps you could say there are four front doors.

After the Second World War when my parents returned to Mas Mistral, and they were living there alone without staff, they felt the need, goodness knows why, to build on a new wing facing east. A third central heating plant was installed so that, on very cold days, all three could be heard thrumming, rumbling and hissing together, turning the house into a furnace. But in spite of this greenhouse temperature, Papa, whose blood cells had been thinned out by fifty years in the tropics, still crept around with a shawl over his shoulders and an anxious look on his face, muttering 'The water will freeze in the pipes if it doesn't warm up soon!' as he tapped the glass of the thermometer on the wall.

The furniture, which my parents had collected from farm-houses and village shops far and wide, was antique Provençal, beautifully made and quite unobtainable nowadays. Everywhere, in all the rooms, were priceless Chinese and Japanese vases and silver objects, all collectors' pieces, which I found perfectly hideous.

My parents' weak spot was pictures. Apart from Papa's own oils and watercolours dotted about here and there, there were none except a few Japanese prints hung from the picture rails high up near the ceiling. But to make up for this lack, there were hundreds of photographs from all parts of the world, going back to the 1850s and '60s, in silver frames everywhere.

Underneath the house and scooped out of the mountainside was the cellar, where in due course the grapes were crushed in the great vat at the time of the *vendanges*, and the barrels in which the juice boiled and bubbled until it turned to wine, stood in rows like Ali Baba's jars. Until very nearly the end of his life, Papa spent whole days down there, presumably quite happy, bottling and decanting, sticking on labels and hiding away from visitors.

At the top of the house, under the roof, was a huge attic which could easily have been made into a large and comfortable flat. This was our favourite place, stuffed with treasures of every kind, and full of ghosts and rats and enormous lizards which crashed about in fearful midnight battles over our heads. And as a background to all this, there were continual orchestral effects of sighing and rattling sounds, and mysterious gurgling noises. We were never allowed up there alone, which naturally added to its fascination and attraction.

Along the whole front of the house ran a balcony, which was soon festooned with begonia, wisteria and moonflowers climbing up from the terrace below, so that for six months of the year at least the whole front was covered with thick clusters of flowers. The begonias were always obscured by a thick coating of ants, which were so addicted to the flowers' heady juices that they came hurrying from miles around as soon as the plants began to bloom.

Ants were an all-the-year-round plague. When on the move, marching sixteen abreast in close formation, they would take short cuts through the house to gain time and save their legs, and you would come across their columns at all hours of the day in the most unlikely places. When their journey happened to take them through the larder, whole legs of lamb and sides of pork would disappear overnight, leaving pink bare bones, and pots of home-made jam were sucked dry and left smooth and gleaming on the shelves. *'Ces sacrées fourmis!'* Marie would splutter as she followed their trail, pumping furiously at her 'Fly-tox' gun and spraying everything in sight. The ants, needless to say, were not in the slightest bit incommoded. But their greatest addiction of all, electricity, fortunately polished them off by the thousand. Swarming into the wall plugs, they clustered there in a drugged stupor, and had to be scraped out with nail-files and meat skewers. (Once, when wanting to do some ironing in the kitchen after the war and finding the plug bunged up with electrocuted ants as usual, I started to scratch away at them with a hairpin, the whole thing exploded in my face, and I was thrown flat on my back on the floor.)

While the new house was being built, we camped very comfortably in the old farmhouse, known locally as *Le Vieux Mas*, my parents, my new-born brother John, who lived in one of those tall gangling prams all made of wire and trembling springs which shuddered in the slightest breeze, myself now aged about two, and Marie, who had joined us from Australia. Marie had brought Papa up in Sydney, where he had been born thirty-five years before, and now she had answered his appeal to come and look after his young family.

All that first summer, while the house was growing, clouds of dust hovered in the hot, still air. The workmen, bare to the waist and with wide red cummerbunds around their middles, churned piles of sand and cement, ran up and down scaffolding and made a great deal of noise. And all through the night, under constant very white moonlight, clouds of fireflies swarmed over the land as far as the eye could see, while a chorus of frogs kept up their monotonous croaking until dawn, when the cicadas and the birds took over for the daylight hours.

chapter two

Both my great-grandfathers, born within a year of each other in Bordeaux, set off more or less at the same time to explore the world in different directions, little knowing that their grandchildren, my parents, would meet and marry in Malaya seventy years later.

Great-Grandfather Fesq, on my father's side, settled in Australia in 1848, after having spent a few years sailing to and from New Orleans with shiploads of wine which he sold there at good profit. He had run away from home at the age of fifteen after his father's death, on the suspicion that his mother, and the doctor whom she married very soon after, had done him in. And there may have been something in it, as his uncles, with whom he sought asylum in Bordeaux, made no attempt to send him back, but instead gave him a job in their wine-exporting business.

After a few profitable years on the New Orleans run, Great-Grandpapa fell in love with a cotton planter's daughter. As the moons of her fingernails were too dark to denote pure white ancestry, he begged to be allowed to take his cargo to the other end of the world, as mixed marriages 'weren't done' in those days. As his uncles obligingly consented to this, French claret was from then on despatched to Sydney instead of New Orleans. After a few years he bought land, including a good chunk of what is now Sydney Harbour, built several villas, married and begat a family, and there have been Fesqs there ever since.

While Great-Grandfather Fesq was busily plying his trade between Bordeaux and New Orleans, his opposite number, Great-Grandfather Chasseriau, had landed in Mauritius, where he spent a few years planting sugar cane. But soon, feeling hemmed in by the diminutive size of the island, he set off again across the seas, and this time landed in Malaya. And the Chasseriaus remained in the Peninsula for the next hundred years.

After I was born, my parents decided to come to Europe and re-establish a permanent home in France. As my mother was a British subject through the accident of her birth in Penang, a Crown colony at the time, and Papa was Australian, they regarded themselves as part of the British colonisation of the South of France, which was then in full swing.

Mamma, whose veins flowed with good, red, pugnacious Gallic blood, was none the less fanatically devoted to England, the Empire and all things British. This completely prejudiced and unreasoning attitude remained with her to the end of her days, and nothing got her French blood up so much as the slightest criticism of England – even its weather she considered the best in the world. But Papa, who knew better, insisted on the sun.

Marie had first joined my father's family when he was three years old. His mother had originally discovered the twenty-year-old on one of her many trips to Europe, and brought her home to Sydney as nanny to her children. There is a photograph of the young Marie, with leg-of-mutton sleeves and wasp waist, but without the gold-rimmed spectacles to which she took soon after. Her hair, which remained pale shining gold until her death and was never cut, was always scraped severely back from her face. Although she was of peasant stock, there was a look of great elegance and breeding about her.

An accident with a merry-go-round had left Marie with only one good eye. She had taken my father and his brother and sister to a local fairground, where she hoisted them onto the wooden horses, then stood back to watch. At that moment a spark from the coal-powered engine fluttered into her left eye, boring right through the bright-blue pupil and destroying the optic nerve. I still have those fierce gold-rimmed spectacles with lenses no bigger than shelled almonds, which scored a deep groove into the bridge of her nose, as she hardly ever took them off, even going to bed wearing them on occasion. Handicapped though she was, she could still see as well as most people with two good eyes in their heads. Moreover, she could see right through people, and claimed that many of them had such murky souls that they left a dark stain on their surroundings.

When my father and his brother and sister reached their teens, Marie had gone to Switzerland for her first holiday in sixteen years, and married a widowed policeman with fourteen children. Some of them, she told us, had been difficult at first, but she soon had them eating out of her hand. Eventually she had a son of her own, who died of meningitis when only a few months old. He was a beautiful baby. The photograph of his little corpse, all draped in satin ribbon, lace and paper roses, hung between our beds in the night nursery. On the anniversary of his death, the picture would be taken down, a candle lit in front of it, and we would all kneel around it weeping at Marie's grief and the terrible sadness of it all, and praying for the repose of his little soul.

Her husband had died soon after the baby, and my grand-mother had no difficulty in persuading Marie to return to Australia. And when, in the course of time, Papa wrote asking her to come and look after his growing family in Vence, she came and stayed until the Second World War scattered us to all parts of the globe.

Marie adored my father, and I suspect that she may have been the first and perhaps the greatest love of his life. Whenever there was a crisis it was Marie he turned to, not my mother. I am quite sure that the relationship was an innocent one, and that they were unaware themselves of anything more than the per-fectly normal bond of trust and affection which habitually existed in those days between master and servant. I have a photograph of Papa as a boy, looking like a Proustian character, with one large and bony hand lying in Marie's lap, while a smug and unconsciously revealing smile plays on her face. Although she may not have been completely aware of the influence which she had over him, the smile certainly indicates some inkling of it.

But when, not long after her arrival at Mas Mistral, my new-born brother John was placed in her arms, he took possession of her heart altogether, so that the vague indifference she had felt for me until then became more marked and I fell out of favour entirely. Perhaps she saw him as the reincarnation of her own son. It made no difference whatever to my devotion to her, and I would lean over backwards to win a smile, swallowing great lumps of gristle, feeding bits of chocolate to John, which he dribbled all over his clothes, and sticking dandelions and daisies in his ears to make him look like those lovely pigs' heads I so admired in the butchers' shops. I even walked ostentatiously *round* puddles instead of splashing straight through them, as I longed to do. All to no avail – my efforts were simply dismissed as 'showing off'.

Soon John was joined by my sister Anne, who appeared quite suddenly in Marie's arms one April day when the palm-trees were being pruned and the terrace was child-deep in razor-sharp sword-like fronds. Having had no forewarning of the new arrival, we stared at this creature in amazement. I was most struck by her fingers, of which she had a complete if minute set on each hand. This *was* a discovery, for babies, I firmly believed, grew like tadpoles in reverse, adding new bits as they grew older instead of dropping them off. But John remained Marie's favourite – after all, he was my father's son, and we were my mother's daughters.

Marie's relations with Mamma, whom she openly disliked and despised, were bad from the start. Their mutual jealousy, of which they were probably unaware, was always aggravated when my father was at home. A sort of truce, uncertain but welcomed by us with relief, reigned when he was away. Another cause of friction was Mamma's impulsiveness and lack of emotional control, which exasperated Marie, who regarded such 'weakness' as lack of character.

Although strong on discipline – particularly where Anne and I were concerned – Marie left us a great deal of freedom. And for the best part of the day we were in the garden, out of her sight and very often out of hearing. During those hours of bliss when we did as we pleased, Marie filled in her time reading French, German and English newspapers. For our benefit she marked paragraphs of special interest, way above our heads, and these she would read to us in the evening. It could be on any subject – science, politics, aviation, motor racing, or anything that featured in the press at the time. As we knew neither English nor German, we found it all extremely boring. But Marie maintained that the best way to learn a language was to read the papers. The rest would come in due course. And because of this addiction to the press, she was incredibly well informed.

But overriding everything else was her passion for natural history. In the evening, when she wasn't reading the newspapers aloud to us, we cleared everything away and helped her to press the plants we had collected on our walks. There were usually a few spiders, scorpions and various other fascinating creatures as well, to pickle or bottle for her insect collection lined up on the nursery shelves.

When she was in a particularly good mood, Marie would tell us stories of her childhood in Switzerland, of her grandmother who had stood by the roadside watching Napoleon and his army trekking over the mountains on his way to fight in Italy. Of her wise, far-sighted father, who predicted a time when carriages would zoom around the streets without any horses to pull them along. We never grew tired of her tales of life high in the Swiss Alps, of the autumn festivals when the cows, decked out in all the flowers of the mountains, came down in long processions from the high pastures, to be tucked up for the winter in the stable under the house. On those occasions dancing went on all night, with the lads slapping their heels and throwing the girls high up in the air. Years later, in Malaya, during our jungle walks, when carried away by the poignant glory of her memories, Marie would sometimes break into a yodel, startling the monkeys in the trees above into stunned silence.

With Marie to look after us, our parents were able to get down to making the garden, planting fruit-trees, and laying out the vine-yards and the strawberry beds. Their longing for roots must have been gratified at last, but when all this began to bear fruit, there was far more than the household could absorb.

The top of the garden, laid out in several terraces behind the house, was planted with vines. For the *vendanges*, all hands were put to work. It was a period of delicious excitement, feverish activity and merrymaking. Memories of ancestral rituals stirred the peasants, and the whole of October was dedicated to grape-picking and wine-making. Neighbours lent their presses and helped to tread down one another's grapes. In due course, when we were old enough, we were allowed to take part in this intoxicating exercise. The feeling of the fat grapes squelching between our toes was infinitely satisfying.

Equipped with secateurs and old kitchen scissors, the neighbouring farmer and his friends who were helping with our harvest would start picking at sunrise, with hods strapped to their backs. We joined them after a hastily swallowed cup of cocoa as the early morning haze hovered over the vineyard, promising a fine day. Dragging baskets as large as ourselves, we snipped and tugged at the heavy grapes all through the day. It was a backbreaking job, as the largest bunches were usually hidden under the leaves low down on the vines, just clearing the ground. When the baskets were full, we staggered with them to the end of the row and tipped them into wheelbarrows, which were then trundled to the cellar for the final crushing in the great wine vat. By the evening, flocks of tipsy birds which had been competing with us throughout the day, rolled over on their backs, literally legless, and an easy prey for the workers who wrung their little necks and took them home for supper.

The vine terraces were divided by sloping banks on which grew thousands of strawberry plants. We were allowed to help with the picking, and gobbled so many that we were invariably sick before the end of the day. Quantities were given away, and the rest went into sticky jams, cakes, puddings and tarts, until the smell of cooked strawberry oozed out of the walls. Peach-trees and greengages grew among the vines, while dotted here and there haphazardly were fig, pear, cherry, pomegranate and persimmon trees. On either side of the entrance to the old farmhouse, our parents planted avocados and tree-tomatoes, which were fed daily with doses of tea-leaves.

The garden in front of the house was devoted to mimosas, oleanders, palms and exotic plants from Malaya, China and Japan. From time to time, and for no apparent reason, Mamma would suddenly descend upon a bed of Chinese lilies, bamboo orchids or Cherokee roses, root the whole lot up and put down rows of string beans, pumpkins or tomatoes. She had probably been given the seeds by a neighbour, and having no other space available, she would ruthlessly sacrifice some of these exotic treasures without a second thought. Papa, suddenly coming across an outrage of this kind, would lift up his thin voice and bleat with distress: '*Mon dieu, mon dieu*, what has happened here? What vandalism! *Quelle horreur!*' Whereupon Marie, hearing his lamentations, would come hurrying out of the house to comfort him, muttering dark things about my mother in German.

One fine day in early spring, soon after Mas Mistral was finished, a large building suddenly began to rise on the hill behind us, on the very frontiers of our land. Marching off to Vence to see the Mayor, my mother learned that it was to be a sanatorium for TB patients. There was outrage in the family, for it had been done in a sly and underhand way, without warning of any kind. Fury was followed by consternation. Safe, as they thought, in having found a dry and healthy spot on which to build their house and rear their young, our parents felt truly cheated. Clouds of germs would now drift downhill on the breeze, pollute the air around us, and settle on our lungs, infecting us all with the dreaded disease, for which there was then no cure.

When the first patient arrived, we were bundled off to Nice to have our lungs X-rayed. And from then on, this became a very boring twice-yearly routine. Soon Vence was crawling with coughing, spluttering strangers. Whenever we came across one of them on our walks, Mamma would command in a loud voice, 'Cover up your face and SPIT! And don't breathe until I tell you.' And Marie would drag us away to the other side of the street.

The area had been advertised as having the best climate in the world for TB. This was perfectly true – for undertakers. Business was brisk, and the church bells tolled non-stop as one funeral followed another, the victims borne off to the graveyard in the old horse-drawn cemetery cart, all draped in lace and with black feathers fluttering in the breeze. In those days it was believed that lying in the sun all day long was the most effective treatment for tuberculosis. It was actually the quickest way of bringing the patient to the end of his misery, by speeding up his death.

In the end word got round, Vence was regarded with increasing suspicion, and the sanatorium was eventually closed down. It reopened later as a miners' rest home, for a disease even more deadly than the last – but as this was caused by coal-dust, it couldn't be spread by germs floating down the hill.

John was growing into a plump and rosy child, satisfactory in every way, and the most beautiful creature I had ever seen next to a new-born chick. But I was becoming difficult, and full of tiresome fads and dislikes. Although I loved bees and their clever way of spewing up honey out of chewed-up flowers, I could *not* stand the taste or even the smell of the revolting stuff itself. This was the cause of endless strife, for Mamma was convinced that honey was a cure for all ills. And John, of course, lapped it up.

Milk was another problem. One of our neighbours was a farmer, who lived in incredible squalor in one room with his cow, his wife and hens, and a clutch of wild, retarded children. It was he who brought his milk every evening to our kitchen door. The poor man was riddled with syphilis (one of his ears had dropped off) and as his cow was certain to have TB, the milk had to be boiled almost solid to make it safe enough to drink. This produced clotted lumps of overcooked skin, which were added to our cocoa every day, since Mamma was convinced it held special virtues. The slimy curds made me sick every time I tried to swallow them.

This daily nightmare ended when the unhappy farmer went down to the railway line in the valley and had himself run over by our little local train. The tragedy saddened the neighbourhood, but for me life brightened up at once. My parents built a cottage at the bottom of the garden and imported a clean-living farmer and his wife, a beautiful shining cow, a mule, a donkey and a pig. The mule, who was never seen to do a day's work, spent his time rolling about in the grass. The donkey jogged us blissfully up and down the garden, and the pig went the way of all pigs. But most crucial of all was that the new cow's milk passed all the tests, and didn't have to be boiled solid any longer.

Madame Rose the farmer's wife very soon took control of our kitchen. She was a large bundly creature always dressed in layers of black skirts, and I loved to watch her at the kitchen range in her long white apron and black straw hat anchored to her bun with jet hairpins. She was at it all day long, concocting delicious stews and pâtés and complicated things out of pigs' ears, bladders and other unmentionable organs. She used every herb that grew in the garden, and the store-cupboards were soon crammed with quince, strawberry and redcurrant jelly, raspberry and cherry jam, and olives in brine, to mention just a few of her famous preserves. Her cassis, plum, apricot and cherry brandy was made with eau-de-vie from Father's vines. In the summer she would sit on the kitchen steps, surrounded by baskets filled with fruit. It was fascinating to watch her flicking stones out of the cherries with a hairpin – a useful trick which I was never able to master. But years later, in Vienna after the war, when faced with the austere rations of the British army, I taught myself to cook by trying to recreate the delicious smells which Madame Rose used to produce in our kitchen.

'Pauvre Claire', the young housemaid, mooned around the house with a feather duster. Her afternoons were spent pressing our clothes with a huge iron like a camel's hoof, filled with live charcoal. From time to time she opened a trap-door at the back and spooned in some more fuel. It was Pauvre Claire who made the hens tipsy one day by throwing them handfuls of cherry-stones which Madame Rose had soaked in eau de vie to make cherry brandy. Dazed out of their minds, they rolled over on their backs with their legs sticking straight up in the air. But as far as I remember, there were no lasting effects after they recovered from their massive hangover.

Pauvre Claire didn't make much impression on life. She lived in a world of her own, and it was difficult to make friends with her. My mother had some natty dresses and stunning little caps made for her. But she remained uninterested. Her hold on life was too tenuous. She was to fade away only a few years later when barely thirty.

Soon a couple of gardeners were added to the workforce. They dug the heavy clay soil and looked after the vines, the strawberries and the fruit-trees. The flowers, which seemed to come up spontaneously, managed to grow by themselves, with scarcely any attention.

Gino, the older of the two, was tall and thin, with a bandage over his left ear and another across his right eye (syphilis again), which gave him a roguish air. He spoke a mixture of Italian patois and Provençal, which was perfectly clear to us but sometimes perplexed mother. She would call out to one of us, 'What on earth is he saying?' And the message was duly translated. Every day he brought a different child with him. He had a large assortment of these, all crippled and suffering from a variety of infirmities. The child of the day, whom he carried all the way up from the village on his back, was settled under an olive-tree, with its poor twisted limbs set out as comfortably as possible. Then a bottle of wine was planted in the grass within easy reach, and throughout the day the little creature sucked away at it, crooning to itself in tipsy contentment.

Gino's colleague, Marius, was much younger, and still unmarried. Short and knotty, he was like a vine in winter when all the gnarls are showing. He came from Sardinia and spoke a curious brand of Southern Italian mixed with some of our local patois. We all understood him, more or less, except for Mamma, and Marie who pretended not to.

Another Italian who never bothered to learn French was Caroline the washerwoman. A small hunchback with a handsome moustache, she screeched and cursed all day long as she whacked the sheets with an implement that looked like an old cricket bat. The washing was done out-of-doors in two great stone troughs filled with cold water, one for soaping and the other for rinsing. Summer and winter the laundry was dried on the grass in the sun, where it acquired a delicious smell, a mixture of ozone and fresh grass which, when added to the verbena of the linen cupboards, gave the beds an unusual fragrance. For me, and despite everything that has happened since, this is still the signature smell of Mas Mistral.

The mattress woman came once a year, when spring-cleaning was in full swing. She set up her carding machine on the terrace under a cherry-tree, and the mattresses were brought out to her one by one. Having unpicked them and pulled out all the flock, she would give the covers to Caroline to wash, then stuff the lumpy sheep's wool into her machine. After she had furiously pumped the handle back and forth for a few minutes, the wool was all fluffed out like candyfloss. Once washed and dried, it went back into the mattress, and she stitched it all together again with a needle the size of a dagger, which went right through to the other side. And small rounds of leather protected the ticking from the sharp knots of string. When the mattresses were done, it was the turn of the carpets. They were tipped upside-down on the grass, beaten free of any remaining dust, then washed with vinegar, and finally fluffed up with damp tea-leaves.

It was after spring-cleaning that the annual storms usually broke out. Apart from causing a good deal of damage to fruit-trees and vineyards, they were truly terrifying, especially when suddenly exploding over our heads after dark. Our eccentric lighting system would flicker on and off, and finally peter out altogether at the first flash of lightning.

All was well when Marie was there. In fact a good thunder-storm cracking about over our heads, with her nodding at her newspaper by candlelight, was quite comforting. But once, when she had gone off to the dentist in Nice and Mamma's youngest sister was looking after us, an instant storm suddenly broke out over the house. Green lights flashed at the windows and we were plunged into instant darkness. Shocked by the unexpected fury of the outbreak, we panicked and became hysterical with fear. Our poor aunt, only seventeen at the time and nearly demented herself, floundered around in the dark, feeling for matches, clattering into the furniture and yelling at us to shut up. The wind raged and howled around the house, and a shutter, broken loose from its moorings, banged against the wall like a battering ram.

To add insult to injury, when Madame Rose finally came in with our supper, *the wrong forks and spoons were laid on the table.*

Instead of our own sets, engraved with our names, which we had used ever since we could remember, we were given huge grown-up silver, as heavy as garden tools. This was the last straw. We flatly refused to eat, driving those poor women mad until they found our own cutlery. When Marie eventually turned up, badly battered and soaked to the skin, she was so glad to be back that no punishment followed our disgraceful behaviour.

Next day a man came up from the village bearing a magnificent lightning-conductor, which he fixed to the highest chimney. As an extra precaution we handed him a celluloid angel, clad from head to foot in white samite (he belonged on the top of the Christmas-tree), to attach to the lightning-conductor. And after this, every morning we would rush out to see how he was faring. His gleaming robe gradually turned from dazzling white to lemon-yellow, then light ochre, but he remained at his post until the next storm, when he took off, bearing away his lightning-conductor with him. We assumed the ordeal had been too much for him and that he had fled back to the safety of heaven, riding his mount like a witch on her broom.

chapter three

When a rather eccentric cousin of my husband's once said to me that he had been getting on with his mother much better since her death, I thought he was being his usual loopy self. But now I realise that you don't even *know* your parents, let alone get on with them, until after their death. The relationship, which is inevitably blurred by long conditioning, doesn't clear until they are no longer there, and their eccentricities, so desperately embarrassing at the time, turn into harmless memories.

My mother's childhood was spent in the country near Bordeaux, at the Château des Charmilles, with her two brothers and two sisters, under the autocratic rule of Grandmother Chasseriau. The children were much left to the care of servants, and from all accounts it was not a happy childhood for any of them.

When Mamma was seventeen, she went out to Malaya to join her parents, and I believe that the next four years until her marriage were the happiest in her life. Her father had by then founded Alma Estate, which was a flourishing several-million-pound concern.

Grandpapa, who was a rumbustious extrovert, loved entertaining, and so numerous were the guests, and unending the stream of people who came for dinner and stayed three weeks, that another bungalow – a visitors' annexe – had to be built in the garden to accommodate them. As the Chasseriaus also ran their own hospital for the benefit of their workmen, my grandmother must have welcomed the arrival and help of her eldest daughter.

According to the *Pinang Gazette*, she and Grandpapa were forever singing duets at charity concerts, and organising balls and fancy dress parties on every possible occasion. There were visits from the Governor, and receptions at the Sultan's Palace, where my grandfather made 'enthusiastic speeches' (which must have been excruciatingly embarrassing for his family). The *Pinang Gazette* described my mother as 'the prettiest girl of Province Wellesley'.

I have never been able to discover how or where she met my father, or how those two human beings, so totally different in every way, could ever have thought they would find happiness together. My father plunged his bride immediately into solitude and loneliness through his relentless discouragement of all entertaining and hospitality. But somehow she kept herself going and her spirits bubbled on for many years, although it must have been very hard for her to be married to a hermit. They say that opposites attract each other, but surely in this case it was a matter of extremes.

My mother was straightforward, honest and transparent as a sheet of perspex, and completely incapable of dissimulation, lying or any kind of pretence whatsoever. Everything came straight out, sometimes to our shame and misery, so that we treacherously disowned her whenever we could, clinging to

Marie, whose reactions were so much more predictable. With her at least you could be pretty certain that whatever happened and whatever the circumstances, she would be harsh and severe, so that you usually had time to prepare yourself for whatever was coming.

Not so with Mamma. Catching you out at some wholly absorbing occupation, such as puncturing a tube of toothpaste with a set of neat little pin-holes, or carefully picking out the yellow centres of marguerites while leaving the petals intact, would drive her into a frenzy of rage. Not only would she revile you for the present crime, but this would remind her of all your past offences, which she hurled at you with mounting fury, as the enormity of your misdeeds built up in her mind. One moment she was in a cheerful and jovial mood, and seconds later she might be screaming at you and chasing you out of the room with the most fearful imprecations. When I was about seven and she tried hard to teach me to read, most lessons ended in tears, while I was accused of deliberately doing my best to exasperate her. It was greatly to her credit that she eventually broke through my mental block and that I was able to read at last. But it was a severe trial, and we were both on the verge of a nervous breakdown by the end of it.

On the whole Mamma was always much happier in England and Malaya than in France. Unable ever to master the English language properly, she was nevertheless insanely prejudiced in favour of everything British. When she went into a London shop and someone spoke a word or two of French to her, she was ecstatic with admiration at their discernment and perspicacity in guessing that she was French. She never tired of telling them how clever and wonderful they were and, not surprisingly, they adored her. It was a great pity that my father couldn't stand the climate, as I think they would have been much happier in England than in France.

When, in Vence, I accompanied my mother on her shopping expeditions, her behaviour sometimes filled me with embarrassment. She would race through the narrow streets, fight her way to the head of the throng (nobody ever queues up in France), and to my amazement people made way for her with good humour. And then, in order to get from one street to another, she would take short cuts, diving straight through people's houses. Housewives looked up from their cooking pots, grandmothers peered up from the stocking they were knitting, children stood up from the table where they toiled at their homework, and said '*Bonjour Madame*', as if it was the most natural thing in the world to have their home used as a right-of-way.

When my mother's father retired from Malaya, he built himself a house in Vence, which he called the Villa Ste Claire, but unfortunately did not live to enjoy it for very long. Those colonials seem to have had no idea of architecture at all, for this house, though not quite so hideous as some of the monstrosities that disfigure the South of France, was pretty unattractive as well, although much improved by the palms and banana-trees which were hastily planted all round. After it was finished, everybody realised that the less you saw of the house the better. But in spite of its inner and outer ugliness, it seemed like a paradise to us, as it was always running with dogs who were allowed *everywhere*. Nobody ever thought of turning them off the beds or the furniture.

It seemed that, unlike our own father, Grandpapa loved young people. Mamma, and her brother Henri (who was very soon to die from the after-effects of war-gas), her sister Isabelle and their friends, danced all the afternoon, sang duets or opera at the piano, and went off to play endless games of tennis. Suzanne Lenglen, who was one of their gang, launched the fashion for a white headband, so that all the females blossomed out in them. Sometimes they all got into open cars and headed for the coast, or a place in the mountains called Peyraccava, to which for some mysterious reason they were continually repairing.

My father having gone back to Malaya by then, and Mamma's spasmodic interest in our welfare being regarded as intolerable interference by Marie, who kept us jealously to herself, there was very little for Mamma to do except to enjoy herself. And I am glad that she had the sense to do it.

For a short time Grandpapa was well enough to come up to Mas Mistral, and joke and chatter with us, then play the piano and sing with Mamma after we had gone to bed. We used to huddle at the top of the stairs to listen to their singing and their laughter and all the cheerful noises from which we were excluded. And I remember quite clearly the resentful sentence which went through my head at the top of those stairs: '*Ils dinent tard, ils chantent tard et ils rient toute la nuit.*'

After a few months, when summer was drawing to an end, poor Grandpapa was taken ill, wilted and died. We had never seen my mother cry before, and it was very upsetting. After she had left for the funeral, Marie dressed us all in white and marched us down to the village, where we took up our position outside the church. When the coffin had been loaded onto the hearse and the family, friends and neighbours had filed past, we tacked ourselves onto the end with the ragtag and bobtail of the town. Mamma, who had not wanted us to go, was very angry when she heard that Marie had taken us. It did not, however, have any traumatic effect on us. We had not known our grandfather well enough to be upset by his death, which we did not really understand anyway. Besides, we knew and greatly admired *le corbillard*, with handsome black ostrich plumes waving on the roof, and enormous springs like hoops which creaked and groaned, particularly on the mountain paths and country lanes deeply scored by the torrential winter rains. It was a familiar sight, toiling and bumping through the country-side, followed by a procession of mourners snaking slowly behind. We often saw the horses, which were black all over except for a white diamond-shaped patch on their foreheads, exercising the hearse between funerals. On duty, they were draped down to the ground in handsome black medieval-style coats embroidered with silver stars, and each proudly sported black ostrich plumes on his forehead. On the whole, therefore, far from being traumatised, we were proud to see our grandfather, dead though he was, riding in such glory.

At the cemetery, my mother and her female relations, all smothered in their weeds, stood at the gates shaking hands, as if receiving the guests at a reception. When it was our turn to go to her own funeral, we could not find it in ourselves to follow her example and behave in such a civilised manner, and instead allowed 'the guests' to pile in helter-skelter, ungreeted at the gates.

One terrible day, when John must have been unusually provoking, Marie, who loved him more than anyone else on earth, having been brought to the boil by his naughtiness, gave him a good spanking. Taking him outside, she walloped his bottom with a slipper under the orange-trees behind the kitchen. Overcome by the indignity of this treatment, he set up such an uproar that Mamma came hurrying out to see what was happening. The sight of John being spanked was so unusual that it must have taken her by surprise and thrown her off-balance. She shouted at Marie to stop at once, which order was naturally ignored, so that Mamma saw red and completely lost her temper.

'Put that child down,' she roared above the din, 'I forbid you to touch my son!' At this Marie dropped John like a hot potato and rounded on my mother. 'In that case, madame, I will leave at once,' she said, in a voice like a corncrake. And she flounced into the house, barked at Marius to bring her trunk down from the attic, and pounded up the stairs to her room.

Grabbing John up from the grass where he had been dropped, I scrambled after her, both of us wailing and keening like banshees, begging her not to desert us. But the trunk was packed and lashed round and round with a stout rope and a variety of leather straps. Alerted (perhaps by Marius?), the railway cart, pulled by the old railway horse, came lumbering up the hill, and the trunk was loaded on.

By then we were in a state of utter despair bordering on hysteria, and clung to Marie's skirts, begging her not to go. My mother had completely disappeared, and I have never discovered what her feelings were at the time. Was it dismay at the thought of losing Marie, or was it relief? In many ways it must have been intensely irritating for her never to be able to be mistress in her own household. Moreover, our devotion to Marie must have been galling, as we never made any fuss at all when Mamma went away. We knew, of course, that she would always return, although we were never informed whether it would be in a few days or a few months. And quite possibly, most of the time, she did not know herself.

Clutching at Marie's skirts and demented with grief, we sobbed and howled, when suddenly the coachman hopped off his perch and, shouting above the clamour, 'Voyons, Madame Marie, vous n'allez pas laisser ces gosses!', dragged her trunk off the cart and swung it onto the grass. Then, scrambling back onto his box, he turned the horse round and clattered off down the hill again. Marie's face was saved, and this, for us, most appalling of all disasters had been averted. The trunk was duly lugged up to Marie's room again.

Shortly after this episode, my mother disappeared, and we learnt later, by chance, that she had gone to Paris to build a house there. But thank goodness, we were never made to go and live in it. Although we never saw it, photographs made it look perfectly hideous. A white box with a flat roof, it looked like a mausoleum.

The reverse side of Mamma's warm-hearted and hospitable nature was that her dislikes were as uncontrollable as her generous impulses. Many years later when we were all back at Mas Mistral with our husbands and assorted children, I dropped a brick which I shall never forget. The man who had rented D. H. Lawrence's house next door had, unknown to me, long been trying to infiltrate himself into our household. As I knew nothing about it, it seemed natural to invite him to tea when I met him in the village one day and he said how much he longed to see us all again.

Forgetting about it at once, I was surprised when he turned up the next day. We were all having nursery tea in the dining-room. My mother, seated in an armchair, had a grandchild on her knee, and eight or nine other small creatures were stuffing themselves with bread and jam at the table. As he minced in through the open door, our neighbour, bowing low, swept off his hat, saying how grateful he was for my kind invitation. My mother gaped at him in utter disbelief, and then exploded. Her fury took us all completely by surprise. She told him that he had no business to take advantage of my stupidity to worm his way into the house, that she had already told him that he was not welcome, and so would he please immediately get out of the house. We were stunned by this outburst, and stared as the poor man turned tail and fled. Meanwhile, my mother had regained her composure and resumed her task of stuffing prunes and baked custard into the face of the baby on her lap.

After the war, when they retired from Malaya, my parents managed Mas Mistral without any living-in staff. Sometimes my father would go off for a whole month at a time to do a cure at

Châtelguyon, leaving Mamma entirely on her own in the house. Marvelling at her bravery in sleeping alone in that huge house, I asked her how she managed not to be nervous at night. Oh, she answered, there was no reason to be nervous, as a strange dog that she had never met before came to the kitchen door every evening and insisted on spending the night on guard by her bed. He departed in the morning after a bowl of tea (so good for their coats you know) and returned punctually at nightfall. He never came while my father was there, but always reappeared during the 'cure' periods.

As he grew older, Papa's mania for solitude grew more marked, and if anybody threatened to pay us a visit he would exclaim, 'What does that idiot want to come here for? We don't want to see him,' and his agitation was such that the prospective visitor had to be put off as tactfully as possible. If anybody had the temerity to call without warning, he would dive into the cellar and remain there until winkled out, only emerging on the assurance that the offending caller was well off the premises.

We were really put on the spot on one occasion soon after my younger sister's wedding, when some of her new husband's friends, who had come all the way from England for the occasion, climbed up the hill to Mas Mistral to see Papa, as they had had no chance to talk to him at the reception. When he saw them panting up the garden path, he shot out of his chair and dashed to the door with unaccustomed velocity: 'Get rid of them,' he squeaked in petulant tones, as he beetled down to his cellar, 'I won't come out until they've gone.' So we had to tell the guests that he had gone up the mountain for a walk, and there was no knowing when he would be back. 'Oh never mind,' they said cheerfully, they were in no hurry and didn't mind waiting in the least. And so for two solid hours they sat and waited, while the family lunch scorched and turned black in the oven, and

Papa fumed in his cellar. But he stuck it out until they gave up and went away.

He really should have been a monk, and I am quite certain that the happiest time of his life was the years that he spent in captivity during the Second World War. His ascetic spirit yearned for austerity, and anything joyful and light-hearted seemed to him frivolous and worthless. Changi Camp in the hands of the Japanese reduced life to basic essentials, and there he came face to face with absolute standards. In a monastery he could have achieved this state with the minimum of frustration. Whereas in the world, he was constantly deflected, so that it was only through the horrors of a Japanese concentration camp that he was able to get anywhere near his ideal. Once he had found it, the rest of his life, after his release, was nothing but a come-down from this higher state.

Above all, no emotional demands of any kind were to be made on him in captivity. These, I think, he dreaded above all else. Reserved and undemonstrative, he was terrified of our youthful, spontaneous affection. This had to be transformed into awe and veneration before he was able to take it. Although I am quite sure that he was fond enough of his children, he could not bear our demands for attention. Emotionally, he simply was not equipped to cope with them. Human relationships panicked him. The fact that as children we worshipped him as God on earth was a great embarrassment to him. Anne, who was always the least neurotic of us all, handled him with a lightness of touch which I envied, but was unable to emulate. When she was eight years old, remarks such as 'I've just seen your wife in the garden. She was looking quite pretty' made him smile, and filled me with admiration at her daring. It worked. But it had to come naturally. And so our great love for him was as much of a burden to us as it was an embarrassment to him – an unwanted commodity.

Quite incapable of small talk, he made a virtue of it and

declared that 'only fools chatter on when they have nothing to say.' Cultured and sensitive as he was, and with all his interests, he could have had a great many friends, but I believe that in the whole of his life he had only two.

His cousin, a painter called Edouard Goerg, whom he had known since childhood, had come to settle at Saillans, a hundred miles or so away on the other side of the Department of Alpes-de-Haute-Provence. Although they saw each other only two or three times a year when he came to Mas Mistral (nothing would persuade Papa to leave the house to visit him), it gave Papa a great deal of pleasure to know that his cousin was so relatively close. And Anne told me that when he heard of Goerg's death, he broke down and sobbed inconsolably, and never really recovered from the shock.

His other friend, who survived him, was Henry Fauconnier, author of *The Soul of Malaya*. He was already a planter when my father arrived in the Peninsula in search of adventure at the age of eighteen. Their interests were identical, and the friendship that sprang up between them lasted until Papa's death. From time to time, we spent holidays with Fauconnier's gifted children, and Hélène, his eldest daughter, became one of my dearest friends.

Once Mas Mistral had been built, and every inch of the garden was laid out and planted, the gardeners took over the daily weeding and general upkeep and there was nothing left for my father to do. Feeling the need for a new activity, he bought the freehold of a corner site on the Place du Grand Jardin in Vence, and made it into a bookshop. A short trip to Paris furnished it with a magnificent collection of art books, all the dictionaries and *Larousses* imaginable, and even, oh joy, a section for children. On that special shelf we found *White Fang*, *The Last of the Mohicans*, *Robinson Crusoe*, *Mon Petit Trott*, *Oliver Twist* and Aksakov's *Russian Childhood*. This last took possession of our souls and held us in thrall for many months. As soon as she had finished it, Marie had to start reading it again from the beginning.

The trouble with the shop was that my father could not bear to sell the books. When he was not actually reading he stood in a trance, in silent contemplation of the shelves. To sell anything would have broken up the collection – a kind of sacrilege. With a little badgering, you could sometimes borrow one, and if you happened to want it very badly, you simply forgot to return it. That was all right as far as it went. But you were never *never* allowed to pay for it.

As might have been expected, the venture was not a success financially. As it turned out, too many people forgot to return the books they borrowed. Replacing them every few months was very expensive, and my mother eventually put her business foot down. Much against his will, my father was finally persuaded to sell the bookshop. It has gone through a dozen hands since then, but it still bears the name he gave it: the 'Librairie Ligurienne'.

After the bookshop came the buses. Le Petit Train travelled from Nice to Marseilles one day and returned the next. It stopped at Vence, and everywhere else, on the way. Apart from that, our only communication with the outside world was by donkey. To remedy this, my father had the idea of starting a bus service. He bought half-a-dozen of these monsters from Messrs Renault et Cie and put them into service. The *chauffeurs* were picked off tables at the Café de la Régence.

It was enormous fun, not untinged with moments of terror, to go to Nice in Papa's buses. Scattering goats and sheep before us, we rattled down the mountainside on what was little more than a track in those days, so closely skirting the edge overlooking the valley that we often had to close our eyes in a desperate appeal for mercy to St Christopher. Having been seen by this much overworked saint safely down to the bottom, we would pass the cemetery at the foot of Haut-de-Cagnes, where we had to dive into our handkerchiefs, as the local stench made the air unbreathable, though it probably came from the village rubbish dump next door and not from the dead rotting in their graves as we then supposed.

The bus was very accommodating, dropping people off all along the road, picking up baskets and letters, and making unexpected detours into side streets in Nice to oblige some elderly party whose feet were killing her. A notice behind the driver's head said '*Défence de parler au chauffeur*', but nobody minded this little bit of officious nonsense in the least. Conversation was general and animated, and the driver took a leading part, conducting it with his hands and swivelling round in his seat from time to time to drive a point home. My father never travelled on his own buses. A taxi drove him to Nice whenever he had to go there.

In the evening, after a long and satisfyingly exhausting day spent in the shops, we repaired to the Café de l'Univers where Marie had a beer, and we restored ourselves with cocoa and croissants. The bus waited patiently until everybody was ready. Then we all piled in and exchanged the news of the day. The drive back into the mountains in the dark was never quite so frightening as the race downhill in daytime, although the spluttering and groaning of the motor made it sometimes seem unlikely that we would ever make it.

chapter four

Great-Grandfather Chasseriau, when he landed in Malaya, had met an Englishman who, over a drink, sold him several thousand acres of jungle. Having picked up a partner on the way, Great-Grandpapa set off at once with a gang of men and elephants to clear his newly-acquired property.

Pirates, alerted by the bush telegraph, were awaiting them by a bend in the river, and the poor partner, taken by surprise, was struck through the heart with a kriss, and that was the end of his adventures. But Great-Grandpapa was ready with his pistol, and within a few minutes the corpses of the pirates were drifting down the river, escorted by a fleet of hungry crocodiles. Undeterred, he carried on with his pioneering alone, and from then on, continually called upon by the Rajahs of the surrounding states to restore order, he became, willy-nilly, the policeman of Northern Malaya, marching his battalion of armed men and elephants wherever a new war broke out.

This was before Ridley had won his battle for rubber-planting in Malaya, and the wars between the invading Chinese and the local Malays over the tin mines were constant and fearful. Great-Grandfather suppressed the bandits and administered justice, and if a few corpses were hanging from the surrounding trees by the end of the morning session, there were no complaints.

After a few years of unremitting hard work and solitude, while still in Northern Malaya, Great-Grandpapa took a trip to Europe to find a wife. In due course, Mademoiselle Bachelier de St Marc, aged seventeen, was wooed and won, and they had a Hollywood-type midnight wedding in Bordeaux Cathedral, with a torchlight procession through the town, and much singing and feasting and rejoicing.

Great-Grandmamma, fresh from her convent, took to pioneering without turning a hair. The stabling of war-weary elephants in her garden could have been part of the nuns' training, so smoothly did she take such matters in her stride. Nocturnal visits from Chinese pirates sneaking up the river only prompted her to grope under her pillow for her pistol in her sleep, and having to turn her bungalow into an emergency hospital after one of the numerous local wars became a matter of routine. There is much to be said for the training of girls by nuns. Above all, they are realistic. The message which comes through, once you have worked your way through all the flummery, is clear and trenchant: 'Be adequate, and let nothing ruffle you.'

In due course, two sons were born to this gallant pair: Emile, a dreamy soul, who eventually sank his all in a mine tucked away in such an inaccessible part of the Borneo jungle that it has remained untouched to this day, and Leopold, my grandfather, who turned out to be a chip off the old block.

On Singapore Island Great-Grandpapa bought several thousand more acres of land but, having cleared it of jungle, discovered that the soil was far less fertile than in Northern Malaya. To remedy this, and having noticed that the streets of

Singapore were littered with uncollected refuse of every kind, he offered to clean up the town free of charge. The Governor, who hadn't got round to this ticklish problem himself, was only too glad to give his consent. So every day a procession of forty bullock-carts and five hundred men set out from Chasseriau Estate at the crack of dawn, and returned later with several tons of odoriferous but invaluable fertiliser, which was then ploughed into the land. And in no time at all the plantation was the most prosperous in Malaya.

The crops included coffee, coconuts, sugar cane and tapioca, which was the favourite food of jungle pigs, who spent their nights rooting up the tasty tubers, thereby causing untold damage among the young trees. Great-Grandpapa's method of dealing with the problem was, against much opposition from the European and native population alike, to encourage visiting tigers to remain, settle down and breed on his land. And in their favour it must be said that they behaved like perfect guests, leaving the labour force intact and conscientiously gobbling up the pigs. The Comte de Jouffroy d'Abbans, who was French Consul at the time, and in whose memoirs I found these stories, relates that, on one of their walks through the plantation, when a tigress ambled nonchalantly past them with her young, my great-grandfather simply remarked, 'These are my cats. They do a good job. There's nothing like a few of them around to keep the mice down.'

D'Abbans' memoirs describe him as tall and broad-shouldered, a pioneer of the old type, indefatigable, sparing neither himself nor others, bellowing orders as he strode about among his men, demanding immediate and absolute obedience; but kind and just, and so never short of labour. Moreover, according to the Count, another reason why Great-Grandpapa, who employed over five thousand men, could always find as many as he wanted, was that he paid better wages than other employers.

As most of his workmen were Muslims, he knew that their dearest wish was to get to Mecca, an expensive trip which they were able to afford after only a couple of years in his service. And so as not to lose them when, as usual, they had squandered their return-passage money, and in order to enable them to get back, he posted an agent at the other end with instructions to lend funds to the improvident pilgrims, on condition that they should work off the loan at Chasseriau Estate on their return. (It was on this very plantation on Singapore Island that my father was interned by the Japanese when they overran Malaya almost a hundred years later.)

Once Chasseriau Estate was running smoothly, Great-Grandfather decided to go back to France on leave. It was his last voyage. As they were approaching Aden, a violent storm blew up, washing a little girl overboard. Great-Grandpapa dived in after her, gashed his knee, and died of gangrene a few days later. And according to the records, the authorities gave him 'an imposing funeral' in Aden, where he is buried.

Meanwhile, at the other end of the world Great-Grandfather Fesq moved with his family from one villa to another, according to the season or the mood of the moment. 'Lentana', particularly, according to Marie, was a scene of continual entertaining and lavish hospitality. Dinner parties, balls and concerts succeeded one another, and the afternoons were given over to those vast picnics to which the Victorians were so addicted.

When Marie joined the family, Papa's elder brother was five and his sister, my Aunt Mimi, was just born. Young Marie took to her like a duck to water, and they were inseparable for many years to come.

Uncle Bunny, Papa's elder brother, was an extrovert, a tomboy, and always in trouble. He ran away from school and was locked up in the attic for several days with only bread and water. My father was totally different – shy and sensitive to a morbid degree. When it came to children's parties, he clawed at the railings, crying and begging to be left at home, and had to be wrenched away and carried to the party in tears. When he was seventeen, and the appalling prospect of dances and balls loomed up, his legs most conveniently gave out and he became miraculously paralysed. Doctors and specialists were called in and massage and mud baths were tried out, all to no avail. Young Emile thankfully took to his crutches, hobbling about the house, feeling safe for life.

But he had reckoned without Marie's fierce determination. She formed her plan. Ordering the carriage one fine day, she took him and the housekeeper for a drive in the country. When the chosen spot was reached, she told the coachman to stop, and they all climbed out for a little walk, my father hopping along quite cheerfully on his crutches, the three of them chatting amicably together. Reaching a grassy bank, they stopped for a rest. Without warning, Marie suddenly seized the crutches and flung them away as far as she could.

'And now,' she said firmly, 'walk back, or stay here by yourself.' And grabbing the startled housekeeper by the arm, she marched her back to the carriage. I don't know how long it took young Emile to join them, or how he managed it, but he never used his crutches again. Within a couple of years the spirit of adventure had taken possession of him, and he set sail for the East, quite literally standing on his own feet. As far back as I can remember, until a couple of years before his death, he was the most indomitable walker I have ever known. When nearly eighty, on his visits to London he used to march me along the Embankment, over Chelsea Bridge, and back by Albert Bridge in twenty minutes flat. I panted after him with aching back and out of breath, but he was undaunted.

My father's search for adventure brought him to Malaya, where he met and married my mother in 1919. There are some splendid photographs of the wedding, taken under palm-trees festooned with creepers hanging over the guests' heads like Christmas decorations. My father, for whom this must have been a terrible ordeal, worse than any of the balls in his teens, looks squashed, diminished, shrunken, half his usual size. I still cannot imagine how he went through with it, and can only put it down to Marie's early upbringing that he did not revert to crutches under the strain.

When I was born, an amah was found who seemed able to keep me, by some special magic of her own, as quiet as a fish throughout the day and night. Nobody had ever seen such a placid and contented baby. It was not until my parents were packing to come to Europe, that the amah's magic was discovered, tucked away behind my cot, in the shape of a bottle of chloroform. That was when Marie, who was still in Sydney, was sent for, and arrived in France more or less at the same time as we did.

chapter five

One fine day Rubio appeared without warning at Mas Mistral. He had been a houseman to Aunt Mimi, Father's sister, who had a villa in Spain at San Sebastián. Whether he had run away or been sacked, and why he came to us, I never discovered. And I don't suppose my parents ever even asked. They simply welcomed him, gave him a room, and put him on the payroll. A Spanish Basque, self-willed and short-tempered, with bright red hair and bright red political views, Rubio had great natural elegance, and bore himself like a grandee. He spoke a peculiar language of his own, probably a mixture of various kinds of patois, and he made sure we all picked it up as soon as possible, since he had no intention of learning any French.

From the start Rubio decided that his chief amusement would be baiting Marie, and he became the bane of her life. He would wait until she was ready to feed her hens, then creep up to the chicken-run, open the door and stand aside to let them out. At the same time he whistled through his teeth a special kind of hen-call which brought them running out. Marie would come staggering up the path with her heavy buckets of food just in time to see her last Orpington vanish into the vineyard with a cheerful waggle of her tail-feathers. For the next hour or so we would try to help her round them up. Leaping about and chasing them only made matters worse. It was a wild scene, with Marie flouncing around purple with rage, glasses flashing in the sun and hat flapping up and down like an eagle's wings. 'Catch them you idiot,' she yelled, as I jumped about, as excited as the hens. And the long bamboo cane with which she conducted operations would come swishing down on the back of my legs.

On two or three occasions, and I don't think Rubio could have been responsible for these, the hens went quite mad, started to pluck one another and laid eggs without shells, which they scattered all over their run in the most untidy way possible. Marie decreed that they needed calcium, bought a dozen oysters a day for the next fortnight and fed them the crushed shells, which meant of course that we had to eat the oysters. After trying one, which wriggled its way down my throat in the most horrible way, I refused to touch another and left the rest for John and Anne, who thoroughly enjoyed the treat. The hens produced respectable shells again, and everything returned to normal.

Rubio decided that his chief job was to watch over us every moment of the day, and to act as my mother's bodyguard. Whenever she went out on her own, he followed, carrying her shopping, her umbrella, letters for posting, or whatever it happened to be. This drove her mad at first, but as he couldn't be shaken off, she came to accept it as inevitable. Marie, who refused to speak his own language, gave him orders in French, which he invariably disregarded. Their relationship never improved.

On the walk to church on Sunday, when my father always had a newspaper ready under his arm to while away the time, Rubio brought up the rear, muttering fiercely all the way, and from time to time shaking his fist when his feelings got too much for him. As a confirmed Communist he strongly disapproved of these expeditions, but for nothing on earth would he have stayed behind and let us go on our own. As soon as we arrived, the curate, who was rather apprehensively looking out for us, would lead us firmly to a side-chapel where we were decently tucked away out of sight. You couldn't really blame the poor man, what with my father rustling *The Times*, Marie nodding and snoring, and Rubio cursing and shaking his fist as soon as the sermon started.

Once a year, when the chimneys were swept and Madame Rose had to let her kitchen range go out, a cooking fire was built outside, between two large stones. Across these was placed a huge cauldron filled with sauerkraut and sausages, smoked pigs' cheeks, trotters and tails. Sitting on the grass around the fire, we all took part in the feast. The farmer came along, and the gardeners left their digging, spat on their hands and rubbed them together, then touched their caps and squatted by the fire. Caroline came croaking and hobbling over from her laundry troughs, her hands all white and wrinkled from years of soaking in cold water, and Pauvre Claire, with her forehead all crinkled with worry and her mouth pursed up like a hen's bottom, handed out plates, glasses, knives and forks. We sat in silence, inhaling the delicious aroma wafting out of the pot, while a couple of bottles of Papa's wine stood 'breathing' in the grass. Then Madame Rose would dish up and we would all fall to.

Rubio never joined us in these feasts, whether by choice or whether he was not invited I have no idea. But once at least he made sure we didn't get our treat. The home-made sauerkraut had as usual been scooped out of its barrel in the cellar, and all the various bits of smoked pork and sausages had been brought up to the house by the farmer the day before. The fire had been lit early in the morning, and Madame Rose had set her brimming pot over the blaze as she always did. But when she came back towards noon to dish up, she found it stone-cold. There was consternation all round. After an inquest, Rubio proudly owned up to *kicking the fire away from the pot* soon after it was lit. There was an almighty row, and everyone turned on him with rich oaths from the depths of their famished bellies. But he just leaned back against an orange-tree, smirking and picking his teeth with a pine needle.

When, years later, war broke out and we were all scattered across the world, Rubio stayed on at Mas Mistral while Marius moved into the old house, which he claimed as his own as soon as Mussolini entered the war and invaded the South of France. One day Rubio was found dead in the garden, where he probably still lies buried, since Marius would never have spent any money on a funeral for him.

As far back as I can remember, we longed for friends. Other children were a rare treat in our lives, and knowing they were regarded as a bad influence by Marie made them all the more desirable.

Our first attempt at friendship was with Clement, one of the flea-bitten brood belonging to the doomed farmer who brought our milk every evening. We did our best, but it was uphill work. Clement really didn't understand anything. We gave him marbles, and lent him our rag dolls. We showed him how to get deliciously giddy by rolling down grass slopes. All to no avail. If he thought anything at all, it was probably that we were even more batty than his brothers and sisters. As his clothes were always falling off him in strips, we stole needles and thread from Pauvre Claire's sewing basket and tried to stitch him together. 'What are you doing!' he shouted, pulling away, as John stuck a large darning needle through his sleeves and right into his arm.

I sat on his legs to immobilise him. 'Can't you see you're falling to pieces? It won't take long. Do stop wriggling,' I implored. 'Get off me,' he yelled, flinging me away. The friendship had no future. We had to abandon it.

Another promising relationship which also came to nothing, entirely through our own fault, was with a boy called Marc, whose parents brought him to tea one day. It was all to do with the zip-fastener on Marc's sweater, which was the first we had ever seen. While the grown-ups were conferring downstairs, we dragged him away to Papa's study for experimental purposes. There we held him down, while each in turn worked the zip up and down in great excitement. As a new invention, it was fascinating. But suddenly there was a fearful scream as a twitch of his neck skin got caught in the zip. He leaped away and galloped downstairs, howling at the top of his voice. That night we went to bed without supper, and we never saw Marc again.

Next door to the house where D. H. Lawrence had recently died there lived a girl of about my own age called Marina, whose wisdom and knowledge of the world dazzled and filled us with admiration. She told us the facts of life, and although we didn't believe a word she said, we were immensely impressed by her imagination and ingenuity in inventing such extraordinary tales. Mamma, who disliked Marina and probably thought her lewd and knowing, discouraged the friendship. She probably wanted to protect our innocence, but she need not have worried. As backward children, we were hard to beat. Although later, in Malaya, we became intimately acquainted with the mating habits of the snakes, mammals and insects all around us, the penny never dropped. These, we thought, were just more of their quaint and fascinating ways. We didn't get the message for a long time to come.

Marina's father was slowly dying of 'cancer of the heart'. Every morning after breakfast she would stump up the path and whistle for us to come and hear the latest news of the advancing disease. We were riveted by the gruesome details, and still more by her detached attitude towards the poor man's agony. We remembered with shivers of horror the time when Papa had stepped on a large nail which had gone right through his foot. So Marina's lack of feeling for her father's suffering was mystifying and confusing.

After a long-drawn-out agony which we shared with him through every stage until the death-rattle, he was gathered at last. A special doctor with a 'suitcase full of knives' came down from Paris to gut and embalm him, and pack him up for despatch to Brazil where he was to be buried. And Marina told us with great pride that she had been allowed to have his heart, pickled in a bottle, beside her bed for the night before the departure of the corpse.

To our grief, Marina soon became too much for her mother to manage, and was packed off as a boarder to a convent in Nice. Years later I saw a photograph of her in a magazine, looking like a film-star in the Fascist uniform of the Italian army.

Another friend we lost, in tragic circumstances, was Gina, the postman's little daughter. Every winter, death and destruction, in one form or another, struck Vence and the surrounding villages. In those days children's diseases often turned into terrible epidemics, which spread alarmingly over wide areas. That year diphtheria raged in Vence, wiping out half the child population of the district. Our postman's daughter was one of them, and the poor man was heartbroken. Trying to cheer him up, we offered him a glass of my father's wine, and led him to our favourite spot under the orange-trees behind the kitchen.

As soon as Marie saw us, she came out with a bottle and a couple of glasses, and they both consoled each other as best they could. She had lost a son, and he a daughter. After that he would stop most days for a chat and a glass of wine. We all became great friends. Although they both detested 'the Boche', he and Marie thoroughly enjoyed a natter in German, as he came from Alsace and knew the language well. This was very boring for us, as we couldn't understand a word they said.

Seated on a kitchen chair opposite Marie, with the bottle between them, the postman would bring out the contents of the mailbag. Every time he fished out a postcard he read it out to us, so we were always kept abreast of local news.

'Ah ha!' he would say, pulling out a plum. 'This is for Madame Bichet, from her son who is doing his service in Algiers. He says his corporal is a pig. I bet he is!' or else, 'Mademoiselle Dupont has just got engaged, to Alfred Béjat of all people.' As we didn't know the young man in question, it meant nothing to us. But Marie would nod knowingly. And from time to time he would exclaim, 'Here is one for you, Madame Marie. From one of your step-daughters. You'd better read it out yourself.'

Marie's suspicion of 'other children' was confirmed when Anne, who was still quite small, nearly met her death at the hands of the local juvenile strangler. Polo, who was about thirteen at the time and had the strength of a man, used to stalk the countryside looking for opportunities to practise his favourite hobby. And from time to time on our walks through the woods, we would come across chickens with their heads pulled off, or the corpse of a lamb without any legs, and we knew that Polo had passed that way.

On the day he had a go at Anne, she had wandered off down the path at the bottom of the garden. Knowing her ways, I expect she was pottering along, picking at the hedgerows and telling herself one of her interminable fairytales. Probably she didn't see Polo until he had pounced on her and got her by the throat. Her piercing yells brought help in the nick of time from a nearby peasant, and she got away with no more than a bad fright and a few bruises on her neck. But after that, whenever we sallied forth beyond our boundaries, we kept our eyes skinned for Polo, and ran for our lives if he ever appeared within a hundred yards.

My mother reported the incident to the mayor, but nothing was done. A couple of years later Polo, by then a hefty teenager, was still striding around the countryside like Frankenstein. One day he burst into the village school and tried his luck in a class-room full of girls. This time the parents got up a formal petition which produced the desired results. Polo vanished from the scene. We never saw him again, and we often wondered what had happened to him. There wasn't much hope of treatment for psychopaths in those days, and the thought of poor Polo, the wild creature of the woods, cooped up in a cell with a ball and chain haunted us for a long time.

From time to time Mamma took us to visit our neighbours, the Hilliers, who lived about half a mile away from Mas Mistral and were the only English people in the area. As a perfect example of the backbone of Old England, they stuck to tradition in every-thing they did, and even managed to create a real English garden in their patch of cracked, sun-baked clay. There were lawns, rockeries and herbaceous borders, and two of those heavenly cyprus trees which continually crop up in early Italian Renaissance paintings, with very smooth pale-grey trunks and close-packed foliage pointing up to the sky like minarets. It was a dream of a garden.

But the Hilliers were not entirely happy. Their Provençal *bonne-à-tout-faire* couldn't manage, try as she might, to produce traditional English puddings, fruit cake, Victoria sponges or first-class steak and kidney pie, so she was replaced by a man who had been a cook in the Royal Navy. All went well until the poor fellow, unhinged by loneliness, took first to the bottle and then to the hills, where he was found three days later raving under a juniper bush.

Throughout all these vicissitudes, Mrs H remained calm and unperturbed. She produced a baby, for which she made a cheerful chintzy nursery – so unlike our own, with the photographs of Marie's dead husband and baby glooming over us day and night. Then she got down to the Victoria sponges herself. I loved helping her in the kitchen, and I enjoyed looking after the baby when Mrs H was busy in the garden.

One fine summer afternoon, Mrs Hillier dropped in for tea. To our surprise, although we were playing quite noisily under the drawing-room window, we weren't called in to pay our respects.

After an hour of earnest confabulation, she reappeared, and as we ran up to greet her, we heard her saying, 'So you see my dear, we must stick together.'

'Of course,' agreed my mother fervently. 'I quite agree with you.'

'If it weren't for the baby,' added Mrs H, 'I would go myself.'

'Don't worry,' said Mamma, 'I will go tomorrow, and the children will come with me.'

After our guest had left, we were informed of the treat in store. A family of Poor Whites had apparently settled in Vence, and were squatting in utter penury in a deserted farmhouse at La Sine. It was generally believed that they came from Ireland, that the husband was an alcoholic, and that the numerous children who ran about barefoot were starving, since the family was totally destitute. Mrs H, having had wind of the affair, and not wanting to get mixed up herself, had tackled my mother, knowing she wouldn't be turned down.

And how right she was! Mamma, throwing herself into the venture full-tilt, made us bring her our rucksacks, and filled them to the brim with all the preserves she could lay her hands on – home-made jam, pickled goose, chicken-liver pâtés, quails in brandy, and all kinds of preserved fruit out of the garden.

Also the last pot of honey from our own bees, whose sacrifice I welcomed as good riddance.

Next morning, booted as if for mountaineering, we harnessed ourselves to our rucksacks, picked up an alpenstock each, and set off down the hill and across the valley to La Sine. Eventually we reached the clearing described by Mrs H. And there indeed stood the old farmhouse with its tiny windows like half-closed eyes, rather battered about the roof and top floor, but spacious enough to house a large family of Poor Whites. A huge chestnut-tree spread its branches over the roof, and all round grew the finest, shortest emerald grass I had ever seen. It could have been a well cared-for bowling-green. Surrounding this fairytale spot were olive-groves, cypresses and orange-trees, and no other house in sight. But everywhere, right up to the front door, were piles of old tins and empty beer bottles and literally hundreds of wine bottles.

As we approached a dog barked and a pack of young children came pouring out of the house, followed by their mother. She stared at us in silence as Mamma explained the object of our visit. As we moved nearer the front door, the dog snarled and barred the way. We didn't appear to be welcome. The woman continued to glare at us without a word, and Mamma said, 'I expect the lady is busy. She wasn't expecting us. Unpack, children, and put your stuff on the grass.'

While we did as we were told, I took a quick look round at the children, a scruffy mob who were milling excitedly about, picking things up and running to their mother, screeching in some unknown language with vaguely English-sounding vowels. Monolithic and silent, the woman continued to stare, until the last pot stood on the ground. Then, in icy tones, she asked, 'And who do I owe this lot to?'

'I am a neighbour of Mrs Hillier's,' chirruped my mother. 'And these are my children. You are Mrs O'Connor, I presume?'

'Correct,' snapped the woman.

'What a lovely family you have,' prattled Mamma, lying in her teeth, as the grubby-looking mob milled around noisily.

At that moment a bulky, lumpy girl, a couple of years older than myself, came out of the house. 'My stepdaughter,' said Mrs O'Connor, mentioning no names. The girl stared in silence.

On the way home after this curiously unrewarding experience, relieved of our load, we skipped along merrily, picking wild flowers and peering into the bushes, looking for birds' nests. This was the end of the Poor Whites as far as we were concerned. But we still didn't know our mother.

'What a charming family,' she said, as I was extricating Anne from a bog into which she had sunk to her knees. 'We must have them round to tea, and you will look after the children, won't you,' she said, tapping me on the head with a hazel twig. My heart sank into my mountain boots, and all joy fizzled away.

When it came to the point, the small rabble, thank goodness, had been left behind, and all I had to deal with was the lumpy girl. John and Anne, needless to say, had vanished, so I took her upstairs to my room and introduced her to my favourite doll. The girl, whose name I still didn't know, stared in bored silence.

'Would you like to see my books?' I tried next. And then suddenly a thought struck me. 'You *can* read, can't you?' I asked tactlessly. She gave me a withering look, but there was no reply. 'Oh heavens,' I thought, 'now I've put my foot in it.' Completely at a loss about what to do with this unresponsive creature, I decided to take things in hand and ask no more questions. 'Come,' I said firmly. 'We'll walk around the garden.'

I showed her our animal cemetery, the goldfish in the pond, the strawberry beds, and the birds' nests in the hedge. By then we had almost reached the top of the garden. 'And here the donkeys from next door come through a hole in the fence to eat our raspberries.' Further up was an anthill. 'If you step on it, the ants will chew your toes off,' I informed her. A little way on we reached an adder's nest, heaving with black, wormlike babies. At the sight of them she sprang back as if she'd been bitten – but still didn't utter a word. By the time we got to the top of the garden, I was at my wits' end. This is my last effort, I thought. After that she can go to hell.

'This is my favourite tree. You can climb it if you like,' I said with the ultimate in hospitality. 'When you reach the top, you get a really good view of people dying in their beds on the terrace over there.' I pointed out the TB hospital, where the poor patients, lying in the blazing sun as was the fashion then, were coughing their lungs out, and giving up the ghost at the rate of two or three a day. Only then did it dawn on me that the girl couldn't understand a word I said because I was speaking French.

After that, I am glad to say, there were no more visitations from the Poor Whites.

chapter six

Not long after this futile expedition my father suddenly and without explanation returned to Malaya, to Assam Java, the plantation he owned at Selangor. Since the reason for his departure was never discussed, we never knew if he had always meant to go back, whether he had lost money in the slump, or was just plain bored with us all and the tame life of the South of France.

To us, it seemed like the end of the world. A feeling of doom settled on the house as the leather trunks were brought down from the attic, Papa's books were gathered from the shelves in the study, and Caroline gave his tropical gear a good bashing with the old cricket bat.

When the dreadful day arrived our grief was overwhelming. Blind with tears, we clung to Papa as he got into the taxi with Mamma, who was going to see him off from Marseilles. And although Marie took us all down to see the animals of a circus which had just arrived in the town, we went on snuffling for the rest of the day. Not even the antics of the king penguins could cheer us up, nor even the news that in a few months we too would be going to Malaya. In those days a few months was like a hundred years.

Another twilight period of gloom and depression settled on the house when Marie, who had never taken a holiday since she arrived in Vence, decided to go and visit her family in Switzerland before we left for the Far East. She would be deserting us for a whole month, while a niece of hers called Frieda took over. Passionately devoted to Marie as we were, her stand-in hadn't a chance.

A buxom blonde with a smooth face and eyes so wide apart they looked like headlamps, Frieda was probably a nice enough girl. And we might have found some of her habits rather quaint in a harmless sort of way, if we hadn't felt so abandoned and miserable. She made us eat on our own, whereas Marie always shared our meals. We had been trained, between courses, to keep our hands in our lap. But Frieda insisted we put them on the table, on either side of the plate. This, we thought, made us look like begging dogs, and lacked dignity. It was a small thing, but we felt it keenly, and when she took us for our first walk up the hill, we had our revenge. Without prearrangement of any kind, we all hurled our straw hats high up into a peach-tree, from where there was no way of retrieving them. Frieda was furious. It was the beginning of a war that continued until Marie's return. From then on there were no more walks, and we were confined to the nursery upstairs, 'doing time'.

No prisoner could have felt his confinement more acutely. Summer was just beginning, and we longed to be out of doors. The sun shone in a cloudless sky, and butterflies hovered thick and heavy over the wisteria on the balcony. Birds were in full song. It was more than we could stand. So when Anne announced she wanted to go to the loo, we decided to take her to a downstairs one instead of the one on our own floor. Even an outing like this would be a treat after the oppressive dreariness of the nursery.

I don't know which one tripped, but we all hurtled down head-first and crashed to the bottom, still holding hands. Frieda burst out of the kitchen, smacked us all soundly and drove us back to the nursery. From then on we were *locked* in. As caged animals often do, we stopped eating, wilted and sickened. It was probably no more than a summer cold, but the full treatment went into operation at once. And this cure was far worse than the passing misery of a sniffle and a cough.

Home treatment for minor ailments was the bane of childhood in those days. Castor oil was a constant terror, dished out at regular intervals, whether needed or not. Bags of scalding porridge were clamped to the chest for coughs, after which came 'cupping'. A glass filled with burning cotton wool was clapped onto your chest. You were lucky when it was left at that. For pneumonia the glass was wrenched off and a cross slashed into the spongy, swollen skin. Blood gushed, letting out the infection, and all symptoms were expected to vanish overnight. We never had to suffer this particular form of torture ourselves. But when John had his tonsils out, the operation took place at home. Marie held him between her knees, his jaws were jacked apart with a clamp, and our local doctor carried out the job as best he could in the night nursery.

When my mother and I returned from the chicken-run to which we had fled from the sound of John's terrible screams, he was lying on his bed in a swoon. Marie, impassive as a Henry Moore statue beside him, was mopping up the blood which oozed from his swollen mouth. And the tonsils and adenoids were floating in a jamjar on the table beside her.

We were only just back on our feet, recovering from our treatment, when Marie returned from her holiday in Switzerland. Ecstatic with relief and happiness, we waited for

her all the morning at the garden gate. And when the railway
cart finally appeared, with her sitting next to the coachman,
we skipped along beside them all the way up to the house. As
soon as they stopped at the dining-room door, we flew into
her skirts with whoops of joy, delivered at last from our
month of purgatory. The shabby railway cart was a chariot of
gold, while the old nag which pulled it was Pegasus in all his
glory!

I never discovered why we didn't all travel to Malaya together.
Perhaps Papa couldn't face the thought of being cooped up in a
boat with his family for three whole weeks. Whatever the reason,
a few months after his departure we travelled to Marseilles and
took ship aboard the *Insulinda*, a gallant long-distance liner sailing under the Dutch flag. I was going back to the land of my
birth, and John and Anne were visiting it for the first, though not
the last time in their lives.

Marie and the three of us were packed into a cabin as small
and cosy as a squirrel's nest, where she managed somehow to
stow everything away with a minimum of grumbling. There was
nothing she loved so much as a good long voyage, rough seas
and plenty of storms. She had even been lucky enough on one
occasion to be shipwrecked, with the boat splitting asunder and
the two halves drifting away in opposite directions. She may
well have been hoping for some dire calamity to overtake us on
this voyage, but disappointingly nothing really exciting happened, apart from a few heavy storms.

Mamma had a cabin to herself, but where it was and what it
was like we never discovered, as we were never invited to visit
her during the trip. We hardly ever saw her, except occasionally
playing quoits on an upper deck or sometimes lying in a canvas
chair with a book. Adults and children occupied different decks,
and we had our meals in our very own children's dining-room.

Every corner of the *Insulinda* reeked of the most divine smells of tar, wood, oil, and all the peculiar emanations which always waft out of a ship's hold. To this was added the sharp tang of the sea, all of which combined in such a potent mixture that every time I have come across it since, the memory of that first voyage comes back with compelling vividness. And although we were almost a month at sea, I don't remember a moment of boredom.

Before the novelty had worn off we were at Port Said, where we stopped to take on fuel for the engines. Thousands of sacks of coal came on board on the backs of an endless procession of men who looked, from the upper deck, like a double line of ants, one coming up the gangway, the other flowing in the opposite direction. For several days after that an overpowering smell of coal hung about, and everything was covered with black dust, as not the faintest breeze blew while we crept through the Suez Canal. Once we saw a mirage, a sheet of shimmering water hanging in the sky, with camels ambling slowly below.

It was a relief to be surrounded by wide horizons again. But the Red Sea didn't live up to its name. This was disappointing, as we were looking forward to cruising over an enormous expanse of blood-coloured water, with bright-red waves crashing right up to the deck.

As we nosed our way into the Indian Ocean the weather grew warmer, and the steward stripped a couple of blankets off our bunks, then showed us how to open the porthole. 'You must always shut it during storm,' he said in his heavy Dutch accent. 'Or you will be drowned in your slip if the sea come in'.

He got on well with Marie. They gossiped in German, and he brought us innumerable bottles of mineral water, as we were forever thirsty – all that salt in the air, and of course you couldn't drink the tap water. He filled our baths to the brim (a luxury never allowed at home), saying there was plenty more where it came from, and the fish wouldn't miss it. He hung about with huge towels, and I think he would even have scrubbed our backs if Marie had allowed it. Sometimes he joined us in a game of lotto, and spoke of his little girl in Holland, saying how much he missed her. He was a kind man, and we invited him to come and live with us in Selangor. Rubio had been left behind at Mas Mistral, and we felt we could do with a man again. But he declined, on account of his little girl.

In the Indian Ocean we saw our first whale, spouting high in the air. Schools of dolphins followed us for days, and flying fish kept up alongside, skimming through the spray at great speed. We all seemed to be travelling in the same direction.

Then the sharks appeared.

An Indian ayah had died on board, and was brought up to our deck, sewn into a sack. We all stood in a circle while the padre read the funeral service, after which a plank was placed on the rail, she was laid on it, and slid straight into the midst of the cruising sharks.

These creatures, Marie told us, had a fiercely clinging hold on life. On one of her voyages across the world, a sailor had harpooned one and hauled it up on deck. He cut out the shark's heart, which went on beating for five hours, long after its body was thrown back into the sea. Marie was convinced that sharks had supernatural powers. She had seen a man paddling in Botany Bay in a few inches of water, where he thought he was safe. Little did he know that a shark, having become invisible through its own magic, had sneaked up close to him for a quick bite. Suddenly the poor man found himself planted in the sand on his ankle stumps, with both his feet neatly clipped away from under him.

The *Insulinda*, being a small ship, pitched and rolled a good deal. In the Indian Ocean we encountered several storms, and since nearly all the passengers were laid low and we were never sea-sick, we had the entire boat to ourselves. Marie would take us up on deck, where we were soon drenched by the monsoon rain and the enormous waves which crashed over us. As lightning flashed across the sky, and thunder roared and rumbled all round, she told us that it was in a storm such as this that she had experienced her first shipwreck.

After a good soaking-through on deck, she would take us down to the saloon, where she bullied the barman into brewing us a strong reviving pot of tea. This was produced under protest, in minute cups, and there was a battle every time over getting a refill. Deprived of her sustaining feuds with Rubio, she was always on the look-out for another sparring partner. Most men were terrified of her, but the Dutch barman enjoyed the fights as much as she did, and stood his ground.

After tea we would return to our cabin and help Marie put her feet up, tucking them into shawls and pillows to ease her varicose veins. Twisted and lumpy, they stood out on her legs like an intricate network of old ivy climbing up a tree. There had apparently been an occasion when one of the veins had exploded, the blood 'shooting straight up in the air like a geyser'. This had been before our time, but we were taking no chances, and always made sure that Marie got her daily rest.

One of the decks had been roped off for the young, in such a way that we were literally inside a cage of netting, up which we climbed, hanging giddily over the water when the boat pitched that way. As our companions were nearly all Dutch, we had to pick up some of their language in order to play with them. Unused as we were to other children, this daily contact completely went to our heads. We threw ourselves wildly at the swings, rocking horses, toy cars and engines, refused to give them up, and had to be dragged away kicking and screaming.

I was completely out of hand, and John and Anne, though more restrained, joined me at meals in catapulting peas with our forks across the table at our equally wild friends. Marie declared she had never seen us behave so badly. The influence of 'other children' was disastrous, and she longed for the end of the voyage, when she would have us to herself again, under control, and well away from the little Dutch terrors.

At last, after days and nights on end with nothing but sea and sky, we spotted a smudge on the horizon. The sight of it threw us into a state of wild excitement, and I am sure this was Marie's own feeling which she was expressing through us. Instead of quelling us as she usually did, she gave us a smile that was a clear sign of approval. And so, hardly knowing why, we whooped and leaped about the deck, yelling 'Land, land,' while she, tense and silent, gripped the rail and stared at the island of Colombo in the distance. Who knows what adventures she was hoping for?

The harbour, when we eventually steamed up to the jetty, was full of canoes with small boys standing up in them, shouting and waving their arms. When someone threw a coin, they all dived in, and there was a tremendous scuffle under the surface. Finally one of them would come up with the coin in his teeth. Among them was a small boy with only one arm, and Marie told us the other one had been chewed off by a shark.

To our joy we were allowed a whole day off the ship. This was our first experience of a tropical island, and it fully came up to our expectations. The white deserted beaches, the waving palm-trees, as soon as we got out of town, were pure Robinson Crusoe. The rickshaw man who jogged us around seemed to know exactly what we wanted to see. At noon we arrived at a small Chinese store made out of flattened petrol cans (this rather clashed with the Crusoe theme) and gorged ourselves on bananas, and a revolting kind of biscuit that tasted like castor oil – the only disappointment in an otherwise perfect day.

When we finally arrived in Singapore, Papa was on the quay to meet us. Our excitement at seeing him again was tempered by a sudden, unexpected fit of shyness. We had never seen him in tropical gear before. He looked odd and unfamiliar in his shorts and white topee. We were dazed by the noise and bustle of the harbour, and our legs felt like boiled cucumbers after our long weeks at sea. Our first encounter with the powerful smells of the East made us feel giddy, and it was a relief to get into a large and comfortable car.

Breakfast at Raffles Hotel brought another surprise. Cutting open what we thought was a luscious cantaloupe melon, we were faced with the little black seeds of the papaya. This was to become my favourite fruit. And there was plenty of it, as it grew like a weed in the garden of Assam Java.

In the afternoon we got onto another boat bound for Port Swettenham. I think at this point I must have dropped off to sleep, for I remember nothing more until we were climbing into Papa's old Fiat for the final stage of the journey, through the jungle, in the dark.

chapter seven

It was several days before a procession of bullock-carts came rumbling up the drive with our belongings, which were packed into several large wooden crates. It took Marie a good deal of grunting and grumbling to sort it all out, and find suitable corners and cupboards for our clothes and toys.

Although Assam Java was quite a large bungalow, there were few rooms as such, since most of its living space had been set out in an early form of open plan. The ground floor, which was built of concrete for coolness, was surrounded on three sides by trellises, over which climbed moonflowers, orchids, fire-cracker vines, reptiles, beetles, and spiders of every kind. Behind the house a covered way led to the kitchen and staff rooms.

A dozen or so stone pillars supported the first and only other floor, which held our sleeping quarters and the sitting-room. It was reached by a rickety wooden staircase steeped in creosote. When going to bed after supper, in the dark, we kept as far away as we could from the hand-rail, as Marie told us that was the way snakes usually got up to the first floor. The thought of laying your hand on the back of a python making for the bedrooms in search of a midnight feast was spine-chilling.

We were never allowed to run, even barefoot, on this floor. No one knew exactly how strong the timbers were, or how far the termites with which they were riddled had wormed their way. Our cousins in Kedah had jumped through their bathroom floor, landing on the concrete below, children, keeper, bathtub and all, and had sustained fearful injuries. After we left, Assam Java did in fact collapse like a pack of cards, but mercifully no one was in it at the time.

The first floor was surrounded by a large verandah and a mosquito cage, only ever used *after* we had gone down with malaria. There were no outside walls, but a few blinds, rotted to shreds by the sun, flapped around, hanging askew on their strings, until one by one they were carried away by the wind. A thick curtain of plants enveloped the house, providing a leg-up for an unending stream of visiting lizards and insects. The landing walls were decorated with krisses, kukris, and all kinds of oriental swords collected by my father over the years. There were also various snakeskins, some of which, cured by local craftsmen, were faded and crumbling. Others, treated in India by experts, shone and gleamed like polished silver.

On the right-hand side of the first-floor landing were our parents' apartments. Marie and the three of us lived across the way, on the opposite side. The night-nursery was made of rough-hewn planks, soaked through with creosote in the vain hope of discouraging termites. There were no ceilings anywhere. We slept under the rafters and palm-leaf thatch, through which wriggled centipedes, lizards and all kinds of insects. An abundant fauna was born, lived and died over our heads. Rats and squirrels peered down at us, various creatures squeezed in and out of the palm-thatch and frequently crashed to the floor with a thud and squelch. I once found a black and yellow snake curled up between my sheets. Another time his twin was tucked up in one of my shoes. I don't know why we were never bitten.

As nobody seemed to worry, we took this constant shower of snakes and scorpions, centipedes and spiders in our stride. Most of them were tossed out of the window. But when a new creature unknown to us landed, it was scooped up and dropped into a jamjar of surgical spirits to join our growing collection of pickled snakes and other creatures on the night-nursery shelves. The handsome array of bright, vivid greens, yellows and reds, sealed in by the spirits, was gay as a rainbow and never faded.

The top shelf of our night-nursery wall was occupied by a row of jamjars filled with various breeds of scorpions with deadly stings, foot-long poisonous centipedes as fat as sausages, and several kinds of tarantulas and bird-eating spiders. These amiable creatures – all very much alive – were fed on grilled insects from the dining-room table twice a day. A huge acetylene lamp hung, roaring like a motorboat, from a rafter and every airborne insect within a mile hurtled into it and dropped sizzling on the tablecloth, cooked to a turn for our menagerie upstairs. A sheet of Bronco, stuck with airholes and held down with a rubber band, covered the jars. And wondrous to relate, none of the menagerie ever escaped.

The day-nursery was open on all sides to anyone who wished to enter. Making free use of the opportunity, miniature owls raised their families on top of the wardrobe. A small ladder was used by Titi, John's tame hen, for climbing into our clothes cupboard where she laid her eggs. John had found her as a very small chick, lying on her side with a broken leg, abandoned by her mother. Clucking over her like a mother hen himself, he picked her up and brought her to the nursery. There Marie put the leg in a splint made of cottonwool and matchsticks, and so expertly did she do it that Titi never had the slightest limp.

From then on we were her family. She flourished on a diet of hard-boiled eggs, bread soaked in tinned milk, squashed flies and minced worms. Marie said the proper way of preparing worms for her was for us to chew them up first, and I actually saw her put this method into practice herself when dealing with a baby owl who was being difficult about his food. But our devotion never quite reached that level.

The nursery door, which looked as if it was made of ships' timbers, was fitted with a huge pig-iron lock and an assortment of rusty bars. The keys, as large as fire-irons, were only ever used by the houseboys as weapons in their fights. The enormous keyhole made a cosy nesting box for lizards, which laid their tiny eggs inside. These we scooped out with a tea-spoon and stored away in matchboxes. Within a few days the babies hatched, wriggling fiercely to get out. Try as we might, we never managed to tame them, and they departed ungratefully as soon as they had learned to open their matchboxes.

The entire household would usually be woken by Papa at five a.m. as he greeted the dawn with trumpetings of hay-fever. He suffered from it all the year round, as John and I did. Soon after that, a houseboy appeared with our breakfast. This was mostly fruit from the garden, including a special kind of mini-banana with such a powerful smell that a clump ripening in the garden would send all the monkeys mad for miles around. Sometimes there were a few dripping stalks of sugar cane as well, but this wasn't grown in the garden as it attracted elephants. The butter, which came out of a tin, soaked like oil into the toast and needed a lot of jam to kill the taste.

After breakfast came the morning walk. This followed a set pattern. We plunged straight into the plantation which surrounded the garden. Marie cruised ahead, with her large hat securely fastened, and skirts billowing all round. Jamjar in one hand and forked stick in the other, with her good eye she scanned the undergrowth for any poisonous creature that might be lurking. From time to time she glanced at the trees above for a possible python or boa constrictor. Whenever she spotted one, she drew out her whistle and blew a few sharp blasts. Instantly Tamils would appear from behind every tree. Their excitement, always on the boil, grew as they prepared for the capture. Shoving, pushing and shouting, they created an uproar that was echoed and magnified by the monkeys all around.

The capture would take a long time. Eventually a stout pole was cut and trimmed, and a length of wire with a noose at the end produced and raised in front of the snake. Its head dodged about it for a few minutes, and then suddenly it lunged forward and plunged straight into the trap. Hauling it down was a slow business. A few brave men climbed the tree to prise the tail loose, while those on the ground tied a rag around the jaws as soon as the head was within reach. From then on it was restrained and thrashed less fiercely. The great coils, loosening and sagging, were tied to a pole with wire and carried back to the bungalow.

The household was summoned to admire and exclaim over the capture and the bravery of the victors. There must have been a price on the head of every snake on the estate, for as soon as one was caught, Chinese tradesmen appeared and started bargaining for the guts before the creature was even dead. We left them to it and resumed our walk. Marie, her hunter's instinct thoroughly roused by success, would march on ahead, followed by Anne and myself, each holding a hand of our tame household monkey.

We had found this little creature on one of our walks, abandoned at the foot of a tree, and she had become our most devoted pet. Her official home was a small box at the top of a long pole behind the bungalow, but she spent most of her time in the house. She would skip about on the floor, then suddenly jump on your back, or hug you around the neck, breathing into your ear. But out in the jungle she cringed with fear at the screams and jeers of her wild relations leaping overhead.

Last in line came John, pushing my doll's pram in which nestled Titi, tucked up to the chin, with her head on the pillow.

When we finally got back from our walk, we knew what to expect. The entire staff would be gathered around the snake in the garden. Looking out of the nursery window, we would see them milling round a huge tree-trunk lying on the ground and, stretched out down its entire length and nailed to it at both ends, the python being sliced open from head to tail. Extracting the gut, one of the men would coil it up like rope and stuff it into a bag. This would eventually end up in Chinese chemists' shops as expensive aphrodisiac. The workmen would get a good price for their catch. I was always horribly sick at these scenes.

Our daily 'jungle-walks' usually lasted two or three hours, according to the heat, the luck of the day, or Marie's mood. When we eventually got back, hot and tired, around eleven, we would be heartily greeted by 'the pack', led by Woo, the family chow. The rest of his gang, a scruffy lot he collected on his rounds, kept in the background, knowing their place. They were constant casualties of the hazards of life, and Woo had to replace them at frequent intervals. They were bitten by snakes, as they would never leave well alone, they gobbled up poisonous spiders, and sometimes I suspect they were kidnapped and ended up in a curry. In the end, only Woo was left. He had finally given up collecting strays, as he was getting too old to control them. His moods grew uncertain, and my mother, with the dread of rabies always at the top of her mind, decided to find him another home. Poor Woo was given to a family friend in Kuala Lumpur, and we were heartbroken when we heard the news. But two days later, to our joy, Woo was back, wagging his tail, telling us what a clever dog he was to have found his way back through fifty miles of jungle on his own.

The ground floor of the house, where we sat on cane chairs around a large bamboo table, was dotted with straw-lined boxes. Here an assortment of creatures were tamed or trained, according to their needs, and the invalids, with broken wings or limbs, mended as best they could in their home-made splints. Baby birds fallen from the nest were wrapped in separate bundles, and had to be fed several times a day with revolting wodges of mashed-up worms. These were stuffed straight into gaping craws with Marie's stamp-collecting tweezers. While the little monkey, who curled up on the first convenient lap, snatched up any food she could get hold of.

Our stork usually joined us for elevenses. He had been found hobbling along a jungle track with a broken wing, and brought home by my parents in the middle of the night. He protested vociferously all the time his wing was in a splint, and went on objecting to everything forever after, even when his wing had healed and he was free to go whenever he chose. But in spite of hating us all, he stayed on and joined the family. Twice a day, down by the pond, Marie threw him fish, and he caught them in mid-air, which prowess he loved to show off by joining a side on the badminton court when my parents were enjoying a game on the lawn after tea, and catching the shuttlecock as it came flying over the net. At dusk he would fly to the top of the house, squawking intermittently throughout the night.

Behind the bungalow was the hen-run, which was wired all over against hawks and other predators. But in spite of this, a ten-foot python, which had managed to squeeze through a hole in the netting, was found one morning trapped inside, unable to get out. There were four large lumps down the length of its body, where the hens it had gobbled had come to rest inside it, and these were now the cause of its undoing. Headed by Cooky waving a hatchet over his head, the house staff came running out of the kitchen whooping with glee. And that night there was a sumptuous feast in their quarters, so much more tasty than their usual bully-beef rations.

But quite apart from the unexpected snake invasions, the hen-run was never quiet. Its inmates were far more exotic than Marie's previous flock at Mas Mistral. Besides the usual hens there were ducks, geese, guinea-fowl, peahens and golden pheas-ant. But most deafening of all were the jungle-fowl. In the morning they flew down from the rubber-trees to join their friends in the hen-run. Unable to get in, they crowded at the door, screeching their heads off, so that everybody knew the jungle set had arrived for the day. Once inside, gobbling up the chicken food, they fiercely stood up to anyone who tried to get rid of them. In the evening all the fuss went into reverse, and they clamoured to be let out, growing more hysterical as night approached. As soon as the door was opened, up they flew in a great flurry back into the rubber-trees where they presumably felt quite safe.

Cooky, who produced all our meals, was a Tamil of uncertain age. Always cheerful, whatever the situation, he had a vast paunch and a jolly countenance. His kitchen was a dark tin hut completely filled with smoke, and there were usually half-a-dozen men and boys crouching on the floor, blowing on the charcoal braziers. Except for a short and blissful period when a Chinese cook took over, and spoilt us outrageously by produc-ing a different menu every day of the week, we had Cooky's curries (mutton or hard-boiled eggs) day after day all the time we were at Assam Java.

The Chinese interlude unfortunately did not last very long. One day soon after his arrival, the new cook gathered the entire staff in the backyard, and the youngest houseboy came to collect us from the coffee-trees where we were lurking at the time. He put a finger across his lips for silence and led us to the kitchen yard, where all the staff were standing in a circle around the new cook, who held a chicken in one hand and a chopper in the other. He sliced off the bird's head, then put it down on the ground. There was a rousing cheer from the whole company as the poor creature staggered forward a few feet, then collapsed in a pool of blood. At this point my mother swooped down into our midst and drove us away, spitting out a few vitriolic words in Malay over her shoulder. And that was the end of a wonderful cook. Next day fat old Cooky was back on the job with his two menus.

Behind the kitchen along a covered passage were rows of white cells, which were the houseboys' bedrooms. A whole settlement of huts and thatched cabins housed the innumerable dependants of the indoor and outdoor staff. It was a constantly changing population, all fed and housed by Papa. Nobody knew or worried how many were in residence at any time. New babies appeared and old people died. We often came across their funerals on our walks, and a jollier sight you never did see. The corpse, painted red all over, would lie on a litter of flowers carried shoulder-high by members of the family, who sang and laughed and jangled bells all the way. A good funeral was a hearty spectacle which set you up for the rest of the day.

Apart from the houseboys who were always changing because of their quarrels and their fights, the *tottegaran* pottered about the garden, squatting in front of a plant here, contemplating a new papaya shoot there, but I never saw him do any actual *work*. He watched the bananas ripen, shooed away the monkeys, picked the mangoes before they dropped to a squelch on the hard earth below, brought the luscious passion-fruit to the pantry, and somehow wriggled in among the spiky leaves to cut the pineapples at the right moment. And perhaps after all that *was* his work.

Our postman (each estate had its own postman) was a bicycle expert. When my parents were at the Club, or in Kuala Lumpur, he would give us magnificent demonstrations of all the tricks he could perform on his machine. Standing on the saddle with one foot on the handlebars, or standing on the pedals on his hands, or sitting backwards on the saddle, pedalling furiously forward. As likely as not, all this would take place on his return from the village, when the bicycle was fully loaded with the mail and mutton rations from the Selangor stores. Since the job of postman occupied only two or three hours of his day, he had plenty of time for bicycle practice, and probably made a little extra on the side by giving performances at fairs and in the bazaars.

The *tanigaran* was the water wizard. Out of a putrid pond he produced drinkable water and filled the baths every day, and so carefully did he ration the monsoon rain that there was enough for hair-washing all the year round. He wore his own hair in a little bun high up on the back of his head – as an outdoor man he didn't wear a turban, but his sarong was always clean and his beard neatly combed. He also did a turn every day at the 'laundry', standing beside the washing slab, trickling water from an old bucket onto the clothes which the *dhobi* whacked with another stone. In this manner, silk shirts and crêpe-de-chine nightdresses were mashed to a pulp in quite a short time.

Sandenam, the chauffeur, was a very superior person. He had his own quarters behind the garage, where his wives and children led a jolly and colourful existence full of song and laughter. His smile, which came frequently, was a dazzling flash of gold, as his savings all went into his teeth. The best way to avoid robbery, he used to say, was to carry your fortune in your head. So whenever he had a few dollars to spare, off he went to his Chinese dentist in Kuala Lumpur to have another gold tooth drilled into his jaw.

He was a very good driver, and understood the car well, never taking it through more flood water than it could manage. With one exception, we never broke down in the jungle – an experience best avoided. When it did happen, luck was on our side. We were free-wheeling downhill on our way back from a holiday in the mountains, screeching round hairpin bends, with the mountain on one side and on the other a sheer drop of several hundred feet into the jungle below. All at once the car dipped forward and we saw one of our wheels gaily bowling down the road ahead of us, making straight for the precipice. As we had no spare on board, we might have been stuck there all night, a welcome feast for the tigers, leopards and mountain bears of the area. There was very little traffic on that mountain road. So it was with bated breath that we watched our wheel approaching the edge.

Suddenly, out of nowhere, a low stone wall a few feet long appeared beside the road. As if guided by an invisible hand, the wheel came to rest gently against that wall. At the same moment, a lorry came chugging round the bend, and the Malay driver, seeing our problem, stopped and came over to help. He had the tools that Sandenam had forgotten to pack, so the wheel was on again in no time. But my mother, who would not let us watch the operation, marched us down the road until the job was done. It appeared the lorry-driver was a leper. His nose and top lip were missing, which gave him the fearsome look of a live and grinning skull. At this point I realised that Mamma's ban on jungle stops might well be justified.

Unlike my grandfather, who rode or drove a carriage wherever he went, Papa walked everywhere. After a cup of tea, he would set off on his rounds of the plantation, the factory, the drainage and the villages. On and on he trudged with only a stick to ward off cobras, for seven or eight hours on end, checking, examining, inspecting everything. At two o'clock he was back for lunch, and after a couple of hours' rest he would go into his office to stir up the sleeping clerks, who snoozed the day away with their feet on the typewriters.

Once a week, the workmen filed past the office window to be handed their pay-packet and rice ration. The queue was long and slow-moving, as Papa had a word with each man or woman as he gave them their wages.

Punishment for wrong-doing was dispensed on home ground in those days. Minor offences (anything up to murder) had to be dealt with on the spot and Father was, perforce, judge and executioner. So many strokes of the *rattan*, according to the offence, were administered on the lawn outside the office. And watching these thrashings from the nursery window, I remember how much more sorry we felt for Papa than for the victim. Sensitive, fastidious and withdrawn as he was, this part of his job was an ordeal. But there was no shirking it if he wanted to keep the respect of his men. The *Tuan* had to do his duty, like everybody else. His reputation as a just and good man survived the war, so that afterwards, when he was released from internment, he was allowed to walk everywhere, unarmed and unmolested, in a bandit-infested country.

Roaming the garden, for us, was the next best thing to jungle walks. We happily spent entire mornings watching the traffic around an ant's nest, or crawling along a hedge hunting caterpillars by scent, as a dog follows a badger's trail. For hours on end we watched the humming-birds in all their dazzling colours, dead still apart from the blur of their wings, 'standing' in mid-air in front of a flower. Birds of every kind fluttered around, large and small, bright and dull, whistling, squawking, screeching.

Moths and butterflies hovered like helicopters in the under-growth, and giant dragonflies scythed through the air in crazy zigzags.

The antics of the monkeys were an endless source of fascina-tion. Continually flying from tree to tree, with shrieks and howls, they would stop from time to time to nibble a twig, peel a banana, have a good scratch, or pee over our heads. Then sud-denly for no particular reason a furious uproar broke out and a glorious battle followed. The audience cheered the fighters with hysterical whoops and wild leaps through the trees. Sometimes a baby lost its grip and dropped to the ground. And you had to pretend you hadn't noticed. As soon as you were safely out of the way, the mother would come down, grab the quaking infant, shake it to a jelly, and take it up into the trees again.

The coffee-trees came into their own at blossom time. Shoulder to shoulder, so to speak, with the humming-birds, which came streaking across the garden from the hibiscus hedges where they normally lived, we hung around the flowers, breathing in the powerful smell, sneezing incessantly but unable to tear ourselves away. It was quite literally a drug, of which we could never have enough. The humming-birds obviously felt the same way, as they remained until the last flower shrivelled and died, when we all returned to our habitual occupations. The coffee seeds would then appear, and very soon turn bright red, when we helped Cooky to pick them. They were roasted in the back yard, and I am sure that there is no more divine smell in the world than freshly picked coffee roasted in the open air.

On the right side of the house was the mud-filled pond round which the stork hopefully paddled all day long in search of fish. But all it contained was a stinking mess of decayed leaves falling off the rubber-trees into the only water supply available for all household needs.

This was made fit for use in a miraculous way through my

mother's ingenuity. Several huge, porous earthenware jars, which stood in a row on the ground floor, were always kept filled to the brim with the slimy liquid. Brought in straight from the reeking pond, it was poured into the first jar, thick, brown and stinking of rotten rubber. All day and all night it oozed through the stone, filtering away, drip-drip into a bucket on the floor below it. When this was full, its contents were poured into a second container from which the liquid trickled into its own pail underneath. And so on all the way down the line, until it reached the last jar. By the time it had worked its way through to this stage, it was as clear as rainwater. My mother then added a few crystals of potassium permanganate, and the job was done. The resulting brew was mixed with fresh lime juice for our breakfast, and my parents added whisky to theirs.

Our daily bath, after the siesta, was another problem. The *tanigaran* brought us buckets of the pond's untreated contents, in which we had to soak. No amount of carbolic soap could kill the smell or dissolve the thick brown slime on our skin. Peeling it off with a towel was excruciating agony. We begged to be let off this daily torture, pointing out that we always came out more dirty and smelly than before. But no amount of pleading did any good.

There were times when a fearful commotion suddenly broke out among the workmen in the garden. The headman would come pelting across the lawn, shouting that one more Tamil had been eaten by a crocodile while drawing water from the river. Among the three or four of these monsters which patrolled our stretch of the stream there was one very old legendary brute well known to all, so gnarled and battered that he looked like a rotting tree-trunk as he lay in wait by the river bank. We often saw him there, snoozing in the mud with his tail hanging in the water, on our morning walks. He was a wily old rogue, and the workmen, who should have known better, walked straight into his jaws every time. It was a matter of constant amazement to us that anyone, especially as experienced as our workmen, could so easily be taken in by the decrepit old devil. On each occasion my father lectured the whole village at great length on the lawn, where they stood wailing and lamenting their loss. They could not believe they were to blame in any way.

Every time, over and over again, one more goat was attached to the hook which hung from the tree under which the croc lay in wait for his prey. Many of these poor creatures had been sacrificed already in the hope of catching the old brute. But experienced as he was, he always managed to pick off the goat and dodge the hook. Then suddenly one morning, soon after the end of the monsoon, the clamour in the garden announced victory instead of the usual disaster. In his dotage, the battered old monster had at last lost enough of his cunning to fall into the trap. The workmen had dragged him up to the garden, and there he sprawled, limp and dead, looking infinitely obscene. The stench of his carcass was overpowering. Somebody propped his jaws open with a stick. There was one green tooth left among the folds of yellow fat which hung about loosely all the way down to his gizzard.

When he was gutted, small bags of coins and a collection of bangles, ear-rings and various other trinkets were found in his vitals. That night there were great rejoicings in the Tamil villages. The tom-toms beat a triumphant tattoo until sunrise.

chapter eight

The tiny eggs used by Cooky for his curries were collected by the houseboys from the jungle fowls' nests in the rubber-trees. They produced such a powerful tang that not even the sharpest spices could kill their taste or smell. This treat, which turned up for children's lunch every other day, was followed by a traditional nursery pudding – frogspawn, boiled baby, squashed flies or bus accident, old Cooky's repertoire. And throughout the meal you had to keep a sharp lookout, as squirrels took flying leaps at the table, helped themselves to whatever they fancied, and were off again before you could catch them. Occasionally, unexpected contributions were added to the menu, as when a fat and meaty tail, shaken off by a lizard on a rafter above, landed in Marie's curry.

As there was no electricity in the bungalow, we had no fans. At midday the heat was unbearable. To make it possible to eat at all, the punkah was in operation throughout the meal. The youngest houseboy, stationed behind a screen, pulled a rope attached to a large palm-leaf mat which hung above the table and swung back and forth, creating a welcome draught.

Our parents' lunch, which they took after ours at two p.m., would be our left-overs. On the rare occasions (such as birthdays) when we had a meal with them, Marie would come in with a bunch of canes, which she slipped into the crooks of our arms to make sure we sat up properly during these orgies of family indulgence. This made eating difficult, and before long the canes were removed, so that by the time the pudding was handed round, we would be flopping and slouching comfortably in our chairs, as Marie so rightly feared.

At dinner the punkah was replaced by a roaring acetylene lamp, which produced our jamjar zoo creatures' supper. As malaria was a constant menace, and mosquitoes were out on their rounds in clouds by the evening, we wore sarongs sewn into bags to keep the scourge off our legs during dinner. Marie, climbing into her mosquito bag respectfully held open for her by the head houseboy, was a solemn sight.

At the end of the meal we would troop upstairs, keeping well away from the banisters as usual, and, bearing our burnt-offerings of fried insects, tip-toe into the sitting-room, where Mamma would be stitching away at her embroidery and Papa playing the piano, with the usual mournful look on his Gothic features. Here was another and smaller version of the dining-room lamp, against which insects obligingly sizzled themselves to death, providing still more treats for our friends in the nursery.

It was a secure and cosy scene, with the black night brooding outside, punctuated by the hooting of owls, the occasional bark of a leopard, or the roar of a tiger, sinister rustling sounds, and sometimes the trumpeting of elephants. And always in the background, the beating of the tom-toms in the Tamil villages. We had to keep still and were not allowed to talk. We could draw or look at picture-books, as long as we turned the pages quietly.

When grown-up dinner was announced, Marie collected us to get ready for bed. We washed and undressed, then sat around the nursery table. We would go on scribbling in our drawing-books, while Marie drowsily read out items from old copies of *Punch* or the *Straits Times*. Sometimes we came across stories and verses written by my father. We always felt very proud of this, even though we didn't understand a word she read. English was still complete gibberish to us. On and on she droned, dropping off to sleep, waking up with a snort to resume her reading with her head on one side, her good eye aimed at the page. Then one day, to our intense amazement, we were fascinated to hear her read a perfectly intelligible account of the King of England's funeral out of the *Straits Times*. This was a revelation. A breakthrough into a new dimension. I have never understood how it happened. One day, suddenly and totally without warning, an unknown language had become intelligible, and we were even able to speak it.

From then on our evening sessions around the nursery table were a new experience every night. We learnt that Chinese pirates, sailing up the river, had forced a Tamil woman to swallow a live snake, and cut off the fingers of several others who wouldn't hand over their rings. While a planter's wife had shaken an arm off her cook, who was riddled with jungle-rot. As well as countless other improbable stories of a similar nature. In spite of this new interest, Anne's head would suddenly fall on her scribbling-pad with a heavy thud, and she would be carried off to bed. Then Marie would start to read again, nod and snore, shake herself awake, and bundle us crossly off to bed.

It was around this time that the rats began to appear. They had a habit, with which nobody interfered, of scuttling nonchalantly around the bungalow, getting to the table before us at meals, and helping themselves to the choicest morsels. They escorted us to the nursery after dinner, snarled, bared their teeth, and bent back their whiskers when we refused to let them in. The final straw came when Marie found her new-born Leghorn chicks nibbled away to beak and claw. She immediately ordered poison from the Kuala Lumpur stores, and distributed slices of toast spread with cyanide all over the bungalow, under beds and wardrobes, on window ledges, and wherever else she could think of. And it was one of these poisoned crusts that Anne picked up one day, and was just about to chew when Marie snatched it from her jaws and threw it out of the window. Anne's life was saved, but it was decreed that someone had to die that day. The little household monkey, who was sitting out-side popping her fleas, picked it up, and was dead within the hour.

The nights were seldom undisturbed. We were quite often woken up by some unexpected commotion or disaster of one kind or another. It might be just the roar of a man-eating tiger prowling round the bungalow or the Tamil villages, the tom-toms celebrating a birth, a death, or the unexpected arrival of a relative from Southern India.

From time to time, without warning, a forest fire broke out in the middle of the night. On one unforgettable occasion we were woken up by an appalling racket – the banging of tom-toms all round the bungalow, and the most terrifying yells and screams we had ever heard. Thinking all the devils of the jungle were converging on the house, we leaped out of bed in a panic.

The factory was on fire, and thousands of tons of sheet rubber were going up in flames. There had been no rain for many months, and there was no water to put out the fire. It was an awe-inspiring sight. A huge barrage of flames rose straight into the sky, bursting and rattling like machine-gun fire. Papa had the gong banged for silence, and harangued the multitude from the verandah. As he spoke in Tamil, we didn't understand much of what he said, but the main message was to chop down all the trees within reach of the blaze.

And off they all went at a gallop.

The chopping and burning went on all night. Nobody thought of sending us to bed. We watched until sunrise, when the flames finally changed to black, reeking fumes, rolling slowly in the still dawn. The awful smell of burnt rubber hung about for days, making us all feel queasy and quite incapable of swallowing our curries and boiled babies.

Another fearful night, the devil whom I had tempted came out of the jungle and grabbed me by the shoulders as I lay on my bed in the dark. I could blame no one but myself. Marie had warned us many times that if we ever looked into a mirror, we would see the devil sitting on our shoulder.

On one of my prowls around the bungalow, I had come across a hand mirror on my mother's dressing-table. Picking it up without much thought, I was surprised to see my face in it. Realising what I had done, I put it down with a shudder and ran out of the room. Next day I found myself creeping back, inch by inch, to the same spot. Temptation was too strong, and I had another quick look. Not the slightest glimmer or suspicion of the devil. And I regret to say that day after day I went back to that confounded looking-glass.

The devil never appeared on my shoulder, but the night of his visit was the most terrifying experience of my life. Poor Marie, who thought I was having a fit, tried to calm me down as I thrashed about on my bed, hysterical with fear, in a state of utter panic. The devil, sitting on my chest, was hacking away, trying to claw the soul out of my throat.

This little interlude ruled out all further experiments with mirrors for many years to come. The abominations were strictly banned from our living quarters. There were none in the nursery, nor (Heaven forbid!) in the bathroom. When I next caught sight of my reflection, many years later, I was surprised to see how different I looked.

Vanity was Marie's bugbear, and she was going to make sure of stamping out its ugly head in our souls before it had a chance of getting a grip on us. People at the Selangor Club, to which we would go sometimes, in the misguided hope of mollifying her well-known ferocity, sometimes passed remarks about our looks, or our clothes, or our good behaviour. This would immediately conjure up her most severe and frosty countenance, and with her piercing blue eye directed at me, she would answer in her coldest tones, 'They are plain, naughty and difficult. A regular handful, and nothing to be proud of.' And with that she would give me a sharp prod and shove me away, in case the speaker should be so unwise as to say anything nice about *me.* And so fanatical was she about this that we were very seldom allowed to wear the delicate muslin dresses which my mother enjoyed embroidering for us. 'Putting ideas into their heads,' she would mutter, as she stuffed them away into the nursery cupboard. As Titi had made her nest there, it was her chicks who eventually enjoyed our embroidered frocks, stamping around all over the delicate fabric and sleeping among their soft folds.

The main reason why the factory had caught fire and gone up in flames so quickly was the terribly dry state of the land and vegetation in our district. After months of searing sunshine, the soil was baked like pottery and parcelled out into sections with inch-wide cracks between them.

On the day when the monsoon was expected to break, we stood outside on the lawn waiting for it. Our excitement grew as the black clouds rolled and merged around like a gigantic cake mixture. Then, again and again, flashes of lightning ripped the sky from end to end and the crashing of thunder grew closer, until it boomed and exploded overhead. Gravel rattled along the drive, and the loose red dust was blown into great sweeps up into the trees, which writhed and groaned and whimpered as huge branches were wrenched off and carried away by the wind. All life was dying off. The animals went to ground, where they would be drowned in their holes and their earths by the thousand.

When the electric storm had thundered around the sky long enough, the clouds opened up and down came the rain. It was as if an ocean in the upper layers had suddenly lost its bottom and was dropping to the earth. Within a few minutes, floods were running through the ground floor, with the cane furniture floating out into the back yard.

The roaring of the sky increased to such a deafening clamour that you could hardly hear the claps of thunder above the general tumult. During a particularly frightening storm one year, when we were huddled at the top of the staircase watching the tables and chairs bobbing about on the swirling waters, we were called to the drawing-room and ordered to get down on our knees and pray for the house to be spared. The great mango-tree on the lawn had just received a direct hit, split down the middle by a thunderbolt. Half of it leaned over and was soon wrenched away by the wind. Marie, who had seen, in our grandparents' house in Sydney, a thunderbolt sail in through the window and scorch its way down the centre of a dinner-party table, knew all about storms and their ways. So down on our knees we went, praying for all we were worth, with one eye open for the thunderbolt.

Bungalows sometimes had their roofs blown off during the monsoon. We were lucky, as the wind only ever swept away bits of our thatch here and there, through which the rain came splashing down all over the nursery. We seldom got much sleep at this time of year; we had to trundle our beds around every time a new hole appeared overhead.

In the morning the ground floor was covered with stinking ooze, and heaving with worms and leeches. Small corpses were scattered everywhere. The houseboys spent most of the day scraping, brushing and swilling away the mud. When it was cleaned up, and order more or less restored, the houseboys placed saucers of milk on the floor, in strategic places, for the snakes who might pay us a visit. Mamma tried to discourage this. But Marie assured her that snakes came in for my father's evening concerts of Bach, Beethoven and Wagner, and *not* for the milk. As I have always heard that snakes are deaf, I don't see how Marie could have been right on this occasion.

If it hadn't been for the monsoon, followed by malaria, our education would have suffered even more than it did.

From time to time, after the morning walk, Mamma would call us in for lessons. The sound of her voice was usually the signal for us to race across the garden and hide among the coffee-trees until all danger was past. So she had to rely on malaria, which usually struck after a sufficient number of bites from the female Anopheles, which swarmed in great clouds at the end of the monsoon. For the first few days we lay flat on our backs, shivering with acute misery, and completely out of action. When the quinine began to take effect, we settled down to a period of 'low fever', singing ears and helpless weakness. It was at this point that my mother saw her chance and grabbed it.

Wobbly and helpless, we were herded into the mosquito cage on the verandah, from which there was no escape. As we hadn't the strength to resist, it was there that education caught up with us at last. We learned to count and add up with matchsticks, and how to measure surfaces. We drew pictures of the Red Sea opening up to let the bands of Moses through. And in the end, we even learned to read – in French.

After this there was no keeping me away from books. I had

broken through to another dimension, and there seemed no end to the joys ahead. I worked my way through *Larousse*, from which I picked up all sorts of fascinating information of every possible kind.

The next step was to read English. Although I could now speak and understand it without trouble, I was surprised how difficult it was to read. In the end, the only way I could make it was by trial and error – pronouncing the written words aloud in various ways until I recognised them and they made sense. From then on I was launched – and constantly in trouble, with my nose stuck in a book when I should have been doing something else.

chapter nine

Ti Vali was the Tamils' annual religious festival. Around midday the entire workforce would gather on the lawn in front of the bungalow. We sat on garden chairs opposite the assembled company, and the headman hung garlands of hibiscus flowers around our necks. There were speeches in Tamil, followed by magic turns, and all kinds of stunts were laid on for our benefit throughout the afternoon. I am not sure if the rope trick was ever performed at one of these shows, or if I saw it elsewhere. But one extraordinary performance was staged by a hypnotised man, who lay flat on the point of a sword which was stuck in the ground and stood straight up in the air. Stiff as a board and hardly breathing, he lay there fast asleep for the rest of the afternoon. The show went on around him, with men swallowing fire and others pushing daggers down their throats – with never a drop of blood to be seen.

I don't think fire-walking ever took place in our garden, but I remember watching it at the Selangor Club. A trench about fifteen feet long and six feet wide was dug out of the ground and filled with burning charcoal. And over this, barefoot, strolled a young man in a white sarong. He showed us his feet at the end of the stretch, and they were not even scorched. Since then I have heard that this trick can be mastered by anyone who really wants to learn it.

Christmas was also a great time for celebrations. Although it never felt quite right, we did our best to make it as convincing as possible. We would set off to the edge of the jungle in the old Fiat, armed with saws and choppers. There we would hunt for the most likely Christmas tree we could find. As there are no pines in the tropics, we had to compromise and make do with the nearest thing we came across. Eventually we settled for the most likely bush, usually covered with thorns, spikes, hooks and claws, all quite useful for hanging decorations. By the time it was finally set up on the verandah under the stars, sprinkled with puffs of cotton-wool, and dozens of candles flickering against the pitch-black background of the rubber-trees, you could practically imagine yourself in front of the real thing.

As we all gathered round, Mamma sat down at the piano and played French, English and German carols, which she sang in French, while Marie piped away in German. Next morning, on Christmas day, the tree looked as if it had been hit by a hurricane. Rats, busy scrambling all over it throughout the night, had nibbled away the decorations, the nuts and the sweets, and every single candle, down to the last scrap of wax they could find.

After the presents were handed out we all trooped down to the dining-room to have lunch together, as one of the special treats of the year.

In the afternoon there was a children's party at the Selangor Club where the tree, probably a fake pine brought over from

Europe for the purpose, was surrounded by mountains of presents for us all. I remember Father Christmas arriving in an open car stuffed with parcels, honking his way through the surrounding jungle. Tea, a magnificent spread of Christmas cake, jam tarts, chocolates and all kinds of sweets and other delights, was much looked forward to, as these commodities were all severely rationed at home. The only sweets we ever got were sticks of barley sugar which came out of square jars, handy for pickling centipedes and scorpions for Marie's collection. And I suspect barley sugar was only allowed because of the convenient size and shape of bottles.

Whether it was Christmas, a birthday party, or any other afternoon treat, Marie dreaded our visits to the Selangor Club as much as we looked forward to them. Once there, it was impossible for her to keep us away from other children. So on the rare occasions when our parents invited us to join them, we were overjoyed. And after they and the other Club members had gone off to play golf or tennis, their little angels looked around for trouble, and drew together to commit their abominations. One of our young friends, Judy Harding, led us into endless adventures. We followed her everywhere, regardless of the consequences. She organised visits to the kitchen, where the houseboys fed us on forbidden grown-up delicacies. She set up blissful paddling parties in the fish-pond. And she would chop up earthworms and swallow the pieces. Pulling down her knickers, little Judy Harding would show us her bottom for a cent a peep, and stuck out her tongue at any grown-up who dared to object.

Her pluck when in pain was awe-inspiring. When she had to have the anti-rabies injections which we all dreaded, and she could only hobble around, doubled-up in agony, she dismissed the whole thing as if it was nothing at all. She was a great girl. But she found no favour in Marie's eyes.

*

From time to time an invitation came up for a fancy-dress party, a social occasion we dreaded beyond all others, as we hated dressing up. But my mother, who was a real needlework artist, enjoyed creating our costumes. Once, much against my will, I was made into a powder-box, and Anne was the powder-puff, with bits of swansdown stitched all over her skirt.

However embarrassed and absurd we felt in our get-up, there was no way out of the ordeal. As for my mother, totally unconscious of our misery, she was delighted when her work turned out to be a success. There were a great many pirates and fairies around, but no other powder-box or powder-puff in sight. To Marie of course, this was nothing more than our usual showing-off and craving for attention. In this case, the last thing we wanted was attention.

At other times, quite as unwelcome, for me anyway, we were rigged out in some of Mamma's daintiest creations (from Titi's nest in the cupboard) and driven over to dancing classes in Selangor. I remember thumping my way through a loathsome number called 'Basket of flowers' to the tune of 'Tea for Two', ground out of an old gramophone. Feeling like an elephant with sore feet myself, I noticed Anne suddenly getting carried away, hopping up and down in all her finery. She looked like a hibiscus flower blowing about in the wind.

Mamma made most of our everyday dresses as well, or rather she cut them out, and handed them over to the Chinese tailor who came once a month to finish them off. But apart from this, and her embroidery, she had very little to do, and time must have dragged for her. The rich life of the garden and the jungle, which sustained us entirely, meant very little to her. All her interests lay in people and human contacts. Given the chance, she could have talked forever. Papa's unrelenting silences must have been very frustrating. In the evenings, when they lay on their chaises longues before dinner with their whiskies, and my father was buried in a book, she would hazard a few remarks, which were invariably answered in the same way: 'Mmm?' And she had to be content with this, as nothing else ever came. During the day she played the piano a great deal. Chopin was her favourite; and we were turned inside out when she played and sang Gounod's 'Ave Maria'. To this day it sends shivers down my spine just to remember it. She also knew all the French popular *chansons*, music and words, by heart, and these she sang when, forgetting she was British, nostalgia for her country overwhelmed her. These songs were mostly stirring and patriotic and had a good deal to do with devotion to duty and heroic death. Some of them reduced us to tears. There was one in which a poor carrier-pigeon, flying over German-occupied Alsace, was shot in the breast by a fiendish soldier, but flew on, bleeding slowly to death, until he reached his post and delivered his message, dying in the hands of the officer who received him. Another described the harrowing end of a young girl dying of consumption, while her small brother, believing that she would die when the last autumn leaf touched the ground, spent his time trying to catch them as they fell.

Sitting on pouffes around the piano stool, we clustered around Mamma, stirred right down to the ends of our toes by her clear high voice and the sadness of the songs, with great tears rolling down our fat cheeks. Then, feeling thoroughly set up by this orgy of sentimentality, and with the unconscious but implacable cruelty of children, we left her to her own tears and clattered down the stairs to race round the garden with the low-flying swallows, or bats, or whatever they happened to be.

Sometimes, when the worst heat of the day was over, we all climbed into the old Fiat and set off for Jeram, our favourite beach on the west coast. This fishing village, a few huts on stilts at the mouth of the river, numbered a dozen or so Malay families, whose entire livelihood came out of the sea. Huge piles of rotting fish-bones all round the village could be smelt miles away. But the appalling stench didn't seem to disturb the residents in the least.

We drove past the huts towards the long white beach lined with mangroves and coconut-trees, some of which grew right down to the edge of the water. The warm sea in which we wallowed was full of life of every kind. It swarmed with crabs and small, extraordinary fish which crawled out of the water and hopped about all over the beach, puffing themselves up to the size of a golf-ball. These were so numerous and generally popular that they were made into toys and sold in all the bazaars of the area. There was also a kind of prehistoric-looking shellfish with a long razor-sharp tail. The fishermen said there was a poison in the end of the tail which either killed you outright or gave you four days of high fever. The Malays cooked these 'handbag crabs', as we called them, on the beach for their supper, placing them upside-down on the flames like frying pans. Their eggs, bright-red and the size of peas, were picked out and eaten one by one.

But most curious of all was a species of silver-coloured fish that wobbled out of the water on their fins. Hopping across the sand, they shinned up the first coconut tree they came across. I have never discovered what they did when they got to the top. Perhaps, like salmon, they returned to their birthplace to spawn, and the trees were crowned with their nests.

The shallows in which we splashed and paddled were heaving with sea-snakes, wriggling all round in the foam. No one ever went into the water without a couple of stones to hurl in self-defence. I made a direct hit once, catching a couple which were gracefully weaving around each other by my knees. The waves suddenly ran red with blood. This put me off bathing for quite a long time. Although these snakes were supposed to be as deadly as cobras, we never had any serum with us – there was probably no such thing at the time. And anyway, the stones we carried were perfectly adequate, as none of us was ever bitten.

There were snakes in the sand as well, so that the delightful pastime of digging and castle-building lost some of its appeal. At dusk we sat on logs of driftwood and watched the swarms of hermit crabs popping out of the sand and dragging their shells down to the sea. After paddling about in the Indian Ocean for a while, they scrambled out again and fussily dug themselves back into their holes.

When the sky began to turn crimson, as the sun dipped into the sea on the horizon, we all climbed back into the car for the long drive home to Assam Java, through the creepy gloom of the darkening jungle. And we were limp and drugged with sleep when we finally made it to the bungalow.

Although we loved our garden and the daily walks through the estate, the monthly visits to Kuala Lumpur were a great treat, in spite of the agonies of car-sickness. And because our parents would never allow the car to stop in the jungle, the dogs and I, crammed in the front seat, spent most of the journey hanging over the side, being sick in the wind.

On one of these trips we suddenly saw a large cobra snaking its way out of the ditch towards the road. The snake and Sandenam, the chauffeur, caught sight of each other at the same time, and both instantly put on a terrific turn of speed. They met head-on in the middle of the track, with the front wheels cutting the snake into three pieces. There was a thump and a hideous crunching sound as the tail came whipping up the side of the car. The chauffeur whooped with glee, and I was sick once more at the sight and sound of it all.

But as soon as I staggered onto firm ground again I recovered very quickly. We got out at Raffles Hotel and swept up the front steps, feeling very grand. They were so different from our own shaky, worm-eaten staircase at home, festooned with centipedes and spiders, and always threatening to collapse under our feet.

A houseboy, all gleaming and crackling with starch, led us to a large bedroom with a private bath and its very own verandah. After soaking in pure, clear water (no stinking rubber slime here) we changed into fresh clothes and were marched down the corridor to the barber's shop. By then feeling quite well again, I was looking forward to the pleasures of the day.

The hair-cutting session was a boring but necessary evil, after which we set out into the glaring heat, which slapped you in the face like a hot pancake. We climbed into a rickshaw for our usual drive around the town and a visit to Whiteway Laidlaw's stores to restock on our crayons and painting gear, while Marie bought yards of elastic for our silk bloomers, cotton for the sewing-machine, and fresh supplies of Zambuk. Stowing all these treasures away in the rickshaw, we told our runner to take us to the river, our favourite spot in town. There we spent the rest of the morning watching the bustling water traffic, the loading and unloading of sampans, rolling up of fishing-nets and sorting out of catches, and men and beasts at their ablutions. It was reassuring for us to see our rickshaw man sitting at peace under a tree, getting his wind back, enjoying the rest, and knowing he was getting paid for it. As everybody knew, he and his colleagues had all had their spleens taken out, so they could run for miles without getting puffed. Until one day, without notice, they would drop dead between the shafts of their rickshaws.

Elephants shambled up to the river and stepped daintily into the murky shallows, where they let themselves down carefully on their knees, then rolled over on one side to wallow in the warm mud. Their small boy-keepers, aged about five, climbed onto their bulging flanks and set to work with scrubbing-brushes. Meanwhile the great beasts obligingly squirted jets of water to rinse away the loosened dirt. They lolled about, enjoying the scratch and tickle and the devoted attention of their mini-grooms.

We would rejoin our parents at Raffles for two o'clock lunch. Marie attended these meals without her hat, which made her feel terribly underdressed. To make up for it, she wore a wide silver-studded black velvet ribbon around her neck. Her blue and white check uniform was so stiffly starched that it stood out around her like a parachute. On those occasions, for some obscure reason, she felt it was 'her place' to speak German only, and pretend to understand no other language.

On one of these Kuala Lumpur expeditions I was taken straight to the hospital instead of the Club. As nothing had been said, I was terrified when a nurse took me by the hand and dragged me away from Marie. I was taken off and dumped on a bed surrounded by powerful searchlights aiming their alarming prongs straight into my face. A mask came down over my mouth, and I clawed away at it in a panic. They managed to fix it on at last, with three nurses holding me down, while I screamed and struggled in a state of absolute terror, until the gas did its work and I mercifully passed out. But I regret to say I gave those nurses a terrible time before they managed to put me under. When I finally came round, one of the nurses was holding up a small object covered with blood on the end of a pair of tweezers.

'There you are,' she said, 'there's your tooth. And you never felt a thing, did you?'

I stared at it in amazement, and fell back in horror and confusion. All that fuss, fear and panic for pulling out one miserable tooth! I liked to imagine afterwards that I might have behaved better if they had told me what was going to happen. But I couldn't be sure.

A totally undeserved reward was waiting for me on the back seat of the car – a beautiful doll, almost as large as myself, with a delicate china face, eyes which opened and closed, and walking legs. I kept her carefully through my teens, and somehow throughout the upheavals of the war as well, hoping that one day I would have a daughter of my own, who would treasure her as much as I did. But by the time this came about, fashionable dolls were made of pink plastic, with fibreglass wigs and high pointing bosoms. Mine belonged to a different world.

On another occasion, after a period of prolonged disobedience and misbehaviour on our part, it was decided to give us a good fright.

There was a boarding school in Kuala Lumpur that Marie had told us about, which she said served as a kind of prison for unruly children. We had been threatened with this on several occasions, and now it seemed the time had come to do something about it. So on our next visit to Kuala Lumpur we were bundled into a rickshaw and off we set in fearful trepidation to visit our would-be jail.

The building itself, all red brick and corrugated tin, was forbidding enough. But the garden all round more than made up for it. Filled with purple hibiscus, banana trees in bloom, and palms smothered in flowering orchids, it was a living paradise. Brightly coloured birds and enormous butterflies flapped around in great numbers. And on the lawn was a group of Chinese and Eurasian children playing a lively game of blindman's buff. And not a whipping-post in sight.

Apart from the head nun who came out to greet us, we saw no other European. She was completely charming, and moved with great dignity and purpose, like a well-trimmed ship. She showed us round the school, and we followed her through the classrooms, the dormitories, dining-room and the kitchen. From time to time we asked, 'And where is the prison?' or 'When can we see your jail?' At which Marie growled, 'Be quiet. Behave yourselves.'

At the end of our visit, the nun took us to a large cupboard and handed out a brand-new toy to each one of us. I forget what John and Anne got, but I was given a mechanical monkey pulling a barrow-load of mangosteens. Feeling puzzled and thoroughly confused, we thanked her politely for her kindness, and Marie whisked us back to our rickshaw in silence. There was no more talk of boarding school after that. Back we went to Assam Java, to our idle, wicked and blissful existence.

chapter ten

Two or three times a year, when we felt even more crushed by the
heat than usual, Mamma and Papa would send us all off to 'the
Hills' to cool off. We would drive to Bukit Frazer, a holiday station
up in the mountains where Europeans from all over the peninsula
retreated whenever they could spare the time. For us this meant
two or three glorious weeks, a change of routine, and most appeal-
ing of all, the chance of meeting 'other children'. We were always
despatched in advance with the luggage, after which Sandenam
would return to collect our parents two or three days later.

We would set off at dawn, before the heat of the day settled on
the plain. The old Fiat was loaded to the roof with trunks, cases
and hampers, picnic baskets and flasks of lukewarm lime-juice.
Our entire menagerie was on board with us as well. This
included the dogs, a mongoose or two (in case of cobras), the
little monkey (until killed by rat poison), and Titi the hen.
Various invalids were strapped in their splints, the tortoises
groaned and scrabbled in their cardboard box, and of course

there were the inevitable jars of tarantulas and scorpions, as the servants couldn't be trusted to look after them at home.

The journey took all day. We would arrive after dark and unload by torchlight. The nights were much cooler than on the plain, and it was delicious luxury to snuggle into pullovers and woolly scarves. Our happiness would have overflowed if it had suddenly started to snow.

On one of these visits, our cousins, who were sharing our bungalow with us, were so wild they had to have a man to look after them instead of the usual ayah. We all behaved so badly that Marie transferred us to a small house on the edge of the jungle, as far away from our lively cousins as possible. But it turned out to be a case of out of the frying-pan, as a panther prowled around the house every night in search of an open window. And we had no idea how long the shutters would survive when charged by a two-hundredweight battering-ram of hungry panther. The houseboys assured us that big cats didn't much like child meat, although they would make do with it if nothing else was available. In this case it was probably the dogs they were after.

The best time of day at Bukit Frazer was the early morning, when huge warm clouds of steam rolled out of the jungle, and the air was so sodden with mist you could almost scoop up the moisture in your hands. The pugmarks of bears which had padded around the house during the night proved how close they had come. When after a short early morning trek we came back for breakfast, we were greeted by the most delicious smells in the world, smoked haddock, fried bacon or kippers. Here at Bukit Frazer we had a real English breakfast for the first time in our lives. Even the coarse and lumpy porridge was welcome and satisfying.

After breakfast came the jungle walks, infinitely more eventful than our tame mornings around Assam Java. On one occasion we walked down the mountain in search of a giant death's-head moth which lived in the darkest part of the forest. For several hours we struggled through the most impenetrable greenery we had ever seen. Giant monkey cups, enormous tree-ferns wrapped in creepers and climbing orchids struggled for space with huge scaly palms entangled in lianas like fishing-nets. By then we were covered with leeches clamped onto our bare arms and legs, while their hindquarters, filled with blood, waved up and down behind them like tassels. And there they had to stay until we got back. For if you tear a leech off your skin you go on bleeding to death, as only they can seal off the wound with their spit, to keep the remaining blood supply intact for future needs.

Suddenly Marie realised we had lost our way. The opening we had made through the jungle had closed behind us, leaving no sign of our struggles.

We were about to turn back on what we hoped were our tracks when the sound of browsing elephant could suddenly be heard among the trees. Frozen with fear, we stopped dead on the spot and stared at Marie. The sounds of tearing and wrenching, munching, rumbling and belching were approaching. I wondered why Marie didn't make us run for it. So far the herd were unaware of our presence. And I thought we could have got away, as they were moving very slowly. But she probably assumed they would hear us crashing through the undergrowth and that this would enrage them. She knew the sudden anger of disturbed elephants and their insane reaction to unexpected intrusion, particularly if they have young with them, when they trample and tear apart everything in their path.

We stood there dead still, hardly breathing, for an extremely long time. At last, gradually and very slowly, the sounds began to recede. The elephants had turned aside, and were moving in another direction. We kept still until they were out of hearing.

Under the stress of their presence, Marie's sense of direction had returned, and we trudged homeward in silence, without seeing our death's-head, but with a multitude of unwanted leeches instead. It took us a long time to ease them off with salt, as we couldn't bring ourselves to sizzle them up with cigarette-ends, which would have been much quicker. That day we fell on our lunch with more than our usual voracity. There is nothing like a good strong Madras curry for setting you up after a fright.

On our next expedition into the thickest part of the jungle, Marie was taking no more chances, and she hired a guide for the day. This time we were after human quarry. She wanted to see the Sakaïs, the last of the Aboriginal tribes who have been living in the jungles of the Malayan peninsula since prehistoric times – and haven't changed since then.

These naked, diminutive people, sometimes described as 'forest dwarves', have survived all the efforts of successive invaders to eliminate them. The Sakaïs now live in small nomadic groups, spread out all over the jungle, isolated from one another and from the rest of humanity. They have found this the most successful way of life for continued survival. Living entirely on the resources of their surroundings, they hunt and ward off enemies with blow-pipes and poisoned arrows, which they have been using since earliest times. The darts are dipped in the sap of the upas-tree, whose lethal qualities last for a couple of months. As the Sakaïs know how to remain invisible, and their arrows are shot through a hollow tube in complete silence, it is impossible to find them unless they themselves want to manifest. According to legend, they have learnt how to vanish on the spot, a trick they picked up in order to escape from the Hantu Hutan, the evil spirits of the jungle.

There are innumerable theories on the origins and present way of life of the Sakaïs. So Marie decided to find out what she could for herself, and off we set in the wake of our guide for the day. Following in his footsteps, we scrambled through a barrage of leaves and creepers so dense that a fly would have had trouble finding a way through. But our man hacked to right and left with his kris, and we wriggled on.

We came across several sites where fires had been hastily stamped out, a sure give-away. But although we searched the clearings and scrutinised the trees, we saw nothing more than the odd python and a couple of sloths hanging upside down, fast asleep with their claws wrapped around a branch. There were also a few bats snoozing the day away, but not a glimmer of a Sakaï. The guide told us that they were definitely around. As they obviously had no wish to materialise, however, we never caught a glimpse of them. And to this day we still don't know what a Sakaï looks like. It was a great disappointment.

For some mysterious reason, it was always in the Hills that the miseries of jungle rot came to a festering head. The trouble, which started with the slightest scratch or cut, was held in abeyance on the plain with regular applications of Zambuk, our magic cure-all ointment. But as soon as we arrived at Bukit Frazer, its power dwindled and the rot spread with alarming speed.

The daily visits to the local chemist for dressings were torture, and would have been quite unbearable but for one bright spot. On the counter, reigning among the cough mixtures, the purges and aphrodisiacs (snakes' guts from Assam Java?), inside a jar of methylated spirits, sat an enormous, horny, mottled toad as large as a pumpkin. This ineffably beautiful and desirable creature kept us going throughout the ordeal of the dressings. Marie ogled it as enviously as we did. And on the last day of our visit to the Hills, she came out of the shop bearing the jar with the toad inside it. I have no idea how she managed to persuade the Chinese chemist to part with his treasure. But it came back to

Assam Java with us and took the place of honour on the nursery shelves. Zambuk's power was restored, and our horrible jungle rot, of which I still have the scars on my elbows and ankles, simmered down to manageable proportions again.

Back at Assam Java, life seemed rather tame and flat after our stimulating jaunts around Bukit Frazer. Our first outing after our return would be a visit to church. And this was no great treat.

The service was held in a wooden hut with a tin roof, onto which rubber seeds falling off the trees above bounced and rattled like grapeshot. We sat on rickety benches in rows around the altar, while the congregation, which the priest had managed to capture that morning, crouched on the earthen floor, chewing betel nut and spewing thin red jets of spit several feet away in front of them. But kindly and considerate as they were, these people aimed at the spaces between the heads, and nobody was ever hit.

The air was hot and steamy, and infinitely smelly. There was no music, no hymns, just the monotonous chanting of the priest, and the nasal responses of the congregation. It was a relief to get out, when small booths and shop-windows strapped to bicycle handlebars arrived just in time to catch us at the end of the service. As this was our only chance in the week of spending our pocket-money, we made a bee-line for them. There were tiny celluloid models of tigers, elephants, and the small puffer fish which hopped about on the beaches all round the coast. And various carved and hand-painted miniature objects – Japanese dolls in kimonos and complicated hair-dos, Chinese sunshades made of oiled paper, bamboo flutes, silk parachutes strapped to toy monkeys, and a multitude of glass bangles of every possible colour. You could get the latter for a cent a dozen. John frequently bought great numbers of them. One day Mamma asked him who they were for.

'They are for my daughters,' he said briefly.

'Oh, you are going to have daughters?'

'Yes,' he replied. 'I am going to have four.' And he did, in due course, have the four very charming daughters for whom he had been collecting bangles since early childhood.

chapter eleven

One fine day without warning, Marie suddenly announced: 'We are going back to Vence, and I want you to sort out your toys.'

Coming out of the blue as it did, it was quite a shock. When we recovered, we realised what she meant. What she was really saying, of course, was 'You will have to give most of your treasures away.' Then she added, 'You can just keep a few of your favourite things. I want you to put them on your bed straight after breakfast, as they will have to be packed by the end of the day.'

We collected as many of our dearest belongings as would fit on our beds, knowing quite well that only a few would be picked out for packing, and all the rest given away to the estate children. But as the thought of going back to Mas Mistral filled us with excitement, parting with most of our possessions seemed small hardship. The only disappointment about returning to Europe was that our father was staying behind. Once more we would be parted from him for months, perhaps even years.

The sad day came only too soon. Apart from a few boring, innocuous storms there were no excitements, and we never got the shipwreck we were all secretly hoping for on the voyage home.

Soon after our arrival at Mas Mistral, Mamma disappeared one day without warning. As there was nothing unusual in this, we took it in our stride. What did surprise us much more was the arrival of an unexpected guest, who had apparently come to look after us during Mamma's absence. As Marie had always done this job herself, and we could never have been happier with anyone else, we were much relieved when she stayed on with us. So we had no real objection to Mrs G's arrival, especially as she came equipped with a small daughter of our own age, and a delightful chow who joined in all our games.

John, who had recently seen a blind man being led by a guide dog, decided to train the poor chow for the job, in case one of us should suddenly need it. And day after day we would come across them padding round the garden, Fang with his black tongue hanging out of his mouth in utter boredom, and John with his eyes tight shut, hanging onto the dog's collar. This went on until the poor creature, finally overcome by the heat, thirst and general weariness, suddenly turned and nicked a small chunk out of John's left ear. Not surprisingly, there was a good deal of bleeding. Marie always maintained that ear lobes were little bags of reserve blood, like spare fat in a camel's hump. From that moment on, poor Fang had to be chained up, as the fear of rabies was always uppermost in people's minds. And according to Marie, this was most likely to strike during the hot summer months, when milk turned sour in the human breast and dogs went mad.

In Molly, Mrs G's daughter, we finally had a companion on the spot. John and his damaged ear were removed to another room, and Moll, as we called her, joined Anne and myself in the night-nursery. It was pure joy to have a friend on tap day and night, and we chattered excitedly for hours on end. No punishment, however severe, could stop our endless flow. Mrs G, who wandered in and out of the nursery as she pleased, was another cause of aggravation for poor Marie, who regarded this as her own exclusive privilege.

Mrs G was kind, serene and equable, and for the first time in our lives we received a daily ration of chocolate – minute red-wrapped slabs, enclosing a picture, which we saved up to stick into a book specially made for the purpose. When one of these books was filled up, the grocer exchanged it for a toy which we were allowed to choose from the storeroom at the back of the shop. Marie deplored this wanton spoiling and could hardly wait for Mrs G, her Molly and her choc rations to depart.

One very hot afternoon in early August we were ordered upstairs and kitted out in our best white clothes, then bundled into one of Papa's buses to Nice. And there we were marched off to a nursing home, where we were amazed to find Mamma lying in bed with a cradle beside her, containing, we were told, our new baby sister!

When they finally came home, Christine was installed in Marie's bedroom, which became the new night-nursery. Her baby days were spent in the wobbly old pram under the cherry-tree on the terrace. But in spite of constant and devoted attention, our new sister did a terrible lot of screaming, especially at night. The noise was so loud and overpowering that it finally came to drown the sound of Marie's snores, to which I had become so accustomed that they no longer woke me up. As this went on night after night, I crept down the corridor in the dark to see what I could do about it. I felt sure that Christine must be desperately unhappy. I rocked her, shook her and tried whistling to her, all without success. Until eventually I hit on a magic formula, which worked from then on without fail. Leaning over her cot, I blew on her face, which surprised her into instant silence – until I ran out of breath, when she set up her howling again. So night after night, for what seemed like months, I managed to keep her quiet. Although by the time I got back to bed I felt dazed, and my head was spinning and aching, I thought it was well worth the effort to stop that fiendish noise. From then on I applied the method whenever and wherever necessary, and the family regarded my influence over Christine with some awe. But I carefully concealed my tactics, as instinct warned me they might not meet with wholesale approval.

When this new pride and joy was old enough to stand and waddle around, Marie dug out of the Australian trunks in the attic the delicate, exquisitely tucked and embroidered Edwardian dresses trimmed with lace that my Aunt Mimi had worn half a century earlier under the skies of the Southern Cross. And we became accustomed to the sight of Christine's short, square, sturdy figure stumping around under the mimosa trees, dressed in flounces of white lace flowing down to the ground and flapping around her fat ankles. I came across her once, decked out in all this finery, in a bed of madonna lilies, standing on tiptoe, holding my paint-box in one hand and splashing with red paint the white waxy trumpets of the lilies, which she could only just reach. The poor things, she explained, had been left out by the Almighty when he dealt out their colours to the flowers of the garden. She was a pious child, and her mind turned naturally to divine intercourse whenever the need arose. Once, when the three of us were due for a routine visit to the dentist in Nice, my mother found her on her knees in Marie's bedroom, praying fervently for Anne to be struck down by some sudden and fearful illness, so that she would have to stay behind and keep her company.

Christine, who knew her mind from the start, was adamant in

everything she said or did, and the only one who could stand up to Marie and get away with it. She simply said No, she would <u>not</u> eat her spinach, and if the plate wasn't whisked away at once, she rapped the table with her spoon, and Marie came to heel at once. If we had tried these tactics ourselves, a sharp smack would have been the answer.

'La vieille et la jeune', as Marie would say, pottered about hand in hand all day long, picking raspberries for the table, checking the linen cupboards, feeding the hens and an ever-increasing army of cats which came from far afield, word having got around since our return from Malaya that there was open house at Mas Mistral again. And from time to time, at dead of night, there was a fearful commotion in the hen-house and you could hear them, Christine with a pop-gun and Marie with her air-rifle, taking pot-shots at the poachers who were raiding the *basse-cour*. These were literally shots in the dark, and I am sure that no one was ever hit, but it served the purpose of frightening away the thieves.

We could not help feeling a little left out, as the two of them, entirely absorbed in each other, paid scant attention to anyone else. But we felt no resentment, as our devotion to Christine was absolute. Strict and bossy though she was, she looked to us like an angel, and we wove daisy-chains to decorate her blonde curls. Queening it regally in her high-chair, she accepted this admiration with calm graciousness as her due, and sat patiently while Marie twisted her hair stiffly around a candle to make the curls last longer. These long sausage curls were always known as '*anglaises*'.

By the time she was three years old, this mane of blonde curls was the cause of one of the great uproars with which life was punctuated from time to time. On a sweltering hot July day, when not a breath of air stirred the leaves of the trees, and the grasses steamed and fermented, while the birds hopped around panting with their beaks wide open, Mamma slyly abducted

Christine and carried her off to the barber in the village, where she was shorn like a French poodle, with a tuft left on top and a couple of hideous flaps at the sides, while the back was shaved like a peasant boy's head. Her chubby face, no longer angel-like, looked like a swollen poppy-bud on the thin stalk of her neck.

'She will feel much cooler now,' said Mamma uncertainly, as she pushed the little monstrosity towards us. We were struck dumb with horror at the enormity of the sacrilege, and saw that Marie was going to 'have an attack'. But to our relief, she went to have it in her room. Her one eye shrunk to a pinhead of fury, she scooped Christine up and turned on her heel, and we saw nothing more of either of them for the next two days. After that, Christine's hair was allowed to grow again, and nobody interfered with it any more. Mamma had shot her bolt, and her fit of courage had spent itself.

Having done her job producing Christine, poor Mamma, feeling underemployed, was once more casting around for something to do. It was then she remembered our education.

With a huge Montessori book on her lap, she collected us around her feet on the nursery floor and handed out great piles of wooden blocks to us, without suggestions or instructions of any kind. And there we sat, perplexed, wondering what we were meant to do with them. In the end, the answer didn't seem to lie in playing with bricks, and Montessori was discarded. It was then that the first governess appeared.

Mlle C was a typical example of what my father called a 'church rat'. She made the Almighty into some awful kind of headmaster hanging about in the sky, waiting to catch you out and pounce with fearful retribution.

A thin gaunt figure, always dressed in black bombazine, Mlle C was the ex-headmistress of a girls' school. Her fierce grey hair, which fitted her head like a stocking, was done up at the back into a little bun which made you sigh just to look at it. Every few seconds her nose twitched like a rabbit's, drawing up one side of her lip and exposing the gleam of a menacing eye-tooth. A stiff black moustache bristled on her upper lip like a third eyebrow. And most off-putting of all, she had a whistling nostril which emitted a thin sound, like a faint hiss of steam, whenever she inhaled under stress. As soon as the nostril began to hiss, we knew an explosion was about to burst over us.

Mlle C's only redeeming attribute was an ancient cat, who always had to have a cork clamped between his dribbling jaws. He followed her everywhere, and sat in the middle of the table, chewing his cork, as he presided over our lessons. We found him a great comfort during our daily ordeal.

Unlike Marie, who was probably just as strict, Mlle C was totally unlovable. Our religious education had nothing to do with her, but she took it over on arrival, so that we were completely under her thumb on every front. Our cosy sessions in the side-chapel, Papa rustling *The Times* and John and I smuggling in the odd conker when in season, were done away with. There was no more going to church with our parents, Rubio and Marie. We had to follow her to another part of the building. Bit by bit we lost all our cheer, and poor Marie nearly had a nervous breakdown. My mother locked herself up in the summer study and we never saw her, even when she was at home.

Our day started at seven a.m., when Marie woke us up and we washed and dressed at top speed. Fifteen minutes later Mlle C stalked in for prayers. After that we trooped downstairs for bread and cocoa. The bread was stale, as Mlle C maintained that fresh bread was indigestible and lay heavy on the stomach, interfering with concentration and keenness. As it was, we were so poorly endowed with these qualities anyway that we could not afford to lose the minutest available scrap. By eight o'clock we were sitting down to work.

Mlle C covered the table with sheets of newspaper to protect it; they puckered and creased under our books. Then she uncorked a bottle of purple ink and handed each of us a pen with a thin scratchy nib whose needle-sharp, pointed ends crossed over with a vicious twist as soon as they touched the paper, flicking sprays of the purple ink all round. If this happened too often we got a sharp rap on the knuckles with a black ruler. My copy-books were punctured with small holes and sprinkled with ink spots on every page. At five minutes to twelve, Pauvre Claire crept in to lay the table, and Marie whisked us away for a quick wash and brush-up. Although she was as grim and rough as could be, we knew quite well that her bad temper had nothing to do with us.

Lunch was eaten in silence, except for the odd sniffle from whoever was still struggling with the last tears of the morning. As children were meant to be seen but not heard, Mlle C had to eat in silence too. That at least was a mercy. There was usually one of us who was made to go without pudding, which we minded much less than being kept in during break. As we got only half-an-hour in the garden after lunch, our school-day seemed very long. Mamma once had the temerity to complain that I had not been out of the house for a week. She was told not to interfere, and reminded that children have to grow pale over their books if education is to be taken seriously. Which we did, in quite a short time.

John had withdrawn into complete silence, and Anne's huge oyster-coloured eyes were usually swimming in tears. I became more neurotic as the weeks went by, caught sight of ghosts floating up the stairs as we went to bed, and sneezed non-stop through a spring which seemed to have no end. This rule of terror lasted one whole and terrible year. The day of reckoning came one fine June morning when my mother burst into the dining-room without even *knocking*, while we were sweating over a dictation. 'Come on, children,' she crooned, 'the cherries are ripe and must be picked at once or the birds will eat them all.'

There was a terrible silence, while we stared at her as if she had gone out of her mind.

Mlle C's nostril whistled like a steam engine as she exploded: 'I must ask you, Madame, not to disturb my pupils.'

'They must come at once,' babbled Mamma. 'They must pick those cherries right away.'

There was a clash of voices raised in anger, and we fled into the garden.

Gino and Marius had placed ladders against the cherry-trees, and we lost no time scrambling up. We could reach the topmost branches, and we were expert pickers. The birds came fluttering angrily down, aiming at our eyes. But we held our own and ignored their bullying.

By the end of the week Mlle C had left, and we were FREE. This was the start of a wonderful new life.

About this time our English neighbours, the Hilliers, who had decided to go back to England, were looking for a home for their old spaniel.

Sam, a friendly, exuberant dog, was perfectly happy with life in general, except for one thing. He loathed, detested and despised French dogs. He attacked, roughed them up and really savaged them whenever he got the chance. This was quite a disadvantage, and nobody else was keen on giving him a home. So, what with one thing and another, Mrs H was very anxious he should come to us. We begged Mamma, who was in two minds about it, to take him on. In the end she gave in, dear old Sam joined the family, and we were overjoyed at having a dog again.

Soon after that Mamma decided that after such a gruelling year we needed a proper holiday. Letters of enquiry went off to innumerable house agents, and finally, one fine evening in early July, we set off for Nice station in a convoy of taxis.

Mamma headed the column, Marie followed in the second cab with us, Rubio captained the third, and the luggage came last. This included several trunks, camping equipment, a primus stove and tricycles, and Mamma's cameras and developing kit. And most important of all, our pharmacy and medical supplies. We might have been heading for the Kalahari Desert. Instead of which we were on our way to the west coast, to enjoy the iodine-laden air of the Atlantic Ocean.

At Nice station we climbed into the night train, surrounded by an army of porters, all shouting orders to one another. Marie went off with them to make sure nothing was left behind. Mamma reclined on one seat, with her head all wrapped up in lavender tulle, while Rubio, who had to sleep in another compartment, clasped to his bosom a heavy wooden chest filled with table silver, and labelled in black letters: '*Argenterie. Service de table*'. Marie tied nets over our heads to keep the nasty soot out of our hair, but did not, for one instant, put down Mamma's very obvious jewellery case.

The picnic we had that night was euphoric – the hampers were stuffed with delicacies from Madame Rose's kitchen. This was an unimaginable feast after our long year of stale bread and cocoa. And then, to our surprise and delight, we were each allowed an inch of Papa's best *rosé* in our Vichy water. This was a rare treat, as wine, along with vinegar, was generally held to bend your bones and dissolve the teeth in your head before they even showed up. By the time we had flicked the last crumb off our swollen bellies, it was nearing midnight. We climbed into our bunks, and Anne and I lay side by side, leaning on our elbows and watching the ink-black Mediterranean slipping by, edged in the west by the lime-green sky, darkening gradually to pitch-dark at the top.

Swaying wildly from side to side, as French trains always did in those days, we thundered along the coast, tearing through Cagnes, Antibes, La Napoule and St Tropez, for this was the Rapide Nice–Bordeaux, not our little coastal train which stopped at every station. Fiery sparks streaked past the window, the whistle shrieked practically non-stop, telegraph wires leapt and plunged up and down, and we rolled over on our bunk and fell asleep.

PART TWO

the road to bordeaux

1930–40

chapter twelve

The journey took all night. We arrived in Royan in good order, and the station-master, who had been alerted on the phone by the Nice *chef-de-gare*, was on the platform to meet us. Our luggage was hoisted onto a caravan of horse-drawn coaches lined up outside the station waiting for customers. We climbed into the first, a *calèche* of ancient design with tufts of horse-hair sprouting here and there, and tattered remains of a hood which flapped about in the breeze. Rubio, still clutching the case of table-silver, climbed into the second coach with some of the luggage and promptly fell asleep.

The drive along the front of this fashionable resort was a revelation. We had never seen such enormous waves, with breakers as high as horses, galloping along the beach. Dead jellyfish as large as bicycle wheels, left over from the previous tide, were lifted up and floated away, to be churned and pounded by the next breaker. How could anyone bathe and paddle in such raging turmoil? 'The sea will be much calmer in St Georges,' said our coachman to cheer us up. 'The beach is much more sheltered there.'

We arrived at the nearby harbour village of St-Georges-de-Didonne at the height of the shopping hour, with the market in full swing. Our convoy, shambling along the main street, caused an unexpected stir. We found this puzzling, as we looked no different from usual. It must have been Rubio who was letting us down, fast asleep in his barouche with his bristly red face squashed onto his chest, his beret over his nose, and the box of silver still clutched in his arms. After him came three more coaches loaded with luggage. On top of the last one were half-a-dozen mouse-traps wobbling rather ominously astride our two Singer sewing-machines (in case one broke down).

Chalet Gaudin had been described by the agents as a large family residence full of old-world charm. It was in fact not only old, but crumbling. When our convoy stopped at the gate, we thought we had arrived at the Sleeping Beauty's castle. You could hardly see the house for the trees. They towered above the roof, vines and creepers swarmed all over the walls, and the wide front steps sweeping up to the first-floor terrace were shrouded in ferns and mosses. Great loops of cobwebs hung about like washing lines; some of the shutters were suspended from one hinge, while others were encrusted into the walls like barnacles. The vapours of the ocean, Marie said, were the cause of it all.

Rubio, still fast asleep in the second carriage, was now prodded awake by our coachman, who poked him in the ribs with his whip. 'Come on, you lazy-bones, give us a hand with the luggage,' he growled.

Unloading our bags and boxes was no joke. Apart from the trunks full of bed and table-linen, kitchen equipment and all the rest, the load piling up in the garden included camp-beds, a field medical chest, a large box full of photographic developing material, trunks stuffed with clothes, toys, games and books, and perched on top of it all sat the two sewing-machines, as well as our swing for Rubio to hang in a tree in the garden.

The so-called 'chalet' was a large, battered old house, built on no intelligible plan. Even in summer, as we soon found out, it was damp and dark as a dungeon. Trees grew through the windows, invading the rooms, and any light that might have trickled in was kept out by a curtain of creepers which swarmed all over the building. The entire house was plunged into the kind of gloom which usually obscures the bottom of an aquarium.

The garden, mysterious and creepy, was full of narrow tunnels between overgrown box hedges and old cedars with huge branches snaking along the ground, all of it so tangled with vines and ivy that it could have been abandoned for a hundred years. The overall atmosphere was one of languor and melancholy decay. All this luxuriant vegetation would at least, I thought, shelter an abundant insect life, which would surely keep Marie happy for the rest of the holidays. But her first preoccupation was cleaning out the cupboards, which were lined all over with mould and mildew. And after a stormy week of scrubbing and scouring every corner of the house, it took her a long time to unpack and store away all our clutter. During this cheerless period we kept well out of her way, spending most of our time in the garden.

A wall seven or eight feet high separated us from the garden next door, which sloped down to the beach. From the top of the wall it was literally child's play to swing into the cedars, and from there to proceed all the way round the garden, cruising along the treetops, creeping from branch to branch in the lime-green twilight like a troop of monkeys. Completely invisible from the ground, we took great care to keep dead quiet, as our treetop life was like another world, a glorious in-between state, subject neither to the rigours of earthly discipline nor to the ascetic standards of heaven. Sometimes Marie would stamp about below, calling and searching, with the broad brim of her hat flapping up and down in mounting irritation.

One day we decided to build our own house in one of the tallest trees, and become established denizens of these upper regions. It took us ages to haul the boards up and nail them down into a firm platform – which in the end was about all the construction was. There were neither walls nor roof, as we preferred to look around through the foliage and up into the bright blue sky above. All the time we were not on the beach was spent in our tree-house. So far we had managed to get up there unseen, until one day Christine, who was about two at the time, caught us at it. 'Me want to go up too,' she announced. We explained why it was impossible. She insisted, and we told her to run away and play. She let out a piercing scream. 'Me going to tell Marie,' she yelled. The little pest was going to sneak, and that would be the end of our tree life.

I slithered to the ground to collect a basket, into which she squeezed. And tying a rope to the handle, I scrabbled up again with the rope in my teeth. We started to haul her up. All went well until the basket began to swing and crashed into the tree. Christine let out an ear-splitting screech. As the rope grew shorter, the whole arrangement began to spin. 'Me going to be sick,' she wailed. Soon she was jammed beneath the floorboards, and the harder we pulled the more we flattened the poor creature into her basket. 'We've got to get her over the side,' I kept saying. 'We can't pull her thro' the floor . . .'

In the end, as she came into view on a forward swing, we whipped her over the edge with a swift manoeuvre. When we finally got her out of her basket she was quivering like a jelly. I sat her on my lap and smoothed her down while John tied the rope around her waist, with the other end firmly tethered to a branch. 'If you fall overboard we can yank you back,' he told her. 'But try not to all the same.'

After that episode we took good care to shin up our tree only when we knew Christine to be well out of range.

On very hot days, Marie, who hated the sand, the sun and the sea, marched us firmly off to the forest behind the sand dunes. There she would settle under some vast oozing pine, which spewed resin from every pore: its fumes, inhaled into our tubes, would keep off winter colds and wheezes. In Vence she frequently made us play in the shade of eucalyptus trees for the same reason. And there she sat, happily knitting away our endless winter socks, clicking and flashing her four steel pins at an incredible rate, while we mooned around, bored to death and longing for the beach. If we were lucky enough to have settled down by an ants' nest, all was well and the day was saved. Another powerful attraction were the caterpillar processions with thousands of them crawling along nose to tail in single file for miles on end. Marie would even put her knitting aside for these and go down on hands and knees, peering sideways at the creatures which humped along in total unconcern. Occasionally she fished out one of her specimen bottles and scooped up a handful to take home for pickling purposes.

Owing to her regrettable thumb-sucking habit, Anne's second batch of teeth, which had lately arrived on the scene, were beginning to poke forward in an alarming way. Quite unintentionally, she was beginning to damage people with them. As they were razor-sharp, she was becoming dangerous. From time to time you would hear John growling, 'Do be careful, you've hit me with your teeth again.'

'I can't help it,' she would wail, 'they stick out too far.'

'Well, keep your mouth shut, then.'

'I can't, my lips won't meet. It's not my fault.' And she would burst into tears.

In the end my mother took the matter in hand. As there was

no dentist in St Georges, they had to go to Royan to find one. And in due course Anne was fitted out with a curious-looking object made of bakelite. This instrument was supposed to stretch out gradually and widen the roof of her mouth. It became known, not surprisingly, as Anne's cleft-palate. Since she couldn't speak through it, she had to spit it out whenever she wanted to utter. Half the time, of course, the wretched thing was found lying around in the most unlikely places. John was heard to say at lunch one day, 'For goodness sake, take this ghastly thing away,' as it turned up in his table-napkin. I once found it in my pencil-box. Poor Anne's life was unmitigated misery during those cleft-palate years. On one occasion, as we were all sitting down to lunch, a loud crunching sound was suddenly heard under the table. 'Who's given Sam a bone?' asked Mamma sternly. 'You know you mustn't feed him at meals.' As we were eating skate and black butter at the time, we could claim, quite truthfully, that nobody had given Sam a bone. 'He's probably scratched one out of his store in the garden,' suggested John.

Peering under the table, we bent down together. Sam glared at us all in turn, and suddenly Anne wailed, 'He's got my palate . . . It's my palate!'

'Really!' exploded Mamma, 'this is *too* much! Why on earth did you give it to him?'

'I didn't give it to him,' whimpered Anne. 'He must have pinched it out of my pocket.'

'Well, get it back at once. I've never heard of such a thing.'

As Anne went down on her knees under the table, Sam uttered a deep growl of warning. 'He likes it,' remarked John. 'He's never had anything so tasty before. He won't give it up . . .'

'Don't be so disgusting,' said my mother. 'And be careful, Anne, he might bite . . .'

'Of course he won't bite,' I said indignantly. 'Sam never bites!'

Anne crept forward another inch, and Sam's lips curled back

in a snarl as his hackles rose. They glared at each other, their eyeballs out on stalks. This seemed likely to go on forever. Suddenly my nerve broke and I exploded in a violent sneeze. Sam gave a start, and Anne pounced on her palate. 'I've got it,' she yelled in triumph, reappearing at table level. 'Well, go and disinfect it at once,' commanded Mamma. 'Ask Marie for some of her pickling spirits, and make sure it's thoroughly disinfected.'

When we next saw the object, it was residing in state in a jamjar full of meths, between a pickled snake and a four-legged chicken on the top shelf of the kitchen dresser. And after a suitable length of time it was duly reinstated in poor Anne's mouth.

chapter thirteen

In spite of the damp, the darkness and persistent smell of mildew in the house, our first summer in St Georges was pure bliss. For three long hot months we lived on a beach of white sand three miles long. We shrimped and 'swam' in the shallows with one foot on the bottom, and so gentle were the waves that we never had to wear life-belts (rubber rings, wings and such-like were still inventions of the future at the time).

The only snag was the daily gym lesson, on which my mother insisted, to 'keep us in shape', whatever that might mean. So every morning after breakfast, the PT instructor, M. Dupont, marched us, along with a gang of other reluctant children, up and down the beach like a battalion in training. Running, jumping, skipping, standing on our hands, whatever he did in front of us we had to copy. This went on for a solid hour, in the full heat of the sun. In the end he chased us all into the sea, to pick out those who sank from the ones who could swim. He left the latter to their own devices, then pulled out the sinkers and flung them on the beach. As we were among this lot, he cornered Mamma and persuaded her that we would all drown before the end of the summer unless he taught us to swim. And from then on, this was one more chore we had to face every day after gym.

After lunch, for which we returned to our sombre villa, came the siesta on the beach. Mamma made us lie flat on our backs, stripped to the waist, and popping seaweed onto our chests, she rubbed the slimy jelly into the skin. This, as everybody knew, being full of iodine and other precious minerals, would be baked into the bloodstream by the sun, thus keeping coughs and colds and wheezy chests away for the whole winter. Then, when done on one side, we were turned over for basting and roasting on the other. How she managed to keep up this boring performance for a whole summer I cannot imagine. But I suppose that her reward came the following winter when we caught nothing worse than measles, plus a dose of pneumonia for myself.

Moved by one of her sudden flashes of inspiration, on which she always acted immediately without a second's hesitation or reflection, Mamma had decided to bring us to St Georges because it was the home of her friends, Pierre and Camille Darlange, whom she had known in Malaya when she met and married my father in 1920. Their own son Jacques was born a few months before I arrived on the scene. We had often been trundled together in the same pram under the banana-trees in the garden. And presumably also received our bed-time whiff of chloroform served from the same bottle by my Chinese amah.

When Pierre and Camille left Malaya for good, they went to live in Paris, but always spent the school holidays at Pierre's family home in St Georges, where his parents had lived since time immemorial. Nostram was a very large house, in which Pierre's five brothers and sisters, and all their children, gathered for the summer holidays, and often Christmas and Easter as well. To have friends we could meet on neutral ground, on the beach, at any time, was a new, exhilarating experience. We made the most of it, and became inseparable. Jacques now had two sisters, Ninette and Nadia, not to speak of their innumerable cousins.

The Darlange children, built on a large scale, were twice as big as we were, and I suspect that our mother, secretly envious of her friends' brood of giants, submitted us to those daily gym lessons on the beach in an effort to stretch us upwards and sideways as much as possible. But I regret to say that although we were put through this infinitely dreary performance for many years, she was defeated in her purpose and we remained just as we were, growing at our own leisurely pace, and as thin as stick insects.

When bored with bathing and castle-building in the sand, we scrambled over the reef at low tide. We jumped about over the rocks, covered with bladderwrack and very slippery, exploring their cracks and chinks, filled with water and life of every kind, from sea-spiders to prawns and baby squid. Right on the edge of the reef close to the sea was a very large pool, where flying squid flicked their way from end to end until finally swept away by the incoming tide. Supposed to be quite brainless, these extraordinary creatures are said to have hearts like a power-station. Whelks glided through the seaweed, curling around any shell they came across, sawing away at it with their long, knife-like tongue, edged all round with hundreds of razor-sharp teeth growing in rows of three. As soon as one set snapped off, another rushed forward to take its place. With this equipment, they had no trouble at all boring through the toughest shells and sucking the unhappy mollusc out of its home. The sea anemone, for all its eyeless, mindless state, is organised beyond belief. From time to time one of them will suddenly split asunder, each half quickly growing into a new, fully-fledged anemone. Should any scraps fall off during the split, these will grow at once into minute members of the expanding family. Nothing is wasted. At other times they go broody and decide to lay eggs instead. And these are hatched within the folds of their own stomach pouch. How the new brood avoids being digested along with the latest meal is a mystery. But having by-passed this fate, they float away with the debris of their parent's lunch, in search of adventure on the high seas. Starfish, the real tigers of the pools and in great numbers everywhere, wriggled along on their tiny tubular feet. They have so many of these that when one set gets tired they tuck it up and let down another lot to take over. These creatures are also equipped with powerful suction pads, which come in useful for prising open clams and oyster shells determined to remain closed. The starfish will then wrap its arms around the shell, switch on the suction, and use all its feet in turn until the unhappy clam, oyster or whatever, exhausted by the struggle, simply has to let go. The big bully will then shoot out its stomach, wrap it round the occupant, and digest it alive in its own parlour.

Sea-cucumbers were another intriguing group, some fat and short, others long and hollow like macaroni. I once picked up a fat one, but dropped it in a hurry as the revolting brute spat out all its guts in my face. Then away it lurched to knit itself a whole new set of insides.

Seahorses, those seductive creatures, swung about in the deeper pools, or curled their tails around a seaweed stalk. I never saw them eating anything. We brought them crumbs, tiny waterfleas, and any other scraps we could find. They swam up, nosed at our offerings with their little snouts, then floated away in disgust. Sea-snails crawled about everywhere in profusion. We once got into trouble for collecting a jarful of them as a present for Marie. Next morning the jar was empty, and most of the snails were swarming all over the sugar, the coffee-beans, the breakfast bread and croissants, while the rest were cruising along the ceiling in search of other delights.

At very low tide the reef was covered with oyster-beds, whose shells, as lethal as broken glass, slashed our gymshoes to ribbons. Cemented as they were to the rock, they seemed to lead a dull life, their sole excitement being their annual sex-change, one year male and the next female. Crowded in dense colonies, they were condemned to the company of their next-door neighbours for life, as there was no hope of moving around in search of new faces.

Our aquarium at home was a large washtub sunk into the ground in the garden, with a wire fence all round to keep out cats. Marie already had a collection of the local feline population under her wing. The aquarium was a faithful copy of the pools in the reef. We had even managed to chip off bits of rock with oysters attached, which we spread around the sides. These were covered with kelp and other weeds for the seahorses, and for the slugs and snails which snuggled in its shelter. For the whelks we brought a daily supply of clams, and for the anemones we went shrimping at low tide. The starfish gobbled up everything they came across, and the sea-urchins hoovered up the sandy bottom, disposing of shrimp legs and soft crab-shells as well as any other debris lying around. After my adventure with the sea-cucumber, we decided to leave the breed alone. Tiny, soft-shelled green crabs scuttled about everywhere, and we even had a baby jellyfish. But he (or she) soon disappeared, probably digested by one of the sea-anemones.

A great pleasure which we enjoyed so to speak second-hand was fishing. Following the top of the cliff above our reef was a narrow path where a number of fishermen had a permanent pitch. At high tide they lowered large square nets hanging from a rope, which was wound up and down on a pulley. When the tide began to ebb, we raced to the cliff to inspect the catch of the day. There were sole, crabs, lobsters, grey mullet, dabs and plaice, and sometimes a clutch of drowned new-born kittens. The first time we were given a batch of these by the fishermen, we flew home to resuscitate them, convinced that they were merely in a bad way. We placed them, all carefully tucked up in cotton wool, in a wooden box beside the kitchen furnace, and tried to force warm milk into their small, clamped-down mouths. On the third day, the usual day for resurrections, we lost all hope when the little creatures seemed to have shrunk still further into themselves, and Marie declared that she would not put up with these stinking cadavers in her kitchen any longer. So we were forced to bury our poor little corpses.

At the end of September the Darlange family went back to Paris. And we had to abandon our thriving aquarium when Marie suddenly told us to collect our belongings, as we were returning to Vence the next day. While we were away, Fred the farmer had died, and Madame Rose, now his widow, had gone back to Switzerland. So Marie took over the kitchen for the time being.

A couple of months after our return, Papa came home on leave, and Mamma decided to do away with the little farmhouse and its stables. Her latest scheme was to remodel it as a 'winter residence', much smaller and warmer, and easier to run than Mas Mistral. And when it was finished, furnished and fit to live in, they called it 'Esterel', after the mountain it overlooked in the west, the Kingdom of the local fairy, Esterelle.

As the distance between the two houses was only about 150 yards, the move was simply a matter of running back and forth with piles of clothes, books, silver, bedding and kitchen equipment. When the day for the move finally came, we spent the rest of the week staggering up and down the path like pack-mules, dumping our loads in the new kitchen where Marie was floundering about trying to bring some order into the monumental muddle.

When everything was more or less sorted out and in its rightful place, Mamma once more remembered our education. The word 'governess' began to crop up from time to time in her conversation. And we all shuddered at the sound of it. Fortunately, it remained as an idea in the back of her head for the time being. Meanwhile, one day in late autumn, an appalling storm suddenly broke out. Mamma and I sat curled up on our chairs in the drawing-room, engrossed in our books and only vaguely aware of the storm raging overhead. With our feet tucked up on account of the draughts, we were oblivious of what was going on around us. It was only when a rug came spinning round on the waters swirling through the room that I took in what was happening.

Perhaps after this the house was damp, or the thought of a new governess was niggling away at my vitals. Anyway, down I went with pneumonia, soon to be subjected to the full treatment. Cupping and hot mustard poultices having done no good, I lay on my bed, shaking and panting for breath, with tears rolling down my face at the pain in my side.   Marie came in every two hours to wrap me up from head to foot in a soaking, ice-cold sheet to bring down my temperature. And as she spun me over, tightening the sheet around me, she growled at my tears and groans and told me to stop behaving like a baby. Her philosophy was never to sympathise, as it only made you feel more sorry for yourself. And as usual, she was right.

I was lucky compared to the peasant children of my generation. They had to put up with far worse horrors, such as swallowing the juice of crushed live snails mixed with sugar, or having a pigeon split in half, clamped, still palpitating, to their heads, or freshly torn-off rabbit skins wrapped round their chests, and worst of all, they continually had to suffer the most dreadful indignities connected with their nether regions. Little pellets, bits of soap, cloves of garlic, were pushed up their bottoms, and most astonishing of all, constipation was treated with the insertion of a violet. What happened when violets were out of season leaves one wondering. Whooping cough, when it resisted snail juice, was cured by pushing the child seven times backwards and forwards under the belly of a donkey. Some of these animals were famous for miles around for their curative powers, and the patients were driven to far-distant villages, bumping along the mountain paths in horse-carts for their treatment. But in spite of all this care and trouble, child mortality was very high in those days.

After what seemed like weeks of painful illness and even more painful treatment, I pulled out of it and slowly began to feel better. One glorious morning Papa, whom I hadn't seen since I became ill, came and sat beside me with a book. This unexpected treat made up for everything. He read me the *Divine Comedy* from beginning to end. And I remember thinking how lucky that it was in French and not Italian. It was pure bliss to lie back in bed, with a large pipless orange in my hands (a brand new invention at the time), listening to his dear weak voice, while gazing out of the window at the pale spring sky and the olive-trees waving slowly from side to side.

When we had squeezed everything we could out of Dante, Papa read me extracts from a huge tome of Rabelais' complete works, and we both rocked with laughter at the adventures of Pantagruel and Gargantua. Papa was in one of his rare frivolous moods, reading the sixteenth-century text with the local accent, which made it sound even funnier. Then he read Lamb's *Essays of Elia* in English, and the mood changed to one of delicate melancholy. Soon after this I got up and went downstairs, feeling weak and light-headed, and Papa once more withdrew into himself and his study. From then on, he hardly seemed to recognise me whenever we met in the hall or on the stairs.

All this time John and Anne had been leading a busy and engrossing life in the garden, and didn't want me either. And so I never knew what they were up to when John pottered about with a busy look on his face or Anne wandered away vaguely with two hats on her head.

It was at this time that I discovered a new, very satisfying occupation. It consisted of sitting in the fork of a mimosa tree in bloom, and trying *to feel like the tree*. Nothing in the world seemed more delightful than having sprigs of mimosa sprouting out of your arms and legs and the tips of your fingers. It was really a question of the time available. If you were called away, or distracted too soon, nothing much happened. But when a long sunny afternoon stretched ahead, you could be pretty sure of plugging into the 'tree-feeling' fairly quickly. Quite soon your own identity floated away, and you became a living part of the tree itself, rippling in the breeze and tingling with the little thoughts and feelings that came rushing up out of the ground, usually so tenuous and elusive that you could never catch them any other way. But when the mimosa went out of season there was nothing more to do than moon around, sitting for hours on the swing Rubio had rigged up for us in an old olive-tree, chewing pomegranates and spitting out the pips for the ants to take home to their babies.

Everything seemed out of joint. So in a way it was a relief when the new governess suddenly appeared, without warning. Spring set in early that year, and the move back to the big house for the summer coincided with her arrival. So her first job was to help us bundle our belongings back to Mas Mistral, and shovel them into their rightful places under Marie's eagle eye.

Since then I have often wondered what the new governess must have thought when she arrived, to be greeted on the doorstep by a mountain of household chattels and her new charges shooting out of the house one after the other, with arm-fuls of clothes, blankets and saucepans. When later she plucked up the courage to ask Marie the reason for this seasonal tidal flow backwards and forwards from one house to the other, the curt reply was that 'the children needed a change of air.'

chapter fourteen

Mademoiselle B, always pleasant and harmless, was, I think, a little bemused by the abysmal depth of our ignorance. She had probably never come across anything quite like it before, and wasn't sure how to tackle the problem. Hoping perhaps to win us over, she did away with the needle-sharp nibs and purple ink, allowing us to use pencils instead. John, being of a practical turn of mind, enjoyed doing sums, nice friendly adding up, with different combinations of the same figures, so he could always rely on the results. At that time he had a passion for headgear, and was never seen without something on his head. It could be an old disused work-basket or a discarded bathing-cap with a strap under the chin. But more often than not he was totally invisible beneath one of Marie's enormous garden hats. As they were far too big for him, the breeze got hold of the brim (we worked under the cherry-tree on the terrace) and the whole thing swung back and forth quite freely on his head. With face all screwed up in concentration, and his fingers uncurling from his left hand for counting, he was quite oblivious of the spinning hat whizzing round his head. But I, with my feeble concentration powers, found it distinctly distracting. As it rotated under my nose, I never quite knew which way round it would go next, or on what side to expect the little black patent-leather bow to reappear. As for myself, I managed to convince Mlle B that my only so-called skills lay in drawing, painting, reading and writing stories. These were the sole subjects I could understand or work at. To my amazement, she fell for it. And so I was able to spend all my 'lesson' time doing pictures for my stories, often before they were even written.

Anne, by swivelling her enormous oyster-coloured eyes all round in their sockets in an unblinking stare, had learnt the useful trick of hypnotising our teacher into letting her get away with doing nothing at all. So there she sat, with her thumb in her mouth, steadily pushing out her front teeth, her huge eyeballs rolling about, following Mlle B's every movement. So lessons, on the whole, were relaxed and uneventful, and I never learnt a thing under that regime.

To encourage at least a degree of self-education, we had the freedom of my father's bookshelves, were we could read anything we liked, except for the *Larousse Médical*, a huge heavy tome which was strictly forbidden. For extra safety it was stored out of reach on top of the highest shelf in the study, so that getting at it was a hazardous, even a dangerous adventure. And if we ever managed to lower it down to the floor without an almighty crash, there was always Marie's ultra-sensitive radar system to be reckoned with. So our only hope hung on one of her rare visits to her dentist in Nice.

This delectable book was adorned on every page with the most appalling diseases and conditions. Many of them, as an extra bonus, were in colour. I remember gruesome tumours, like Californian sunsets, ears that really looked like cauliflowers, strawberry noses, some without nostrils, and Siamese twins glued together at various parts of their anatomy. There was one really sickening case of elephantiasis, in which the patient's penis had grown all the way down to his feet and looked for all the world like a third leg. And I remember looking at John with my heart all twisted with pity at the thought that on account of his sex he too, poor boy, might end up stumping around in this condition one day.

But summer and winter, whether we were going through a period of education or idleness, the afternoons were always free to feed our animals and tend our own gardens and our private graveyard. It was there that we buried our dead friends, domestic and otherwise. Tastefully laid out, with gravel paths and mini-tombstones, it followed the same pattern as the village cemetery where our grandfather was buried. It contained a great number of birds, several large lizards, two cats, a tortoise bitten through the heart by a dog, and a porcupine.

These activities kept us going until tea-time, after which we would return to the nursery for drawing, painting and Marie's reading sessions. There was at that time an exciting new mania for flying. It was the kind in which you had to lean over the side of your plane to see where you were going, counting the steeples as you went, to make sure of landing in the right field. Turned into a mystical experience by St Exupéry, that high-priest of the air, it became a cult, and no one was immune from the craze, least of all ourselves. We throbbed along fervently, with Marie leading the way, when Charles Lindbergh crossed the Atlantic in 33½ hours in a 200-horsepower monoplane. She read us the books of St Exupéry, and although a lot of it was above our heads, her own suppressed excitement created an unforgettable impression.

Special leather coats were devised for pilots, for keeping out the terrible cold in the windy heights of the sky. Mamma, reacting in her own individualistic manner and never giving a damn for other people's reactions, acquired one of these garments, so sensible as a protection against the icy blasts of the Mistral. It was a great thrill when we saw her rigged up in this, with the addition of one of her more fetching cloche hats and a stout pair of golfing shoes. Thus attired, she would set out to do her shopping, visit her friends or sort out her lawyer, the village priest or the mayor. And whatever it was she wanted, she always got her way.

At about this time, a couple of English ladies, Helen Hill and Violet Maxwell, rented rooms in the old farmhouse. They wrote books about the South of France and the local peasants, involving a good deal of regional history. Miss Maxwell wrote the stories and her friend drew the pictures.

By then Mlle B had moved on to a more rewarding job. And before my mother had time to find her a successor, Miss Maxwell came to the rescue. She had a sweet white lined face, and seemed infinitely old (she must have been about forty at the time). Her short stiff grey hair stuck out like straw on either side of her cheeks. She invited us to tea under the fig-tree by the pond, and over the bread and butter and cherry jam, she started to tell us the history of Vence. And it was not till much later that I realised we were having *lessons*! After tea we had to go and write it all down – in *English*. This took some doing, as my spelling was still largely phonetic, and all kinds of foreign words from early childhood kept cropping up. In the end, my essays, if they could be called that, were sprinkled with bits of Provençal, Malay, Italian, or just plain patois. Miss Maxwell never turned a hair. She simply remarked, 'I think the English word you want here is probably this, or that,' or whatever seemed most likely. And where the story was concerned, she would just say, 'Actually it was the Saracen invaders who were the pirates. The French knights were trying to defend the coast . . .' And with all the barbarian invasions throughout the centuries, poor Provence had more than her share of invasions to cope with.

June was now back in all its glory. The animal and vegetable life of the garden was heaving and bustling with activity. The nightingale had started to sing in the cherry-tree, and Miss Maxwell declared that nobody should be allowed to grow up without sleeping at least one night out of doors at this time of year. My mother had no objection, but there was serious opposition from Marie, who said that the night dew would leak into our bones and set up rheumatism which would stay with us for life. As an early heatwave made the grass steam by day and the stars quiver through the heat haze at night, her arguments were unconvincing. Little Miss Maxwell, brave as a lion, carried the day. She sent us scuttling up to the attic to collect hammocks, and poor Marie looked as if she was having a seizure. Strung up in the fig-trees by the pond, our bedding dangled over our animal graveyard. Taking care to avoid the tiny tombstones, Miss Maxwell tucked us up in our rugs and left us to experience our first night out of doors. Listening intently to the noises of the night, we were so excited we could hardly breathe. The deafening sound of the cicadas gradually died off, and the field crickets set up their plaintive dirge. Then suddenly, sharp as a knife, came the first notes of the nightingale. He tried out a few trills at first, then finding his voice, got going in earnest. On and on he went, gaining confidence, changing the odd note here and there, then settling down to a truly magical performance.

Pungent smells began to ooze out of the ground. A field-mouse squeaked, and fireflies flickered in and out among the fig-leaves, taking their time, allegedly searching for a wife, but in no great hurry to find one. From time to time a fig flopped into the pond, a goldfish leaped at a firefly, while above our heads the dark-blue sky displayed its myriad stars. Squelchy, thumb-sucking noises coming from Anne's hammock announced that she had dropped off. But John and I stayed awake a long time, riveted by the revelations of the hot June night.

It was still pitch-dark overhead, even though a mustard-tinted light edged the horizon over the sea, when we were woken up by the hysterical chatter of the birds. This was the first time we realised that birds tune up *before* sunrise, and by the time the sky turned milky at the approach of dawn, they had switched off their racket and gone dead quiet. For about fifteen minutes, a strange new warmth puffed up all round, while not a sound was heard. The world seemed wrapped in cotton-wool. Then gradually the air freshened as the sky grew lighter, twigs and leaves began to rustle as insects got on the move, and not till the sun was well up did the birds begin to sing again. But this time it was in a quick and chatty way, as they hopped about their business, clearing out their nests and bustling around for grubs.

When Miss Maxwell came round a little later, she listened to our excited comments in silence but offered none of her own in exchange. And later that day she made us write it all down, so we should never forget the experience of that wonderful night. All through the war I followed the army around the Mediterranean theatre of war with Hill and Maxwell's little books about Vence until they, along with all my gear, disappeared during the Italian campaign. But that is another story.

Since our return from Malaya I had been regularly visiting Mrs Hillier's kitchen and nursery, and this helped to keep my English going; it would have completely withered otherwise. In another effort to keep up our English, Mamma took us to an English children's 'club' in Vence run by 'Auntie', on the first floor of her tea-room on the Place Peyra. There we played Happy Families, Hunt the Slipper, Postman's Knock and Hide and Seek.

'Auntie' was a middle-aged English spinster, who had lived in Vence from time immemorial and befriended painters and writers. Norman Douglas always stayed with her on his way through (presumably to and from Capri), and after D. H. Lawrence had come to die at the Villa Keja next door to Mas Mistral, Auntie rooted out his gravestone and stored it under her kitchen sink for safe keeping. It was always fascinating to slip away from Happy Families upstairs and sneak into the tea-room on the ground floor to listen to the grown-ups' chatter. Auntie, who always insisted on speaking her atrocious French to my mother (who invariably answered in her equally atrocious English – but as neither listened to the other it didn't matter in the slightest and everybody was perfectly happy), returned from Nice one day after an appendix operation, firmly convinced that a pair of forceps had been left inside her. She could feel them rattling, she declared, as she shuffled around her tea-room. And insisting on being opened up again, she was proved right, and the instrument, which she proudly kept under a glass dome, was always produced for her guests' inspection.

Vegetarians and nudists ('cranks', as we called them) frequently dropped in for tea and toasted buns, and we sometimes came across their camps during our country walks. Given to beards and sandals and fringy garments (when they wore anything at all), they were the forerunners of today's hippy communities. One of them, whom we called 'Jesus Christ', was a great favourite of ours. Gentle and harmless, he drifted about the streets in long flowing robes, with curly hair and beard, looking noble and prophetic, a character straight out of the Bible.

We often met the stage-designer Gordon Craig, swinging

along in his black cloak and hat, and he and Papa politely bowed to each other, while a civil exchange of 'Morning Craig, Morning Fesq' passed between them. But as far as I know, the friendship went no further. Matisse, who lived on the route de St Jeannet, hardly ever left his house, whereas Chagall was often seen, prowling around the market stalls.

Another character who also flourished at that time, and floundered about the streets of Vence carting buckets of raw, bleeding meat, was a wild-looking woman who lived in a large house in which she harboured five or six dozen cats. Her downtrodden husband was miserably eking out the last days of his life under the same roof in total neglect. His wife and her trusty serving wench crouched all day long over the kitchen fire with a bottle of wine between them, while the cats spat and hissed at one another over the buckets of meat, and the wretched husband lay dying in his soiled, unchanged sheets. The cats, which he feared and hated, spent long busy nights with him, conducting passionate love affairs, fighting one another to the death, and leaving their messes all over his bed.

At the end of the war when, after a long and protracted agony, the poor man was eventually hustled out of this world with the cats' assistance, his wife packed up all their mutual belongings and trundled them up to Mas Mistral, to be stored in the attic for safe-keeping. Why my mother, in the unthinking kindness of her heart, permitted this is hard to tell, but Anne's husband, who was there at the time and was press-ganged into helping with the operation, told me recently that even the largest pieces of furniture were heaved up the attic stairs.

The poor woman was eventually taken off to an asylum when her behaviour, even by Vence standards, became too eccentric. Before that I often passed her sitting on a stone at her garden gate, upbraiding her geraniums in accusing and reproachful tones.

chapter fifteen

The happy arrangement with Miss Maxwell and her 'tea-lessons' under the fig-tree every afternoon was not to last much longer. It was the village priest who ruined it all one day when he tackled my mother about our education. I think our impending confirmation was the reason for his presence at lunch that day. Mamma, who was usually on good terms with him, only occasionally told him how to run his business. This time the roles were reversed. He suddenly turned to me and asked what class I was in.

'We don't have classes,' I explained. 'It's a kind of holiday.'

'Indeed,' said the priest with interest. 'Other children aren't on holiday at the moment, as far as I know.'

'Their governess has left, and I haven't found another one yet,' said my mother.

'But why do they need a governess?' he asked, surprised.

'Well,' said Mamma reasonably, 'they have to have *some* sort of education. Mind you, they can read and write,' she added hastily.

'What about the village school? What's wrong with that?'

'The *village* school?' Mamma looked startled. That was one thing she hadn't thought of. Always open-minded, she was quite prepared to consider this new idea. Inwardly, I cursed this priestly interference. What had it got to do with him? Why didn't he mind his own business? And keep out of our affairs . . . Life was difficult enough with governesses, and if school was now going to be introduced, it would become quite unmanageable.

And so it came to pass that we were enrolled at the Ecole Communale, on the far side of the village. Mamma, determined to do the right thing now that she was launched, took a long searching look at the other children to see how they were turned out. And so a few days later we were rigged out as little peasants, with wooden-sole, lace-up boots and rough-haired navy cloaks reaching down to our ankles. This bulky garment, so useful to shepherds high up in the icy mountain passes of the Alps, was much too hot and heavy on balmy days. And in a raging wind, when the Mistral was roaring down the railway cutting, our cloaks flew high up in the air as we crossed the bridge, then came crashing down over our heads, knocking us off our feet.

As it turned out, school was not so bad after all. Although we were forty-strong in my class, silence and order reigned throughout the lessons. We were split into two sections, the dumb and the not so dumb. I was in the first category. The teacher promised to move us up to the higher level as soon as we proved worthy of it. I decided to concentrate on literature, the Greek and Roman civilisations, history and geography. Maths and fractions would have to take care of themselves.

To begin with, following Mamma's decision that we would conform in every way, we had lunch in the canteen, where soup, the only course, was dished up in army mess tins together with half a loaf of bread. The boys, whose playground was on the other side of the wall, joined us for lunch, but we were forbidden to talk to them. John, whenever I caught sight of him, looked so gloomy that it made me want to cry. But Anne seemed to have found her feet, and was the centre of an animated group obviously hanging on her words. I often wondered what stories she was telling them.

We never knew what went wrong with this arrangement, but it soon came to an end. From then on we were given a packed lunch each and forbidden by Marie to go near the canteen again. As the classrooms were locked up during the lunch-hour, we had to sit in the schoolyard, disconsolately munching our sandwiches. I am quite sure that none of us complained about the soup, as we were quite used to taking things as they came, accepting discomfort when inevitable and heartily enjoying the goodies whenever they appeared.

Without explanation of any kind, this joyless period suddenly came to an end. We were simply told one day that we wouldn't be going to school any more.

Intoxicated with our restored freedom, we galloped up and down the garden, yelling our lungs out, rolling down the sloping banks and climbing trees, perching at the top, enjoying the view of the sea in the distance, the hot sun, and the birds singing all round. After a couple of days we sobered down and returned to our private occupations, so boringly interrupted by school. The graveyard, badly neglected, was buried in weeds. Some of the crosses had fallen down flat, and a quail's sepulchre had been desecrated by a cat. When it was all cleared and tidied up and we were wondering what to do next, Mamma announced that we would be leaving for St Georges as soon as possible. A villa was booked, and the leather trunks came thumping down the attic stairs, propelled by Rubio's rope-soled espadrilles.

Papa, who was coming home on leave, met us in Marseilles as usual. We were once more overjoyed to see him, knowing we would have him with us for three whole months.

The journey to the Atlantic coast went off smoothly. The midnight feast which Marie had prepared was up to its usual standard, nobody was sick or got trapped in the loo, and the train arrived at Royan on time. As the horse-drawn coaches now plied their trade along the sea-front for tourists only, we hired a fleet of taxis and set off for St Georges.

Although just as uncomfortable as we expected, Pépé was the least smelly of the villas we had lived in so far. In the yard at the back was a companionable two-seater loo, with round windows cut out in the door for callers to peer in and see who was at home. Marie, who was once more in charge of the cooking, had to sweat over the usual furnace to make the merest cup of tea. The whole house was shrouded in the dust of the preceding winter. We all managed to fit in somehow, an achievement, as it was much smaller than anything we had ever lived in before. Rubio was squeezed into a kitchen cupboard. Anne, Christine and I all squashed together into a tiny bedroom. John moved in with Marie, and our parents had a room to themselves, while poor Sam whimpered the nights away in the dining-room.

We spent all our time on the beach, or with our Darlange friends at Nostram. As long as we turned up on time for meals, we were allowed the most blessed freedom – apart from the morning when we had to resume gym lessons with M. Dupont. And, of course, the swimming lessons had to start again. On and on it went, until he announced we were at last ready to take the swimming test, which included the dreaded, all-important life-saving certificate.

The ordeal, almost a national event, took place in the harbour in front of the entire population of the village, with the aid of the fire-brigade's brass-band, which blared rousing marches throughout the afternoon. The judges sat in a rowing boat at the end of our 'run', where we had to turn and go back to the starting-point. There had been a heavy storm the night before, and the sea was dark and murky. When we lined up at the starting-point on the pier and looked down, we saw that the water was bubbling with huge jellyfish. With a gasp of horror I turned to M. Dupont and said we couldn't possibly swim in *that*! His answer was to push me in.

We all flopped on top of the soft yielding mush and went under, thrashing about among the jellyfish. It was like trying to swim in tapioca pudding. Within seconds their tentacles were twined around my arms, creeping round my neck and trailing across my face. Somehow or other, most of us managed to make it to the judges' boat. Those who couldn't get there had to be hooked out from the mass of jellyfish.

We then had to turn back and start on the return journey. As we scrambled up onto the jetty, we were all pushed in again to do the life-saving part. This consisted in dragging an inert body along, making sure the head was well out of the water, as far as the judges' boat once more. Having made your mark there, you had to haul your unhappy victim all the way back to the jetty. There you handed him or her over to M. Dupont, who confirmed that the job was successfully done and the poor wretch was still alive. After that it was your own turn to take the victim's role. As my own 'saver' was in an even worse state of panic than I was, she pulled me under much more than above the surface. So that when I reached dry land at last, my mouth, full of jellyfish, felt as if I had chewed a hornets' nest.

The ordeal was over at last, we had our 'pass' badges, but we were covered with stinging weals on every inch of uncovered skin. By evening we were puffed up all over, as if blown up with a bicycle-pump, with eyelids painfully glued together. Marie, grinding her teeth in disapproval, dumped us in a bath of boracic water, and spent the next few hours sponging our throbbing faces.

After this, Mamma, ever pursuing her aim of trying to improve our physique, devised a most terrible, lolloping walk for us, which was designed to arch the feet, loosen up the joints and tone the muscles all in one go. It was, according to her, the best possible exercise for developing young growing bodies, so two or three times a week we were marched off to the pine-woods along the beach, thereby getting double benefit from the performance, as we would be breathing in all those valuable essences at the same time.

Completely unselfconscious as she was, our mother broke into her lollop, enjoining us to do the same, before we had even left the village. John and Anne followed her, doubled-up with giggles, while I hobbled behind, with tears of shame and humiliation running down my face, as people stopped, stared, and exclaimed: 'Oh, poor things, do look! Whatever is the matter with them?' We looked like a family all cursed with the same strange affliction. Curiously, Mamma minded the giggles much less than the tears, which she said I produced on purpose to draw attention to myself and make people feel sorry for me. And so we lolloped along, rocking from heel to toe, flexing the knees, flinging out the arms ('From the shoulder, I tell you! Those feeble little wiggles are no good at all!') and thrusting out the hip-joints this way and that like a school of belly-dancers. When this performance was over, and we had hobbled disjointedly back to Pépé, we rushed off to the beach as fast as we could, in case Mamma should think up some new form of body-building exercise for us.

It was a great joy to be able to swim really well at last. No breaker, however huge, was frightening any longer. We dived straight through it, gliding in the glassy water, and learnt how far we could go before coming up for air.

Twice a year, at the time of the Equinox, the tide went out much further than usual, and the sea withdrew for miles. The harbour was drained to the dregs, exposing all the treasures of its bottom. Old prams, cartwheels, toy boats, broken bidets, and so on. The firm wet sandline came to an abrupt end, and the primeval oceanic mudflats stretched out for miles ahead, bubbling and wriggling with their own private life. Lugworm, like strips of raw liver, dived head down into the slime. Razor shells peered out of their holes, tiny green crabs scrambled frantically into the mud, and all kinds of nameless, shapeless blobs of jelly wriggled about, waiting for the sea to return. And all this snapped, crackled and popped, as millions of tiny bubbles continually burst everywhere for miles around.

The first time we saw the tide go out so far we ran along the edge, breathing in the deep rich smell which came wafting out of the ooze. Suddenly, overcome by an irresistible urge, I threw myself flat on my face in the mud. John and Anne followed at once, and we rolled about, slapping and whacking the slimy sludge with flaying arms, unconsciously reaching back millions of years to our original home in the warm Cambrian seas, where our ancestors, all those bits of quivering jelly, first came to life. Black and dripping from head to foot, we jumped back onto solid sand and raced home to show Marie, who we knew would be fascinated by the look and feel of this extraordinary slush so seldom seen.

'What do you think of this?' John asked her as the three of us, still black from head to foot, stinking and dripping all over the floor, burst into the kitchen. She ran a finger down his arm and rubbed it on the palm of her hand. 'Good, rich stuff this,' she said. 'Very fertile. There's nothing to beat it. I'll get Rubio to fetch a few pails of it for the herbs in the garden.' Then she hissed fiercely: 'Get back to the beach at once and wash all that filth off in the sea. And don't let me see you again before dinner.'

*

When the tide was rising, ah, that was when our spirits soared, and a strange new elation took possession of us all. This reaction to the advancing tide seemed to hit everybody along the beach like an electric current. And the higher the tide rose, the more delighted we all were. On very special occasions, freak waves even swamped the tents and carried away bits of underwear and other belongings, and we dived in like retrievers to restore their sodden property to the distracted owners. It was then that the *plongeoir*, a high wooden structure planted in the sand and used for diving when the tide was high, came into its own. Now that we were expert swimmers we enjoyed plunging into the heaving swell and swimming underwater, among the fish who wriggled through our hair, our hands, and nosed into our ears. They revelled in it all as much as we did.

It was so absorbing that we didn't always notice when the tide was going out. On one of these occasions, I dived from the very top and landed flat on my head on the sandy bottom. Had it been stones I would have broken my neck. As it was, my backbone merely slipped out of joint. But this was bad enough to keep me flat on my back for the rest of the summer. Plunged into despair, I think I would have died of boredom and frustration had Jacques not come every day to sit by my bed for hours, reading aloud, playing rummy, the hanging corpse and the battleship game. He came straight from the beach, smelling of seaweed and dripping sand everywhere. My gratitude for all those hours of swimming ungrudgingly sacrificed, to sit with me and keep up my morale, was unbounded, and my devotion and admiration for him grew as the days went by, and he still came, patient and forbearing, while the others simply put their heads round the door to say hullo and were gone. So that by the end of the summer I was totally, unquestioningly in love with him, as a dog is in love with his master.

At the beginning of September I was allowed to sit up in bed for a few days, and then to stand up and come downstairs. But there was no more swimming that year.

At about this time my mother had another of her fiendish inspirations which could turn one day after another into a ghastly nightmare, when the high tides of the autumn Equinox revealed, upon retiring miles out in the bay, the largest oyster beds imaginable, clinging to a vast shelf of rock, usually hidden by the sea. Mamma spotted them at once, and day after day during the *grandes marais* she sent Rubio hotfoot with a sack and hammer and chisel to collect as many as he could before the tide returned and swept him out to sea. So for days and days he came home with his sack heavily loaded with huge oysters as large as Marie's gardening shoes.

Apart from me, the entire family was delighted with these oysters, which they gobbled up by the dozen. But for me it was torture. The mere sight of the obscene creatures glistening and writhing in their shells made my insides heave. The minute you stuck a fork into them, they wriggled and squirmed so much that I had to clasp my napkin to my face, howling, 'You don't realise, they've even got kidneys . . .' And I was sick every time. It was a repeat of the daily milk and honey tea-time dramas at Mas Mistral all over again.

By the autumn I was strong enough to get back to all our normal activities. One day Marie despatched us with Rubio to collect wood for her furnace. And off we set with all the saws and choppers we needed for the job.

John, on the whole, was a calm and placid person, wise beyond his years. When people approached him with their problems, as they often did, his advice was always judicious and succinct. But once in a while the devil managed to get into him. Whenever that happened, it was best to keep as far away from him as possible.

On the fateful day when Rubio tried to kill him, the weather was perfect. We had rucksacks on our backs and we skipped along in high good humour. Even Sam, who was getting on in years, was trotting along quite briskly. When we reached the spot where we knew a lot of dead trees would be lying around, we all got down to work. Rubio wielded his axe, and we helped by breaking the sticks into suitable lengths. It was then, with a sinking heart, that I noticed John's mood was changing. He was beginning to snap the sticks with exaggerated effort, flinging out his arms so that one of us got scratched or poked in the eye every time. When he caught Anne's skirt, lifting it high on the end of a branch, and roared with laughter, she whipped round in a fury. 'I'll hit you with my teeth if you're not careful,' she snarled. Rubio, coming in for the next round, got a sharp sting on the back of the neck. He missed a stroke and went sprawling past his target, landing on his knees with his beret over his nose. Again John hooted at the sight. Rubio's fierce Basque temper flared. He scrambled to his feet with a growl of rage and made straight for John with his chopper held high. I yelled, 'Run, for heaven's sake, run!'

John, leaping like a goat, bolted through the trees, with an infuriated Rubio staggering after him. But owing to his weak sight (his eyeballs had been seriously damaged by lightning during a thunderstorm) he kept stumbling over stones and stumps which he couldn't see. John got away. After that incident, and though we all pleaded for his reprieve, poor Rubio was sent back to Mas Mistral in disgrace.

That summer, out of the blue, Mamma took me inland to Barbezieux to stay with her friends the Fauconniers. Hélène was there with her three brothers, all of them cool, detached and haughty, like highly-bred hawks. François Fontaine, who was later to become Hélène's husband, was also there. *He* was less of a bird of prey than a stag, and God knows how *I* looked to them! Anyway, after a while the ice melted, and we all played noisy and rumbustious games in the garden. There were swings and a trapeze and parallel bars, and that peculiar overriding melancholy, insidious and seductive like a kind of lotus-eating, which broods over the region around Bordeaux and which pervades all the novels of Mauriac. I felt even then that it could, if allowed, soak into the bloodstream and fix in it a permanent mood of languid melancholy for life. More than ever did I sympathise with those full-blooded adventurous pioneers, my two great-grandfathers, for getting away from this cloying, dreamy, enervating miasma.

Henri Fauconnier's sister, Geneviève, who wrote that blissful book about her farm, *Pastorale*, and got the Prix Femina for her novel *Claude*, lived a long way out in the country. We went there one fine day, to find a scene straight out of *Le Grand Meaulnes*. The farm and its grounds had been given over for the day to some charity or other, and there were booths, merry-go-rounds and coconut shies everywhere. Children in crinolines and knickerbockers bowled hoops along the paths and raced around, laughing and shouting.

We then went into a barn smelling of warm cow and hay, and there, of all unexpected things, two American ladies, who lived in a caravan in the grounds, danced a ballet to Debussy's *L'Après-midi d'un faune*. The whole thing is so nebulous and dreamlike in my memory that, much as I would like to, I can't remember anything more precise. There was a great deal of old-world courtesy around and Mamma was continuously having her hand kissed, which she didn't seem to mind in the least.

chapter sixteen

A few days later Mamma received another flash from On High. She announced at breakfast that we would not be going back to Vence for the winter. Instead we would return to Malaya, and she would take us all with her. This was unexpected, wonderful news. We whooped and danced with joy. But our euphoria was not to last very long. Next day she told us she had changed her mind, and we would all stay in St Georges instead. And off she went to see the headmaster of the College in Royan about our wretched education. It transpired from this interview that he would take us all, on condition that *I* should learn Latin before the beginning of term. There were two weeks to go . . . Mamma assured him that this would be done, and set off at once to find me a Latin teacher. This turned out to be more difficult than she expected. The local priest, who should have been a natural, flatly refused to teach girls.

In the end she unearthed a very ancient scholar who was busy writing a history of medieval heresies in Latin. I never discovered how she persuaded him to take me on. As for me, I was delighted at the chance of learning such an ancient, noble language. Sanskrit would have been even better. Anyway, I plunged into it with much enthusiasm. My new teacher greeted me in Latin when I arrived for my first lesson, and from then on never addressed a word to me in any other language all the time we worked together. We were confined to his study for six hours a day, while my poor untutored brain reeled in complete bewilderment. By the time I was released in the evening, all I could do was stagger down to the beach for a quick swim. And after that, still bemused, I tottered back to the villa to do my Latin homework.

When school started two weeks later, we did not, thank goodness, have to take an entrance exam. A rough guess was made, and we were placed in classes suitable to our respective ages, if not our intellectual level. As it turned out, we managed, through a great deal of hard work and a certain amount of copying from our neighbours, to scrape along at the bottom of the class. Our delight at finally being in a proper school, with mature, grownup children of our own age, kept our spirits up, so that our low marks didn't depress us *too* much. Apart from maths, I enjoyed all the subjects very much, and came across some fascinating facts. In biology, for instance, I learnt that the human eyelid has the only muscle in the body that makes a noise. If you bang your eye shut, you can hear a click. But you have to listen carefully, as it is a very faint click. On the whole we were regarded as harmless freaks by our companions, whose judgement we accepted without question. In fact, enjoying school for the first time, we lived through that term in a kind of dream, floating a good six inches above the ground.

We had to be at school, four miles away from home, at eight in the morning. The tram, as we called it, was a small open train with curtains along the sides. It picked us up every morning in

St Georges at seven a.m. and dropped us at the college gates at seven-thirty. We just had time to dash through the hall and out to the sandy schoolyard to line up with our classmates. The teachers, known as '*professeurs*', were all men. The boys were called by their surnames, but the girls, right down to the little eight-year-olds, were *Mademoiselle*.

Each *professeur* had his own classroom, so that we were constantly on the move from one room to another, according to the lesson coming up next. This caused an enormous amount of traffic on the stairs and in the corridors. Endless crocodiles trudged in opposite directions, with a great deal of banter and witty exchanges on the way. Little notes, *billets-doux* changed hands, assignations were made, and life was very exciting. English boys become gallant at a much later age (if ever) than the French. Most of the boys in my class, though savage in their fights with each other, were gentle and considerate with the girls. They carried our books, gave us sweets, and let us copy their maths homework. And they chatted us up endlessly during break, with gracious compliments on the colour of our eyes and hair. The schoolyard, where a lot of this went on, was an extension of the beach beyond, shaded by umbrella pines. And the sound of the sea was always in the air.

At midday we climbed back into our tram which was waiting for us outside the college gates. And off we puffed and whistled our way through the woods, back to the villa for lunch. After which, stuffed and bloated with one of Marie's ample meals, we returned to school to snooze the afternoon away in the over-heated classrooms. Fortunately the *professeurs* had also had a substantial lunch, and a great deal of their morning ardour had evaporated with the fumes of their daily bottle of claret or burgundy.

Some of the wilder boys flicked ink pellets at the ceiling with impunity, or quietly unscrewed all the bolts of the bench in front of them, so that its occupants would suddenly crash to the floor with a frightful clatter. Sometimes a stink-bomb would go off in the aisle, creating total chaos, with everybody rushing to the windows for air. The four-o'clock bell caused a stampede, with all order gone to the wind, and everybody pelted down the stairs, swinging satchels, bellowing and whooping with released high spirits.

One of the clever girls in my class took me under her wing and helped me tirelessly with homework and moral support. Day after day she encouraged me to keep going, and when I took her home to tea, she even talked wisely to my mother about my work. A year older than me, she had a cool and perceptive brain. Remembering her with affection and gratitude, I have often wondered what became of her. She should by rights have gone to teach French literature at a senior French girls' school. Her parents were abroad, and she and her sister shared a small house with a governess. It was a very pleasant household, calm, cultured, sensible, and with all the right values. The three of them, I realised even then, were born spinsters.

Another girl in my form who could not be ignored was a little hell-cat half my size, who had all the boys in the class under her control. I used to watch her giving them orders to persecute me, then waiting to see what would happen. As I was totally unpractised in this kind of warfare, my only defence was to emulate animals who feign death in the face of danger. When I saw it coming, I simply looked as defenceless as I felt. And this was no act. What is more, it seemed to work. Even her most devoted slaves hesitated to attack such a terrified-looking creature. As they approached, I dropped a handkerchief or a ruler. One of them would pick it up with an embarrassed grunt and hand it back to me. After which they slunk away to take their punishment. And although she kept this up for a whole term, I wasn't molested once. After the holidays she either got bored with the game or found another victim, and I was left in peace.

That autumn the film star Danielle Darrieux had launched the fashion for black ciré (an early form of plastic) raincoats, and we all wore them, boys and girls alike, whatever the weather. Those black raincoats, black gumboots and black berets were the uniform without which we would not allow ourselves to be seen, so that in a school where there was no regulation uniform, we put ourselves into one of our own free will.

That year we started a weekly magazine, for which we soon received so many orders that we had to spend most of our time working on it. There was a children's newspaper called *Benjamin*, to whose editor we sent a copy of our first number. He gave us a glowing write-up which started the ball rolling, and the subscriptions came pouring in. This was the last thing we expected. The wretched thing, which was such fun to start with, got out of hand, and became a menace. Had we been older and more experienced, we might have been able to run it efficiently on a businesslike basis. As it was, we wrote it all out by hand in block capitals with a special ink. The master-copy was then pressed down onto a kind of solidified jelly which absorbed the print. And from this we could pull off as many copies as we needed. We ran two serials, one short story, a crossword puzzle, nature notes, a fashion feature, and a page of ads, fake to start with. As the whole thing was copiously illustrated, it took a great deal of time to set up. And thinking of the work involved, at 50 centimes a copy it was cheap at the price. We managed to keep it going for six feverishly hard-working months, at the end of which, distracted with exhaustion, we had to give it up. Heartbroken, we wrote to our subscribers that we had to stop publication as, alas, school-work had to come first, and there was no time for both in our lives at the moment. And for several weeks after that I continued to wake up at night in a cold sweat, thinking I still had to dash off a couple of chapters for the serials before breakfast. Worst of all were the crosswords – for months we had never dared be out of sight of a dictionary. But on the whole, in spite of the frenzy, I think we got more fun out of it than misery.

Our next craze was for bicycles. The little tram was suddenly considered cissy, only fit for toddlers and grandmas. So my mother obligingly bought us a bicycle each, and from then on, come rain or shine, we cycled to and from school every day of the week. We either took the path through the woods, where we had to cross a stream over a creaking, worm-eaten wooden plank, or else we went by the sea-road, which took longer, but was magic on sunny days.

Going home after school, we often trundled our bikes onto the beach at low tide, and raced round and round on the hard wet sand, like low-flying swallows at sunset. We devised a game of 'bicycle polo', in which we dealt one another the most murderous blows and crashed headlong into each other's front wheels. We often had to carry our cycles home on our backs with a wheel twisted into a figure-of-eight. That winter all our pocket-money went on repairs and 'new' second-hand parts for our battered bikes.

Another sport that we longed to practise, but could seldom afford, was sand-sailing. Small boats made of canvas, with three wheels, a mast and two enormous sails, could be hired by the hour in Royan. In a high wind these thistledown sand-craft simply flew along the beach, and you needed skill and a good deal of nerve to control them and prevent them from taking off like a kite in a high wind.

chapter seventeen

When the Darlange family arrived for the Christmas holidays, we all set off to the woods with saws and choppers to collect the finest tree we could find. We came back with a magnificent ten-foot-high specimen, which we planted in sand, in the biggest wash-tub we could find, and then set up in front of the dining-room window. As we stood around admiring it, my head, which had been aching all day, suddenly felt as if it was going to split. My throat was on fire, and the air hissed and whistled as it rattled in and out of my tubes.

'What's the matter with you?' my mother asked suspiciously. 'Nothing at all,' I wheezed, and hoping to distract her, I asked what she thought of our tree. But this triggered a choking fit of coughing, at which my mother dragged me away by the hand. 'Come with me,' she said firmly, and produced her dreaded thermometer, with which it was never possible to argue. And off to bed I had to go. The next day I was covered with spots all over and my eyelids were glued together. Lying in bed all day long, I wept and sobbed into my pillow at the sound of the revels downstairs.

To cheer me up, Jacques brought me a copy of Kipling's *The Light that failed*, which he had received as a Christmas present. It was the first full-length English book I had ever read. And if it hadn't been for the chickenpox, and the terrible boredom it produced, I would probably never have got through it. But it came in useful at the time, and convinced me that I could really read English at last and even enjoy it.

The rest of that school year went by in a flash. Lessons, totally incomprehensible to begin with, were becoming easier. My Latin teacher told me that I now knew enough to keep the headmaster happy, and that our lessons could stop. The poor man, who had worked even harder than I, was worn out, and longed to shed his dim-witted pupil and get back to his heresies. Our daily lessons had even included Sunday morning after church, and for those who can take it, I recommend the method as the best way of getting the hang of the language, its peculiar syntax, back-to-front constructions and divine rhythm. But not everybody will think it worth paying the price!

And then the term was over, and the Easter holidays brought the Darlanges back from Paris, and we were all in heaven once more.

On the beach, half-buried in the sand was a black, square shooting box known as a *tonne*, which had broken away from its moorings in the marshes, floated out to sea, and subsequently been washed up by the tide. This was one of our favourite meeting spots at the time. Crawling through the narrow shooting slit (the door was on the opposite side, buried in the sand), we huddled inside where we felt cosy, safe and quite unassailable.

The Darlange children, who had grown even larger in the last few months, only just managed to squeeze through the slit. It was touch and go, but they finally made it, and we all squashed up inside as tightly packed as sardines. We were growing up and the boys, whose voices were breaking, uttered the most comical squeaks, which reduced us to helpless fits of giggles. Ninette's hair had grown into beautiful glossy waves bouncing down her back, much to Nadia's disgust, as she herself was never able to produce anything more than a few fluffy tufts around her ears, in spite of all the bottles of castor oil she poured over it. Her hair, far from being her crowning glory, was her despair, the kind of wispy fuzz that usually grows on babies.

We would talk in the tonne for hours on end, mostly about what we had done and the books we had read; we formed plans for the future, set the world to rights, and when talk dried up, we made up stories, no one being allowed more than a five-minute stretch at a time.

One day John produced, as a surprise, some pipes which he had made for us out of bamboo canes, after which he handed round the tobacco, a careful blend of Indian and China tea. We stuffed our pipes with this concoction and lit up. Within a few seconds we were coughing and spluttering as a thick cloud of smoke filled the tonne, kippering our eyeballs and scorching our tongues. By then, as we could hardly get any air through our tubes, we raced home, where we found Mamma safely anchored to her wireless. As usual at that hour, she was trying to capture the six o'clock news through the squeaks and crackles of the 'atmospherics', as Marie called them. Creeping up to her bedroom, we each took a swig of her eau-de-cologne, good strong stuff that went down like fire and would obliterate all traces of tea-smoke on our breath.

The pipe craze only lasted for a week, after which we gave up smoking, all but Nadia, who progressed to Gauloises, for which, from then on, she scrimped and saved, and on which she spent every sou that she could get hold of.

At other times, as a change from the tonne, we went to the *palombière*, which was a pigeon-hide perched on top of the tallest pine-tree that ever grew. The local farmers and vineyard workers used it for shooting wood-pigeons, or *palombes* as they were called, which is to me one of the most beautiful words in the French language. The tree, which was as smooth and straight as a telegraph-pole, could only be climbed by swarming up nails which stuck out at either side and took you all the way up to the hide in the topmost branches. These nails, mostly old and rusty, worked loose in the bark of the tree, and often came away in your hands, if they didn't snap clean off under your feet. This once happened to me as I was nearing the top, so that I was left suspended, clinging for dear life to a couple of rusty nails, with legs flailing wildly in search of some support, thirty feet above the ground. Jacques, who was just above me, vaulted onto the platform and hauled me up by the scruff of my neck.

The hide was made for two people at the most, but we were seldom less than six, and it is a wonder that the worm-eaten floor-boards didn't crumble under our weight. This possibility did occasionally cross our minds, but being perched up there above everything else, with a view of the whole forest and miles of coastline, with nothing above our heads but the clear blue sky continually streaked with flights of wild geese and duck, was so exhilarating that it was well worth taking the risk, while extra excitement was added when a high wind blew and tossed us about like a ship on a high sea.

The following term we made friends with a girl in my class called Yolande, and she joined in our bicycle polo games with great gusto, which surprised us a good deal, as she had a mature and dignified look which utterly disguised her inner wildness. Completely hemmed in by her family life, she lived in a small château on the hill behind Royan, a lonely, tidy, repressed life in a wing of her own, with an aquarium full of goldfish and a governess who neglected her dreadfully, only appearing at meals, when she gobbled her food in a way even we found revolting, then disappeared to her room without ever offering to help with our homework.

One spring evening, after leaving Yolande to her own homework and the silent company of her goldfish, we were freewheeling downhill on our bicycles. As we had enjoyed a particularly lively game of polo the day before, my front wheel, which had a pronounced twist, scraped the mudguard with a hideous noise. The brakes had dropped off during a head-on collision, and the only way I could attempt to slow down as we approached the main street running at right angles at the bottom of the hill was by pressing my foot down on the front tyre as hard as I could. This usually worked well enough, but in this case, under the strain, the wheel flew off and bounced away into the traffic. My bicycle pitched forward and crashed on its nose, and I was hurled against a passing car, from which, to my surprise, I bounced off and hit the corner of the house across the street. Luck was on my side. I landed on my hip-bone instead of my skull, but the bicycle was smashed and flattened under the wheels of the car, which drove on as if nothing had happened. There was no point in scraping up the remains of the bicycle, and we left them there for the dustmen to collect. Dazed and shaken as I was, I could not have managed to walk the four miles back to the Villa Pépé, and John kindly gave me a lift on his luggage-rack. It was difficult to explain to Mamma the nature of the accident which had written off my bicycle but had left me without a scratch. Willing to suffer almost any amount of pain rather than have to go to the doctor, I did my best not to limp under her nose. She told me to go and get myself another second-hand bicycle, and to try and look after it better in the future.

*

It was about this time that my mother threw another of her bombshells into our midst. Now she really was going back to Malaya, taking Christine with her. John would return to boarding school in England, and I would go to a convent in Paris, also as a boarder. Marie assured me that this fate would be worse than being exiled to Devil's Island. I believed her absolutely. Anne was the only lucky one, who would stay on at the college and live with Marie in St Georges.

From now on, every single day would be precious and unique, to be packed with all the fun and pleasure that could be squeezed into it. We got up at dawn and ran down to the beach to swim, roll down the dunes, and build enormous sand fortresses, real models of the Bastille, the Tower of London, Richard the Lion-Heart's *Château-Gaillard*, until breakfast. On our way home we bought fresh rolls and croissants, hot and crackling from the baker's oven, and these, split in half and spread with butter, eaten under the mulberry trees with mugs of café-au-lait, made a welcome and satisfying breakfast. Then back to the beach we went.

That summer we had a craze for the 'hanging corpse' game. Sprawling shoulder to shoulder in cartwheel fashion, we would scrape away a nice pitch of damp sand, flat and smooth for drawing on. Then each of us in turn drew a line or a squiggle or whatever, until you had a gibbet, with a rope and corpse hanging from it. As with 'old maid', the idea was to avoid at any cost being last, so that all sorts of curlicues and appendages were added, nails and screws to the gibbet, twists to the rope, eyelashes to the corpse, and a fierce argument arose when someone gave him earrings. Pirates and sailors sometimes wore *one* earring, but who had ever heard of two? When bored with the hanging corpse, we played the word game. This consisted of writing the first and last letter, and as many dashes as were necessary to make up the word in-between. You could cheat as much as you liked by changing the word in your mind, as long as the letters already down corresponded. Then sooner or later someone jumped up and ran down to the sea, and the whole pack leapt up and followed with whoops and yells and piercing screams.

One day John and Jacques locked themselves up in the garage at Nostram. We could hear them hammering and banging away inside. But they would neither let us in nor tell us what they were up to. Eventually they flung the doors open, and there on the floor lay the most elegant little white canoe you had ever seen. They had made it themselves, to John's specifications. (Later he was to build his own ocean-going yacht, which he sailed for many years in the China Seas.) In a state of high excitement we carried it down to the beach, where it rode the waves like a swan. But what was the use of only one boat? We clamoured for more, and they went back to work. Eventually we each had our own, which we paddled in the bay from dawn to dusk.

But the greatest excitement came with the high tides, when we raced out to where the rollers began to heave out of the sea. Once there, we swung our canoes around with a violent flip of the paddle (which often capsized the boats), but with luck we sometimes managed to climb onto a roller at the crucial moment when it was gathering speed, and then we simply flew into shore on the huge wave – our own home-made version of surf-riding. Sometimes our canoes were smashed in particularly heavy seas, and we were churned up, wrapped in yards of canvas, in the raging breakers, often bruised by the flaying woodwork and gashed by exposed nails. But these small accidents were of no importance when compared with the thrill and excitement of the sport. Our great ambition was to take our boats further up the coast to the *Grande Côte*, where for hundreds of deserted miles the empty beaches faced the open Atlantic and the undertow sucked you far out to sea before washing you up again several hours later, quite drowned, unless some lucky shark had managed to catch you on the way. But we were forbidden to paddle, let alone swim, on that stretch of coast.

Beach picnics were another joy, as Marie, remembering her early training in Australia, produced the most fantastic spreads, for which she took a great deal more trouble than for ordinary meals at the villa. Laden with baskets and followed by Rubio, until his exile, equally burdened with hampers and boxes of table-silver, she would settle down at the foot of the dunes, where the tamarisks dispensed a thin feathery shade, and under her orders Rubio spread out the cloths, the rugs and the food. There were always fresh rolls and several kinds of *saucisson*, cold roast pork and chicken in aspic, big fat juicy tomatoes, egg and salmon pies, and cucumber and potato salads. Then came plum tarts and meringues, and bottles of fresh lemon juice were dug into the sand to keep cool.

As summer progressed, we noticed a change coming over Jacques. He was growing moody, and for no apparent reason he would suddenly snap at one of us, then go off for long walks by himself. It was very tiresome, as it broke the harmony which had reigned until then. The most stupid things would set him off. If he suddenly came across Nadia and myself giggling helplessly over a croissant which we were nibbling at both ends, or reading the same book aloud in different accents, he burst into a rage and stamped away, banging doors. Finally one day he took me aside and lectured me on the subject. It was time, he said, that I should start behaving in a more grown-up way. It was all very well for Nadia to go on being a silly little girl, but I should begin to grow more serious-minded. I was, after all, a whole year older than her. This put me into a painful quandary. Loving him devotedly as I did, and knowing that one day we would be married (this was assumed, as a matter of course, by everybody), I naturally wanted to keep him happy, but the thought of giving up all the fun that Nadia and I had together was more than I could bear. This developed into a guilt feeling, and whenever she and I went off together in one of our dotty moods, I knew that I was in some way letting old cross-patch Jacques down.

Nadia always went to bed in great style; her ample and voluptuous form was superbly designed for undulating between bath and bed. To ensure a maximum audience, she retired very soon after dinner and got into one of her sophisticated nightdresses, with shoulder-straps and sides split up to the thighs. As we had never seen anything but our own long-sleeved high-necked Vyella or Tobralco night gear, these glamorous garments of hers dazzled and enchanted us. A great deal of time was spent in the bathroom, with dogs perching and sprawling everywhere and Anne, Ninette and I sitting on the edge of the bath like a row of swallows on a telephone wire. Our role was to admire, advise and exclaim as she puffed out those few hairs of hers, darkened her moles, sprayed herself with scent, and tried out interesting expressions in front of the glass. When we were satisfied that perfection had been reached and no further improvement was possible, she swept out of the room with one of those well-practised expressions on her face, and closely followed by the snuffling, snorting dogs, we escorted her to her room. We never knew until the last minute which bedroom would be selected, or which one of her young cousins would be turned out and sent off to sleep in her bed.

When a decision had been reached, Nadia would get into bed and pick up whichever book was in the running at the time, Victor Hugo or Racine or Corneille (she was particularly scornful of these three), and she would read aloud in mocking tones as we sat on her feet, in fits of laughter. Sometimes, when she was feeling very magnanimous, we would be invited to squash in with her, squealing and giggling, with all the dogs scrabbling and scratching on top of us, barking their heads off, not quite knowing why but feeling they had to. If she happened to have chosen a four-poster there was plenty of room, but when she occupied a short narrow child's bed it was a tight fit, and we screeched and squirmed and giggled in a lunatic frenzy. Sometimes, attracted by the noise, Jacques would walk in, shoulders and eyebrows raised in outraged disapproval. He would glare at us, and stalk out growling, 'You're all quite, quite mad', and I knew that I would be in for another lecture in the morning.

Sometimes he would tackle my mother, or she him, I never knew which way round it was, but I hated those long chats they had together, as it was perfectly obvious that they were discussing my shortcomings and Mamma was trying to enlist his help in improving me. Lectures invariably followed these dreaded tête-à-têtes, and although I knew he was quite right, it was intensely provoking to get the same kind of pie-jaw from him as from my mother. I suppose they thought it was high time for me to become a tidy, responsible and domesticated young woman. This had, alas, the opposite effect, and my efforts to improve slackened rather than increased. I knew I was untidy, lazy, selfish, terribly absent-minded (a great crime, this) and did not take enough trouble with my appearance – but whose fault, pray, was that, when I still wasn't allowed a looking-glass in my bedroom, and had to wash my face with scrubbing soap?

Once a young cousin of Jacques, who had lived in the Dordogne, came to stay at Nostram for a few days, and joined in all our activities. Tall, with dark curly hair and dreamy black eyes, he wore a brown shepherd's cloak reaching down to his feet, which gave him the romantic look of a nineteenth-century poet. We all got on very well.

After he left, I was surprised to get a lecture from Jacques.

Papa looking very Proustian, seated between Marie and the housekeeper.
The three of them often took decorous walks together

Papa's mournful countenance could
never be cheered up by anything.
The jongleur of Notre Dame would
have been hard put to get a smile
out of him

Mamma soon after I was born. The dog is defending
his place – no room for smelly babies here

Assam Java

Papa off to work during a flood, with his friend Henri Fauconnier, author of *Soul of Malaya*

Children's party at Kuala Lumpur,
Anne as a powder-puff –
skirt covered with swansdown –
and I as a powder-box

First day at St Georges

A picnic in the hills behind Vence; Marie in one of her large hats as usual, Mamma in the
dashing cloche at far right

Basic News, Psychological Warfare Branch, Algiers, 'the nerve centre of the Mediterranean Forces'. A solid hour was spent tidying up the usual mess for the benefit of the photographer

Rome, 1944. Dinner at the Nirvanetta Club on the Via Veneto with an officer on leave from the Gothic Line

...tting up the type for the *Salerno Times* during hostilities. Captain Beauclerk calmly smokes his pipe under heavy enemy shelling

Firing PWB leaflets in two-inch mortar smoke-bombs over the line at Alife di Piedimonte

Law court in Venice, July 1945. Covering trials of Italian nationals charged with collaboration, I am indignant at the summary nature of the proceedings (me, seated, top left-hand corner)

Mine-spotting with the captain of a minesweeping fleet in the Mediterranean, summer 1945

'You were flirting with him all the time,' he said. 'You shouldn't encourage him like that, you know. It isn't fair.' I was stunned. *Had* I encouraged him? I tried to remember. We had once sat in the dunes together, chatting about school. Another time, on the way back from a long walk, a cold wind had come up and he had taken me under his cloak with his arm around my shoulders. Was *that* encouraging him? I suppose I could have insisted on freezing all the way home instead of snuggling under his cloak. At which I probably looked guilty, as Jacques said kindly, 'Don't worry, never mind. He won't come back.' And he never did.

When Jacques was in one of his moods, the best way to revive his happy, creative self was to fetch our stories and paints and start scribbling away. In a few minutes he would come and sit next to me and pick up a paint-brush. I would read out the last chapter I had written, and he would produce one illustration after another with amazing rapidity. His figures and animals were so alive that they practically jumped off the page. When a chapter was finished, we reversed the roles. He wrote the next instalment, while I struggled with the drawings. We were writing a long rambling story about a caveman, his hunts, his fights, and finally the capture of a beautiful girl clad in a bearskin.

Sometimes we worked at Nostram, but the constant interruptions irritated Jacques beyond endurance, particularly as he knew how much I enjoyed them. One small cousin after another would burst in with a fishing-net in need of repair, a request for sticking plaster for a lacerated knee, or even an offer to help with our painting. And best of all, Nadia would make an occasional pounce and drag me away to tell me some utterly fascinating secret. So on the whole, Jacques much preferred to work at our villa.

We spread our clutter on the garden table, and Marie would soon appear with glasses of lemon juice or cups of tea. And into these Jacques constantly dipped his brush, just as he often took a swig of the paint water, without ever noticing the difference. When we ran out of inspiration, he took a book out of his pocket and began to read aloud. After the Mowgli books, which we both loved, had been read several times over, he brought Selma Lagerlöf's *Nils Holgersson*, and this Nordic tale kept us under a spell for several weeks.

The summer was fast coming to an end. As my dreaded fate grew closer, I began at last to grow more serious-minded, and to detach myself from the others and accompany Jacques on his lonely walks. His temper improved noticeably, and he became much kinder and more patient. That was a great relief.

chapter eighteen

The day finally came, at the end of September 1935, when Mamma delivered me to my new school in Paris.

For the first time in our lives we were split up. Anne was packed off to a dark and gloomy dungeon in a small provincial town in the Gironde, which it was amazing she survived, John went off to Sarlat, a Jesuit college, where he had to wear plusfours and a peaked cap like a chauffeur, and I was put down for Sévigné, which promised to turn me from the wild country creature that I was into what a *demoiselle de bonne famille* ought to be. And judging from the others' tales, I was by far the luckiest of the three.

The building, an eighteenth-century château which had belonged to one of the royal mistresses, was entirely surrounded by enormously high walls, within which a formal garden consisted of gravel paths snaking through clumps of evergreen bushes and magnificent, grandiose, noble-looking cedars, at least three hundred years old; beneath the enormous one in the main courtyard, we were told, La Fontaine used to come and read his fables to the noble châtelaine before they appeared in print. But there were no flowers, no colour anywhere. A severe, formal harshness prevailed everywhere.

Gloom and depression settled on me that winter, and bored into my spirits, which had never been so low before. It was not only the dreary lack of anything interesting ever happening, but also the fact of being watched and supervised every moment of the day, and the knowledge that we were all expected to lie and cheat at all times. The misery of that year stands out like a black tunnel.

When we arrived, we were led to the *salon* where the head-mistress was waiting for us. Standing in the middle of the room, drawn up to her full height of at least five feet, she stared in silence as we walked into the room. Her long black gown with leg-of-mutton sleeves and high lace collar made her look formidable. Since the split between church and state had taken place in France nuns had been forbidden to teach, so they got round it by wearing mufti. Everybody knew of the deception, but as long as appearances were kept up, and the nuns wore what they thought was ordinary modern dress, the Ministry of Education allowed them to carry on in peace.

As I shook hands with the head, I felt my wrist being wrenched downwards in an iron grip. Within seconds I was down on one knee. My mother, who had never seen me do such a thing before, stared in amazement. This was my first introduction to the perpetual round of curtseys which went on all day long throughout the school. The 'worker-nuns' curtseyed to the pupils as they handed the dishes round at meals or when we met in the corridors. We curtseyed to the teachers, and everybody bobbed to the headmistress and to Monsieur le Chanoine, who now slowly emerged from the shadows of the *salon* where we stood. By then I realised I had to curtsey to him as well.

We were then read the rules. 'Internees', as we were called, were only allowed to receive letters from their parents. All correspondence was read and censored by the head herself. If anyone was caught smuggling a letter out of the school, immediate expulsion would follow. After this we were dismissed, and a worker-nun led us to the hall where I said goodbye to my mother. The nun then took me upstairs to the dormitory, kindly saying that I could cry until the dinner-bell but that after that no further 'signs of emotion' would be allowed.

The dormitory, as vast as a warehouse, had small square windows, high up near the ceiling, which let in practically no light. The eighty beds were surrounded by curtains, and at all four corners of the room were supervisors' cubicles on twenty-four-hour duty. The wash-rooms at either end had their own watch-dogs. No talking was allowed of course, either in the dormitory or the wash-rooms, where we each had an enamel bowl and a can of water. These were placed on a shelf running all the way round the room, so that we decently faced the wall as we washed. This had to be somehow achieved under the dressing-gown, so that not an inch of bare flesh could be seen. A supervisor stood in the centre of the room to make sure that no indecency (such as a dressing-gown accidentally slipping to the floor) should occur.

Friday was footbath night, held in a crypt in the basement. Worker-nuns scuttled around pouring hot water into tubs in front of each of us, as we sat on benches in silence. Keeping our skirts well down, we soaked and scrubbed our feet. And after this we all trooped off to the dining-room, still in silence, for a Friday dinner (no meat of course) of turnips and boiled cod.

The morning and evening wash and the Friday footbaths were the only scrubbings that most of the girls got throughout the term. I, along with five other privileged boarders, was allowed a weekly bath. This was an extra, and considered dangerous to the health. The school doctor, a very old man with a little grey beard growing out of each ear, had to be consulted every time. 'And why, *Mademoiselle*, do you have such a mania for baths?' he asked me once. 'It's not normal to be so obsessed with them.' But he refused permission only once, when I had a sore throat and wheezing tubes.

The dining-room down in the crypt had no windows at all, and only a few light-bulbs dotted around the ceiling. A long table like a horseshoe ran all the way round the room. Plates only were laid, as our own table-silver was wrapped in our napkins, tucked away under the table. Everybody fussed about the food, but compared to all the other horrors, it seemed to me perfectly acceptable. Soup came first, then meat on its own, handed round by the worker-nuns. This was followed by vegetables, cooked as a separate course. Finally, cheese and fruit were set down on the table. Bananas had to be eaten with a spoon, peaches and pears with a knife and fork. The senior school (from twelve upwards) had a carafe of wine and water as part of the menu. But butter was additional and, Mamma in her kindness, had ordered it for me as an extra. But the rest of the school ate their bread dry with their morning coffee at breakfast-time.

After a long day's work, after dinner we all trooped into the school chapel to gabble our way through the entire rosary on our knees. Some of the smaller girls fell asleep, and occasionally someone fainted. Brought back to their senses with a sharp prod, they had to carry on with prayers.

At six-thirty next morning we were back in church, after which came a quick breakfast, then straight into our classrooms. The form-mistress always started the day with '*Mesdemoiselles*, I am ready to serve you.' Like all the other teachers, she upheld the fiction that the teaching staff were our paid servants. This was infuriating, and they knew as well as we did that nobody was fooled. Why and when this theory was launched I have no idea. It may have been true in the early Middle Ages. But by the time I was there, it was certainly a big fraud.

Two male teachers actually penetrated the establishment and taught the senior school. One was the literature master, and the other taught Greek and Latin. Each would come into a class-room flanked on either side by a couple of lay-nuns, who both sat beside him throughout the lesson. We often wondered what these old men might have got up to if left alone with us, but this was beyond the imagination of even the most knowing of my classmates.

After lunch and tea we were allowed out into the garden when the weather was fine. Otherwise we stayed in the prep room which, as in schools all over the world, reeked of dust, ink and pencil shavings. For the last half-hour before supper we were inflicted on our form-mistress, who was about to become a secret nun. We were convinced she had been 'disappointed in love'. Seductive, with a lovely fresh face, she didn't look like someone who wanted to run away from life. At the moment, her job was obviously to dig deep into our souls and fish out any secrets she could find, all of which would be reported to the authorities. We very much resented all this prying, which only taught us how to deceive and dissemble.

In the garden we played croquet or quoits, on what had been at one time gravel but was now dust or mud, according to the time of year. We were forbidden to gather in groups of less than four, and when only two were caught conferring together, they were sent indoors to learn a fable. Consequently it was very dif-ficult to make friends. I tried to chum up with my next-door neighbour in the dormitory, but the only idea she had in her head was to get married in order to beget as many sons as pos-sible, for the sole purpose of killing Germans. This, she was convinced, was her patriotic duty, and she was determined to accomplish it. Circumstances thwarted her, however, as the war came far too soon for her plan to be carried out.

Our uniform was the same winter and summer so that, as it was adequate in winter we simply sweltered in July, which can be *very* hot in Paris. It consisted of a sailor suit of heavy blue serge, with a pleated skirt and black stockings. For Sunday we had the same, but in white. Navy-blue felt hats completed the ensemble.

Our gym gear had to be seen to be believed – navy-blue knickerbockers to just below the knee with over them a wide flounced skirt like a lampshade, banded with white, a sailor-suit blouse also banded with white, and for the head a triangular piece of cloth tied up in front like a turban, into which all the hair had to be tucked. Decked out in these incredible togs, we marched round and round the footbath room, from which the benches had been removed. The gym nun, whose teeth kept falling out so that she constantly had to catch them in her hand-kerchief, clapped her hands together as we marched. And that was our gym lesson.

Christmas that year was a dismal failure. Mamma and Christine had left for Malaya after dumping us in our various schools, and apart from the joy of seeing Marie and John and Anne again (all of them were even more miserable than I), the Villa Pépé was cold and gloomy beyond belief. Poor Marie, who missed Christine dreadfully, did her best to raise our spirits, but she was too low herself to do any of us much good. The Darlanges stayed in Paris, so that we were alone in St Georges. We went for listless walks, and quarrelled incessantly. We would really have been much happier in Vence, and I can't think why it didn't occur to Marie to take us there. The only bright spot during the holidays was Kipling's *Captains Courageous* which I received as a Christmas present, and which transported me far,

far away into a completely different world. I read it three times before going back to school.

Then suddenly, one glorious day in early spring, a telegram arrived from Malaya, ordering me to go to England on the next boat. As I found out later, it was dear old Mrs Hillier who was behind this move. It was high time, she wrote to Mamma, that Anne and I went to an English school, as no proper education existed outside England. Mamma, who would have had no trouble at all in swallowing that, acted at once. I could imagine her writing out the telegram and despatching the estate postman off with it on his bicycle.

Anne and I were bundled off to Rosemead, in Littlehampton, as boarders. Our new school was a revelation. The relaxed relationship between the staff and the girls never ceased to amaze me. When my desk neighbour once said in a geography lesson, 'Oh, Miss Stewart, you *are* a pig!' I nearly fell off my chair.

And then we were *trusted*. It was always assumed we would speak the truth. Another amazing factor was the spirit of cooperation that reigned throughout the establishment between staff and pupils. The teachers were tolerantly accepted as brainboxes with a tiresome job to do, and the girls ran the school. It was the prefects and the 'subs' who organised games, outings, walks, runs and rehearsals, who assembled the school for prayers and who devised and enforced punishment for breaking the rules. 'Walking round the cabbage patch' for half-an-hour at a time was one of their favourites, as it was healthy exercise, kept you out of doors, and the culprit could be watched from the dining-room windows.

There was a girl called Anne Sainsbury, half-French like us, who had the great good fortune of being able to put her back out by bending over and touching her toes. Whenever she wanted to slide out of anything tiresome like church, or a spell around the cabbage-patch, she would surreptitiously slip away, touch her toes and come back crowing 'All's well, it's out again, girls!' She would then retire to the sanatorium for a couple of days with a bundle of books from the library and a pocketful of tuck. We very much envied her this useful talent. During the war she was to distinguish herself by doing heroic work in the French Resistance, and once, when shot in that back of hers, stoically submitted to the extraction of the bullet without anaesthetic. She was in Anne's form, and they were great friends.

Unbelievably, the gates were open at all times, and we were allowed out in the town, in groups of three. There was no censoring of mail, and we could write to anybody we liked. It was like looking at the world upside-down. The greatest treat of all was being allowed to have as many baths as I liked. So I went overboard, with a quick dip in the morning before breakfast and a blissfully long soak later after games. And nobody ever said a word about it!

There were two heads, one who taught divinity and the other who took English literature in the sixth form. As a great treat I was allowed to attend her lessons while I was still in the fifth. All the teachers were friendly and easy-going, and their methods were perfectly adapted to the various age-groups. That year I really took to Latin and Greek, and was rewarded with a special classics master who came over from Lewes to teach me. We worked in the heads' drawing-room, and romped through Sophocles and Plato, Virgil, and of course Julius Caesar. My teacher seemed to enjoy the lessons as much as I did.

Some of Rosemead's habits remained strange to me until the end. For instance, the girls always drew their cubicle curtains to say their prayers, which to me, used to kneeling in the dust in public as I was, seemed curious to say the least, particularly as they happily stripped to the skin, exposing themselves quite bare to one another without the slightest qualm. I soon learnt to say my own prayers behind drawn curtains too, but never, *never* was I able to undress in front of the others.

Another thing that has remained incomprehensible to me to this day was the effect of the King's abdication, which swept over the school like a catastrophe of the greatest magnitude. Girls sobbed on their beds all the afternoon, and the head girl, a vast mountain of flesh who terrified the lacrosse field, wept loudest of all, and cancelled all games for that day. Such was their grief that some of them could not even eat their evening cornflakes and I, the stony-hearted frog, dry-eyed and puzzled beyond words, gobbled up several extra suppers. It seemed to me no tragedy that the gentle-faced new King should take over a job which his brother so obviously detested. Had there been murder or foul play, as, for instance, in *Macbeth*, that of course would have been a different matter.

Half-way through our career at Rosemead, Mamma suddenly decided to bring Christine back from Malaya and submit her to the civilising influence of Europe. Bright, active, quick-witted, and as ignorant as the usual run of Fesq children, far more enterprising than we had ever been at her age, and unrestrained by Marie's ever-watchful fierceness, she lived, in Malaya, a life of great freedom, and made full use of her opportunities. Nimble as a wild-cat, she could run up a coconut-tree as well as any of the native children, whom she had dragooned into a well-disciplined army which she marched around the plantation, training them in jungle warfare and survival. Herons and other birds, killed in full flight with well-aimed stones, were roasted on camp fires which spread underground along the infinite network of dead roots and rotted vegetation, creating the most appalling risk of forest fires. So, what with one thing and another, the time had come for poor Christine to be tamed and deprived of her wild-animal freedom.

They arrived at Christmas, and Mamma rented a small house

two minutes away from the school. The idea was that we should live there with her and Marie and go to school every morning after breakfast. This, we knew, was meant as a great treat, but by then we thoroughly enjoyed the life of the school and hated the thought of being day-girls. Neither Anne nor I ever discussed this, but we both knew what the other was thinking. And of course it was impossible to mention it to Mamma. The dreary little house she had rented had one redeeming feature – a piano in the drawing-room. So her musical evenings were resumed, and those who could sing joined in heartily.

John, who had managed his affairs remarkably well, had found his way to a very easy-going, happy-go-lucky cramming establishment run by a foreign baron in Arundel. This suited us all very well, as he could come home whenever he liked, any time during the week as well as every weekend.

That winter I caught a cold which dragged on for weeks. One evening, as I was coughing over my homework in Marie's sitting-room, she suddenly said, 'I'm sure you've got TB. It's not normal to go on and on like this.'

I stared at her in alarm. 'Isn't that a deadly disease?'

'It certainly is,' she replied. 'I've seen hundreds of cases in Switzerland, coming over to be cured. Lovely girls from all over the world, coughing their lungs out, all dead within a year. Nothing you can do about it.'

My insides turned over. 'You mean that I shall be dead in a year's time?'

'Most likely. Mind you, it's a painless death. They even say the worse you get, the happier you feel.'

This was no consolation at all. My spirits dropped to zero. 'Never mind,' said Marie, as she saw me drooping. 'We all have to die sooner or later, and I will lay you out myself, and let nobody else touch you. My mother taught me how to do it, and she learnt it from *her* mother. Nowadays people don't bother any more. They let total strangers lay out their dead.' And unconscious of her pun, she added, 'It's a dying art, and no mistake.'

Gradually the cough cleared up and my usual health and appetite returned, thereby robbing poor Marie of her treat. In fact she never had the chance of laying any one of us out.

chapter nineteen

Towards the end of the summer term Mamma announced that we were going to St Georges for the holidays, and we were all much looking forward to it. Papa was coming back on leave to spend a few months with us. And we would meet him at the station in Marseilles as usual. We still looked forward to these long train journeys through the night as much as ever, especially if there was a good thunderstorm raging, with forked lightning ripping across the sky from end to end.

Continental railway stations in the days of steam had something which, once experienced, could never be forgotten. As we clanked into one of these at dead of night, with a great rattling of brakes and couplings and the screech of released steam, Marie would spring to her toes, straining out of the window to sniff the heady fumes of sulphurous smoke rolling slowly under the roof. She would then call the trolley men, buy ham sandwiches, great slabs of Swiss chocolate, and fresh supplies of white pillows. All this was handed up to her through the window, then chucked into our waiting arms. Dogs howled, and small children whined as they were dragged along the platform, followed by tough-looking porters belted into their tunics like Russian moujiks.

Having left his ship at Port Said, my father and a couple of friends had bought a boat and sailed round the Greek islands for the last three months. As the train drew into Marseilles station, our excitement grew to fever-pitch. We could hardly believe that such an arrangement would work out yet again. But there, on the platform, to our delight and amazement, stood my father, aloof, patient and remote as a resigned and elderly camel. Chocolate brown from the tropical sun and his three months sailing round the Mediterranean, he looked different, and we were overwhelmed by our usual fit of shyness when seeing him again after several years.

A squad of porters was press-ganged by Marie, who marched off at the head of our column to the platform where the Bordeaux train was waiting for us. This time my parents shared a compartment, and we all piled in with Marie next door.

When we arrived in Royan next morning, we found Jacques and his father waiting for us. They had brought their own cars and booked several taxis, knowing from experience the amount of luggage they would have to deal with. We hadn't seen our friends for a couple of years, and since then Jacques had grown at least a foot in height. He looked like an Olympic athlete in training. He gave me a bear-hug which squeezed all the air out of my lungs with a loud hiss, and which I bore without protest. I realised how much I had missed him, and it was bliss to be back.

As soon as we arrived at Villa Cobalt, our new summer residence, Jacques grabbed me by the hand and dragged me off to the beach where we flopped down in the dunes under the tamarisk-trees. For a while we sat in silence, filled to the brim with utter contentment and peace. I looked around quickly to see if anything had changed, at the cove where the fishermen let down their nets, the rocks uncovered by the retreating tide, at the diving contraption which had nearly broken my neck, and at the huge sweep of white sand all the way to Suzac. No, nothing had changed. But it seemed that I had.

'You look different,' said Jacques accusingly.

'That's all the worry about exams. Lines and wrinkles,' and I smiled to show that, though wizened, I still *felt* the same. 'Anyway, you've changed too.'

There was a silence, and he added, 'I expect you will look better when you're brown.'

'Let's go and help Marie with the unpacking,' I said. 'It's not fair to leave it all to her.'

'Us' helping Marie meant that Jacques sat on a bed, shunting the odd trunk out of the way or heaving a new one forward, into which Marie and I dived, emerging with armfuls of sheets and towels, blankets, linen hats, bathing things, first-aid kit, card games and all the paraphernalia indispensable to a well-run seaside holiday.

Villa Cobalt, directly opposite Chalet Gaudin (which was now completely engulfed by the tangled vegetation of the garden, and very decrepit), was as bare as all the summer villas we had ever occupied, but less smelly, as the 'convenience' had a little hut all to itself in the back yard. The front garden, shaded by mulberry trees, became our studio, where we spent all our time when not on the beach writing and illustrating our stories. During that summer holiday we discovered Katherine Mansfield's short stories, which Jacques read aloud, and when we had come to the end of her output, somebody produced Rosamund Lehmann's *Dusty Answer*, and we fell under her spell for the next few weeks.

To supplement my income of three francs a week, I put a

card in the local tobacconist's advertising English lessons, to try to catch a few holiday students. This brought me several pupils and became a modestly lucrative occupation, which swallowed up two hours every morning and elicited a great deal of grumbling from Jacques, who averred that I was wasting the best time of the day in this useless occupation. We started at eight a.m. as we were all (pupils and teacher alike) keen to get finished as early as possible. One morning, as we sat by an open window toiling with our *the*s and aitches, a pebble hit me in the small of the back.

I guessed that Jacques had arrived, and turning round, saw him standing in the garden, immensely tall and golden brown, square-shouldered and grey-eyed, and quite unconscious of his looks. Suddenly I realised how lucky I was, how much I would miss his solid and reassuring presence, which even made itself felt in his letters, if he were suddenly to disappear. And there and then I made a vow to bear with his moods and his possessiveness, and never to be impatient or uncooperative again. I made a face and said, 'Nearly ready. Won't be long', and finished the lesson in a new kind of glow. Behind me I heard him crunching back and forth on the gravel, whistling through his teeth, trying to be patient. When I finally joined him outside, he was in a surprisingly sunny mood. 'You gave me a lovely smile just then,' he said.

'Really?' That was unexpected! 'Don't I always smile when I see you?'

'There are smiles and smiles,' he said darkly, and went all gloomy again. I never seemed able to say the right thing. We trudged off to the beach in silence, and it was a relief to find the others already there, giggling over a game of hanging corpse. A great number of small cousins were there too, squabbling and rolling about in the sand. My new-found glow of loving-kindness was already wearing off as I watched Jacques stumping down to the sea to bathe, knowing by the way he walked that he was in a black rage again. Would we never be able to understand each other?

It was not until a long time afterwards, when it was much too late, that I perceived the cause of our malaise. He wanted me to grow up and enter into an adult relationship with him, a natural wish considering that I was eighteen by then; but immature and backward to an incredible degree, and mulishly clinging to the world of childhood, resisting every attempt to be dragged away from it, the last thing I wanted was to grow up. And so we were hardly ever able to tune in to the same wavelength.

The summer weather went on and on, and I loved getting up early when the sun, coming up over Suzac at the far end of the bay, slanted through the morning haze, and the garden, shaking off the torpor of the night, was stretching itself awake, with buds opening up and petals unfurling. Dew-soaked grasses raised their heads as the heavy drops evaporated, spiders tightened up their slackened webs, and early birds pounced on the stupid, brainless worms. It was exhilarating at that hour of the day to sniff the heady scent of the damp soil, herbs, plants and trees all round.

We went for long walks through the woods, the vineyards and the fields, and along the sea-shore, where the beach, starting at the Spanish border, reached uninterruptedly northwards for hundreds of miles almost as far as the English Channel. And behind the dunes we came across flocks of sheep and goats with shepherds, cloaked and hooded in long brown capes, who staggered around among the trees on stilts, stalking the land like Frankenstein. The great trees creaked and groaned in the sea winds, and the smell of resin oozing from the bark filled the air. Sometimes we took sandwiches, or else we stopped at a farm for bread and cheese, and (behind Mamma's back) great jugs of cider which made our legs wobble. And when we finally got home at dusk, we were loaded with mushrooms, wounded birds for Marie to mend and heal, giant sea-shells and sharks' teeth or dogfish eggs.

One evening at the end of summer, Mamma and the Darlange parents suddenly appeared out of the pine-wood through which they had driven in a station-wagon. They looked grim. War had broken out, they said, and we must pack up and return with them at once. '*C'est la guerre.*' It was the first time we heard these words which were to become infinitely boring, repeated at all times by so many people who seemed to relish them, and of which the English equivalent, no less boring, was 'There's a war on.'

The beginning of the war, I regret to say, made very little impact on us except as far as it affected our own lives. Our interest in it, as far as it went, was entirely selfish. The fact that Poland had been invaded by Hitler's armies confirmed our belief, implanted in our minds by Marie as far back as we could remember, that the Germans were a bad lot, and what more could you expect. It was hard luck on the poor Poles, but how they could be helped by a world war was a profound mystery to us. It was one of those things you just had to accept, because the grown-ups, who had launched the war, said it was inevitable. And of course they knew what they were doing.

There were still three weeks to go before the Darlange family had to return to Paris. It was only Jacques who would be going back this time, while Nadia and Ninette and all the young cousins would stay on at Nostram, and go to our College in Royan till the end of the war. As far as our family was concerned, John would go back to England, to his crammer in Arundel, on his own, while Anne, Christine and I would sign on at the College in Royan once more.

Soon after the start of the war the autumn rains began to

crash out of the sky, as implacable as any monsoon we had ever known in Malaya. We were trapped indoors, which suited me fine, as I was perfectly happy to paint, scribble and play dotty card games with Nadia and the rest of the gang. But Jacques prowled up and down the drawing-room until even my mother's patience began to wear thin. She asked him to sit down and read aloud to us. The book she handed him, *Le Grand Meaulnes*, was a perfect choice, as it fitted his mood like a glove. We were all mesmerised by the story and the dreamlike world in which it took place. So the remaining days of our 'last summer' were so imbued with the atmosphere of the book that it feels almost like an autobiography when I read it again.

When school started once more, Anne, Christine and I would call at Nostram early every morning to collect the Darlange clan. They would be in the middle of breakfast when we arrived soon after seven, crowding around the table, all shouting together, and in a state of utter confusion. The hot, steaming room smelt of woodsmoke and cocoa, with dogs cluttering up the fireplace, scarves and satchels strewn all over the floor, while Anne and I hunted around trying to sort out their books and their coats. Somehow or other we managed to get them all out and on their bikes by seven-thirty, our irrevocable deadline.

Pedalling furiously down the sea-road, we battled through wind and rain, our headlights flickering on and off all the way there. Because of the war, and the number of children who had stayed behind instead of going back to Paris, school ended for us at two o'clock, after which the poor *professeurs* had to take on the second batch, who worked from two till eight at night.

By then I was in the top class, doing philosophy, with huge hairy boys of nineteen and twenty, all immensely polite and urbane, and there was no more fighting in the schoolyard. Instead we discussed the theories of Kant and Nietzsche, and moaned about the intricacies of physics and astronomy. Our homework was horrific, but we soon cut it down when we realised that the teachers never had a chance to mark half of it. So we spent the afternoons sprawling in the drawing-room at home or in one of the bedrooms at Nostram, gossiping, giggling, or playing our usual idiotic card games, which we invented as we went along. Without Jacques always around to nag and find fault, we were able to be as silly as we liked. And so the days went by, the weather grew colder, and the edge of the sea became encrusted with ice. The war was beginning to make itself felt. Meat, we were told on the radio, was becoming scarce. The butchers were ordered to close every other day in an effort to cut down consumption. So that, as stands to reason, everybody bought twice as much on open days. By Christmas, Marie was drying out used tea-leaves for a second brewing. Soon coffee beans were made of roasted acorns. Bit by bit we settled into a 'war routine'.

It had always been Marie's practice to cut up large lumps of scrubbing soap (*savon de Marseille*) with cheesewire, and we would each be given a piece of it to wash with. Made for laundry and floorscrubbing, it invariably scorched the top layer of your face off and roughed up the skin on your hands like a cheesegrater. One day my mother, who had not really looked at any of us for some time, suddenly caught sight of my sore face and asked suspiciously, 'Why is your skin so rough? What have you been putting on it?'

'Just ordinary soap,' I answered, surprised. 'Why, what's the matter?'

'You look like a crocodile handbag,' she remarked. 'You ought to start using night cream.'

Night cream indeed! I was not going to spend any of my precious weekly income on such useless, unnecessary stuff. And it was certainly not the sort of thing that Marie was likely to provide. We both conveniently forgot about it and no more was

said. We went on scouring ourselves with *savon de Marseille*, and
it was not until this became one of the commodities that was in
short supply, when soap all but disappeared from the shops,
that our complexions lost their crocodile texture and showed
remarkable improvement.

Jacques and his parents arrived on Christmas Eve with some of
their cousins who lived in Belgium and had foreseen the coming
disasters, in spite of the government's repeated assurances that
the Germans would never step over the Maginot Line. The
Belgian cousins took over Chalet Gaudin which, because of its
crumbling condition, was the last available house since St
Georges was now stuffed to the brim with refugees from the
North.

We all gave a hand with the painting and wall-papering, and
John did wonders for the woodwork with his hammer and fret-
saw and all the other complicated and nameless tools which by
now he used with professional dexterity. And by the end of the
Christmas holidays Chalet Gaudin was a very desirable residence indeed. It was a strange feeling to be back in our first St
Georges villa with all its memories, and now we had an extra
port of call for playing cards, or reading aloud, or painting and
writing, or whatever else.

One night when we had all gone to bed, and I was snuggling
down under my eiderdown and a pile of coats (the weather was
fiercely cold, there was no heating in the room, and anyway I
kept my window wide open), a shower of pebbles suddenly rattled on the floor of my bedroom. Then I heard a low whistle. I
struggled into one of the coats lying on top of my bed and
padded over to the window. The night was bright as tempered
steel, and the moon, like a high white Camembert cheese pasted
onto the Prussian blue of the sky, dispensed an eerie light, so dif-
fused that it cast no shadows. Jacques, who had come for a

late-night chat, was standing beneath my window all swaddled up in an enormous muffler. I leant out and said hello, and how nice of him to come, but he mustn't stay as it was so very cold. This did not go down very well, and he went all silent, standing there leaning against the wall with an outstretched hand, pawing the ground with one foot. I cursed myself, but could find nothing else to say. It was desperately cold, and I longed for him to go. It would only mean another sore throat, a tight chest, and a week in bed. Oh, why didn't he *go*? A little moan escaped me.

'What did you say?' He looked up sharply.

There was another long silence. Suddenly he said, 'You'll be ready at six?'

'Heavens! I'll never manage to wake up. It's nearly midnight now.'

'Good heavens, so it is. Well, I'll come round and throw gravel at your window until you wake up. And please don't be late. I don't want to miss the sunrise!'

'Okay. Goodnight,' I said firmly.

'Goodnight, and you will be quick in the morning, won't you?'

I felt as if I had hardly dropped off to sleep when the dreaded shower of pebbles was bouncing on my floor again. I struggled to consciousness, scrambled into my clothes and boots, and tried to wash my face, but gave up when I realised that the water was frozen solid in the jug. Rapidly brushing my hair, I screwed it into a tight knot which I skewered to my skull with all the pins I could find. As we still had no private mirrors in our rooms, there was no point in even trying to titivate. Creeping through the sleeping house, I grabbed my cloak from the coatstand in the hall and slipped outside, where Jacques was waiting for me.

'You've been ages,' he said. 'We'll have to hurry if we want to catch the sun before it comes up. Come on, let's go,' and grabbing my arm, he dragged me through the gate and out to the cliff path, stalking along with such huge strides that I had to break into a brisk trot to keep up with him.

We covered about five miles at this pace, and by the time we reached the high dune we were making for I was exhausted, breathless, famished and wondering whether it was really worth all the effort. However, we made it in time. The sandy hill on which we stood was planted with young pines and the tall grass all round, frozen stiff, stuck out of the ground like knife blades. Standing still and puffing out little plumes of frosted air, we stared expectantly at the orange horizon.

The colour gradually mounted in the sky, picking out little specks of cloud, and spilling out onto the wet sand and mud-flats of the bay. The sea was miles out and the tide was still retreating. Flocks of waders picked their way delicately about in the ooze; there were plovers, curlews and avocets, and another kind on high matchstick legs as large as storks which even Jacques could not identify. The sky changed slowly to gera-nium red, and then deep ox-blood, and the sun emerged from behind the sea. Jacques heaved a great sigh. It really meant a great deal to him to be present at this daily ascent of the sun, almost as if he did not trust it to do the job properly without his personal supervision.

'Better than any painting in the world, isn't it, little one?' I *loathed* being called 'little one', but let it pass.

'Well yes, I suppose so,' I answered, but secretly thought his own confections rather better. He got a great variety of colour in, and branched out into lovely streaks of lime and primrose which a real sunrise seldom produced. We stood still as the sun slowly climbed out of the sea and the colour faded in the sky.

'One day we will build a hut here, on this very dune, and we will live like hermits, right away from the world,' he said. 'I will chop down trees' (he waved at the saplings around us) 'and we will have huge log fires. I will fish, and shoot rabbits and wild duck, and you will make clothes for us out of their skins.' *Duck skin?* Unnerved by the cold, I felt a ghastly fit of giggles, as so often happened in church, begin to rumble inside me. Mercifully, I managed to keep it down.

Carried away by his vision, he put his hand on my hair and started to poke about in it. The pins began to rain down past my face. I gritted my teeth, but said nothing. Soon the twist of hair began to slip down the back of my neck, and would be blowing about wildly all the way home. He saw my expression and looked contrite, but it was too late.

'Let's go back before you catch cold,' he said solicitously. 'We'll cut across the fields.'

The 'fields', a euphemism for what was normally bogland into which you sank hip-deep, were now frozen stiff into ruts and troughs over which we staggered and stumbled, disturbing volleys of snipe and hundreds of teal and mallard. We crossed a frozen pond, and a slow creaking sound, beginning by the sedges, crept all along the edge and a long crack appeared on the ice.

'Run for it!' shouted Jacques. 'Quick, or we'll sink.' We belted across as the ice slowly began to dip on our side. One enormous leap (M. Dupont's early training came in useful here) and we were on firm, crusty bogland again.

'You realise that if we'd gone under we would have drowned, don't you?' Jacques said, as if I were responsible for our near-miss.

Everyone was in the drawing-room of the Villa Falaise when we returned from our sun-watching expedition, and wondering what to do with the rest of the day.

'Shall we go to Royan and have tea at the pâtisserie?' suggested Nadia, with a Gauloise hanging from the corner of her mouth.

'No, it's too expensive. I've no money left this week,' said someone.

'Let's go and see Yolande then, she's always good for a slap-up tea.'

'We've seen her three days running. Let's think of something else.'

'Let's go skating,' drawled Robert, one of the Belgian cousins from Chalet Gaudin, and the laziest of the entire tribe. He was lying on his back in an armchair with his feet stuck up on the chimneypiece. We all stared at him unbelievingly, and he was already regretting his suggestion.

'Yes,' shouted everybody. 'We'll go to old Goddard's pond. The ice is very thick there.'

Jacques banged a book on the table and stamped out of the drawing-room.

It was – apart from Jacques – a cheerful, noisy crowd that skated on Goddard's pond that afternoon. Jacques' face was like thunder all the way home, and I kept well away from him. When we reached Nostram, however, he thawed a little and said, 'Come in and have tea. You needn't go home yet,' and he generously included John and Anne in the invitation.

Nine small faces were munching in silence around the vast dining-room table. This silence, so unexpected from the usually tumultuous small fry, surprised us considerably. It turned out that they were all sickening for measles, and the poor things spent the rest of their holidays in bed in the dark, in case of blindness.

We went to the sideboard and helped ourselves to cocoa and cake, and large slices of rye bread and butter. Pots of honey and blackberry jelly were dotted about the table. A dozen or so gun-dogs lay in front of the fireplace, with their noses poked right into the ashes. From time to time fleas hopped from one dog to another like circus riders changing horses.

We squeezed in among the ailing ones, and Nadia related our adventures of the afternoon. Her grandmother, serene and composed, sat at one end of the table, while facing her was the other old lady of the house, who had been somebody's godmother in the distant past. Fluttering and dainty and full of little exclamations, she had lived with the family as far back as anyone could remember. With only two living-in domestics, these two ladies between them ran the house, which sometimes sheltered up to thirty beating hearts, not counting the dogs.

With markedly less enthusiasm than usual, the young cousins nibbled their slices of bread and honey, and sitting beside Jacques, watching them, I loved them all so much, every one of them, down to the minutest midget, the infamous two-year-old Antoine (who, when annoyed with someone, lurked around until they had gone for a swim, then peed in their shoes), that my chest positively ached. Quite overpowered by the feeling, I put my hand on Jacques' knee. Unused to such demonstrations of affection, he turned round in surprise. 'Are you all right?' he asked anxiously.

'Yes, quite all right, but I think we ought to go.'

He walked back with us, and we sang '*Malbrouk s'en va-t-en guerre*' all the way home as we crunched along the frozen beach under the white moonlit sky.

Jacques and I continued our sunrise expeditions, not abandoning them even in gale conditions. One morning, when we reached our sand dune, with the wind lashing around us like a whip and the sun having duly risen, Jacques said: 'Let's get into that hollow. It should be more sheltered there.'

We jumped into a kind of sandy bunker at the foot of a great pine-tree whose branches bounced about like a captive balloon straining on its leash, while it creaked and groaned all the way down its trunk like the mast of a ship. Out of the wind it was really quite warm, a real little sun-trap and as cosy as could be. Woodpigeons, annoyed at being blown out of their trees, complained persistently, while lapwings and plovers pecked around us like domestic fowl.

'Why don't you lie down?' Jacques said. 'We can do a bit of sunbathing,' and we stretched out side by side. It was delicious. I closed my eyes and basked luxuriously.

Suddenly and without warning he bent over and kissed me. I sat up with a jolt, and our foreheads clashed together like fighting stags. Taken by surprise, I leapt away in fury. 'How dare you trick me like that!' I yelled, with tears of rage shooting out of my eyes. 'Now you've spoilt everything!' And I stumbled away, making for home as fast as I could in that confounded wind, scattering the birds as I went. It was a very sullen walk home. And I would not speak to him for the rest of the day. He had indeed spoilt everything. After that I was much more wary, and would not go on walks with him any more. Poor John, whom he bored to death with his grievance, finally came to me and said, 'For God's sake, can't you be decent to him again? Aren't you making a lot of fuss about nothing? What's wrong with a kiss anyway?'

'It's not the kissing so much as the way he did it. He tricked me. It was a mean thing to do,' I said, still feeling sore.

Eventually I allowed our old relationship to be resumed – on the absolute condition that there would be no more soppy stuff – and we went on our walks along the sea-shore again, collecting shells, spotting birds, and even fishing.

chapter twenty

With the coming of spring, suddenly and without warning, came the beginning of the end. The first blow leading up to the complete collapse of France was dealt on the 10th of May, with the invasion of Belgium. This trap, craftily devised by the Germans, worked according to plan. The British Expeditionary Force, backed by the First and Seventh Armies, swept forward to the defence of Belgium. This made it possible for the Panzer Divisions, breaking through on the River Meuse where least expected, to rush up behind the Allied forces, surrounding them and splitting the French army in half.

I am still convinced that the fall of France in 1940 was caused by the same factors as those that caused her defeat at Agincourt. The knights of the time, once immured in their armour, thought themselves invincible. In the same way, the French army of 1940 didn't realise that with its slow-moving tanks and other outdated equipment, it was no longer able to deal with the fast-moving, up-to-date methods of the enemy. Relying on the so-called impregnability of the Maginot Line and still thinking in terms of trench warfare, the French High Command were completely taken by surprise by the lightning attack of the Panzer Divisions. Having burst through the defences, they thundered along towards the sea, mowing down any opposition in their path. Too late, the Allied forces in Belgium realised what had happened, and Hitler announced triumphantly that he had fooled the West.

Calais fell on the 26th of May, and the next day Churchill ordered the evacuation of the BEF. The world held its breath during the next nine days, while under fierce bombing from the Luftwaffe, 338,000 men were embarked in every possible kind of craft which came floating over from England. And the miracle of Dunkirk was accomplished. At the time we didn't believe a word of all this, assuming it to be a story put out by the government to boost the morale of the country.

On the 10th of June came the 'stab in the back', when Mussolini declared war on France. We were then told by the French Government that there would be 'fighting to the last' at the Somme and Aisne rivers. When these battles were lost, organised resistance was over and Paris was declared an open city. After that the Germans spread in all directions. On the 13th of June, when Churchill flew over unexpectedly, the French Prime Minister asked to be let off his undertaking not to make a separate peace with Germany.

By then, thousands of refugees were flooding through St Georges, all day and all night, bringing with them fresh stories of the latest captured towns, and of German fighters divebombing and shooting up the endless crowds trudging south along all the roads of France. We offered to help, and soon found ourselves in charge of the Citizens' Advice Bureau, handing out blankets and cups of coffee, and trying to find sleeping quarters for the homeless thousands. People who had been machine-gunned on their long journey south arrived pushing prams stuffed with saucepans and suitcases and exhausted scruffy babies. Lines of cars and horse-drawn carts, loaded with wardrobes, armchairs and potted plants, staggered along the streets, and nowhere could food or petrol be found. Wounded soldiers done up in dirty, blood-stained rags hobbled in, begging for aspirin and brandy. Having long ago lost their regiments, they said the enemy were sweeping through the land at unbelievable speed.

Marie, who 'knew' the Germans, said they would rape the girls at once, and we must all be put into glasses and scrape our hair back in rubber bands, then hidden in the attic for extra safety. Nadia and Ninette, with their smooth brown faces and flirting eyes, were considered to be in greatest danger, although even Anne and I, straight-haired and scrawny though we were, need not think ourselves safe either. As my sole acquaintance with this fate was the Rape of the Sabines, the whole topic seemed lunatic and unreal.

When the loudspeaker in the market square announced that the Panzer Divisions had reached La Rochelle, poor Mamma, who was quite distracted, went off to ask the Mayor's advice. 'Get out,' he shouted at her. 'Get out immediately. I will give you all the petrol you want as long as you go. I don't want any British around when the Germans arrive.' Following the well-laid plans of the German propaganda machine, fifth-columnists had been spreading panic with claims that 'the Boche' were shooting all British civilians on sight.

And so Jacques' father, collecting our petrol ration from the town hall, said he would drive us to Le Verdon across the estuary, where a British destroyer now lay at anchor, waiting to gather up any stray Britons still left on French soil. At eleven in the morning, just as we were about to leave, the destroyer was struck by a torpedo, and disappeared from sight within half-an-hour. There was only once place left to go, and that was

Bordeaux, where the British Consul would take us under his wing. Jacques was to come with us to London, where he would join the Free French forces of Colonel de Gaulle.

And now comes the most painful part of the story. Mamma announced that only British subjects with UK passports would be repatriated to England. And so Marie, with her Swiss passport, *would have to be left behind!* We were thunderstruck! In a passion of grief and fury we turned on our mother and said many terrible things, which I, for one, much regretted later. We were no better, I told her bitterly, than a bunch of rats leaving a sinking ship; our duty was to stay on and carry out as much sabotage as we could until the Germans were finally defeated, and leaving Marie behind was the basest deed ever perpetrated by any human being. And many other things as well. Dreadful, shameful things, which only an adolescent, suddenly plunged for the first time into the hell-hole of utter desolation and despair, is capable of uttering. The fact that Mamma had arranged for Marie to go and live at Nostram with the Darlange family didn't improve the situation in any way. Marie's home was with us, and no one else – not even our dearly beloved friends!

As none of us could swallow anything, Marie made us a packet of sandwiches, and we piled into the Darlange car, all of us sobbing helplessly. Throughout the afternoon we inched along the road to Bordeaux in bottom gear, hemmed in on all sides by thousands of refugees, fleeing they knew not where. The noise and the heat, with the scorching June sun blazing down on us, were almost unbearable. As we could take no luggage, Mamma had insisted we all wore two sets of clothes, and we sweltered, while Christine, who was still under eight, howled all the way, crying for Marie. Dusk fell without the faintest breeze, as the heatwave stretched on into the night. Altogether it was as near a nightmare as real life could ever be.

On the edge of a small village, whose name I shall never forget, St Jean de Cubezac, and overcome by the general horror of the situation, the car broke down to a full stop and refused to go further. Leaving it by the roadside, we walked to the *auberge* at the entrance of the village, and there met with luck for the first time in weeks. The innkeeper, who was astonishingly affable, said yes, we could spend the night in her attic, if we didn't mind sleeping on the floor, or object to mice, rats and owls. This sounded like a corner of paradise. It was well after midnight when Jacques, Christine and I toiled up the attic stairs, while Mamma was trying to wheedle a loaf of bread out of the management. But there was no food about, not even at black market prices, and apart from a few plums we managed to buy in the morning we had to go hungry for the next three days.

The attic window, wide-open as it was, formed a perfect frame for the spectacle of a burning town in the distance. Bordeaux was on fire. We rushed to the window. Christine, who was so tired that she had only just managed the stairs, gripped the window-sill and jumped up and down with excitement. 'Look,' she yelled. 'Fireworks! Lovely fireworks!' And she leaned out, balancing on her middle to get a better view. Clutching her by the waist, I dragged her back. From where we stood, we had a sharp, clear view of the raid on the town in the distance. Zooming and sweeping in circles, the German bombers, lit up from below, looked like gigantic fireflies among the exploding bombs.

'Oh dear God,' Jacques groaned. 'What are we going to do? Whatever is going to become of us?'

I looked at his perplexed, uncomprehending face, at Christine struggling in my grasp, and thought of our great-grandfathers who had so confidently set out over a hundred years ago from the town which was now smouldering like a jungle fire under the sticks of bombs falling out of the sky, of Marie, abandoned to

her most hated enemy in her old age, of the thousands of homeless people all over the country frantically fleeing from the
invading armies. And I knew that whatever was to become of us,
it was going to be *our* war, in which we would soon have to play
our part. And that our childhood was now over for ever.

PART THREE

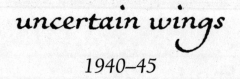

uncertain wings

1940–45

chapter twenty~one

We reached Bordeaux the morning after it had been bombed. The British Consul had left and the town had been declared an open city. We rushed to the station, and with hundreds of other refugees struggled onto the first train going south. With people fainting all round from exhaustion and starvation, the scene had all the elements of a first-class nightmare.

At Bayonne, the end of the run where everybody had to get out, loudspeakers attached to the plane trees announced that the Germans were established in Bordeaux, and that an advance Panzer Division was now on its way to the Spanish border. All British refugees were to find their way to St Jean-de-Luz immediately and board the Channel boat anchored there, scheduled to sail at midnight.

On the quay at St Jean-de-Luz, to our immense relief, the British army was in charge of operations. And oh, the relief of seeing those cheerful, efficient soldiers at last, and no sign of panic or confusion *anywhere*! We were waved on to the pier, where groups of lost souls huddled together in silence, peering at the sky in the north, dreading the black crosses which came sweeping down firing at the slow-moving crowds trudging southwards. Here, herded together along the waterfront, we were sitting ducks for them. If they came down over the harbour, they would make short work of us all.

About a mile out at sea, HMS *Ettrick* lay at anchor, while a fleet of small fishing boats were taking the refugees out in groups of about twenty at a time. As darkness fell, the soldiers came champing through the waiting groups, hissing to left and right, 'No more talking please. The harbour is full of U-boats and they can hear you *breathing*, so keep your traps shut.' By the time it came to our turn, poor Christine was wilting, as we were by then into our third day of starvation. As soon as we started to move and our rowing boat began to bounce on the churning waves, she turned pea-green and set up a wail of distress. A pullover was quickly stuffed down her throat. As we reached the ship the sea was running so high that it was almost impossible to jump onto the gangway. We were all dreading Christine's turn. When she flatly refused to budge, a sailor grabbed her, protesting vociferously. No U-boat could have failed to hear her, had one been around at the time. But we were lucky.

Finally, we were all on board. It was like waking up after a long and very bad dream.

While the ship was gathering up her skirts and generally preparing to sail, Anne and I hung over the rail, not wanting to miss anything. Heavy steel chests, which looked like ammunition boxes, were hauled up on deck. The sailors told us that they were King Zog of Albania's gold reserves; he and his court were already on board. And standing on deck beside me was his golden-haired young queen, only a year older than myself. Little did I know then that a few years later I would be presented to her at a London dinner party under very different circumstances.

As the crowds gradually drifted off, Mamma and Christine were led away by one of the sailors. They were both to share a cabin with several other women and children. Two thousand Polish troops, who were going to carry on the fight wherever they could, had already settled down, lying all over the deck, surrounded by their packs, rifles, hand-grenades and tin mugs. Climbing over them, Anne and I set off in search of sustenance. We finally settled down in the sailors' sleeping quarters below deck, where we were handed large mugs of hot, sweet tea, and an enormous chunk of bread and margarine. No feast could have tasted better. Gradually more women joined us, herded below deck by the sailors; we realised they were making their own sleeping quarters over to us for the rest of the trip. Our guardian angels, as we came to see them, set up trestles covered with boards, to be used as tables, above which they hung innumerable hammocks for us all.

We slept most of that first day at sea. Towards evening a group of sailors came clattering in with buckets of sweet tea. The sea was now quite rough, and the contents of the buckets sloshed and splashed all over the floor. From time to time a whole mug of boiling tea shot into someone's lap. Longing for some light relief, Anne and I greeted this with squeals of mirth, which went down very badly with the ladies.

As soon as we had finished helping the sailors to collect empty mugs and mop up spilt tea, we escaped up on deck, where we were surprised to see how rough the sea had become. Along the edge of the horizon, and blending with the general greyness all round, the destroyers of our convoy were speeding along within their own individual smokescreens; but all so far away that had we been hit we would have sunk beyond recall, long before they had a chance to fish us out. And now that one of our childhood wishes, that longed-for shipwreck, was a possibility at last, the prospect no longer seemed so attractive. Not that there was much time to think about it. Except for Anne and myself and three or four others, most of the women, now laid low with severe sea-sickness, kept to their hammocks day and night. The sailors had placed empty buckets along the tables under the hammocks, and the women made ample use of them as we sat there with our tea and bully-beef sandwiches. In answer to their cries of distress, Anne and I ran around with towels and bottles of drinking water. As this went on round the clock, throughout the ten long days of our crossing, we got very little sleep. Some of our patients seemed to be rather ill. But our friends the sailors, when we asked them for advice, said that nobody had ever died of sea-sickness.

As nobody seemed to know where we were heading for, we lost all interest in our destination. So it was quite a surprise to hear one morning that we would be landing at Southampton around midday.

After all the upheavals of the last few weeks we were truly amazed, trudging along the neat, tidy English streets looking for lodgings, to see posters everywhere advertising Saturday dancing in the Town Hall. Nobody seemed aware of the chaos, the thousands of homeless, starving wounded, the corpses lying along the roads, and the total disintegration of normal life which reigned barely twenty miles away across the Channel. It was like landing on another planet. The June sun blazed on this lovely afternoon, cheerfulness and good humour bubbled everywhere, and the shops were bulging with food. It was all very strange and wonderful.

Years later, after the war, I met the captain of our ship again, and he told me that after long and gallant service on convoy duty, HMS *Ettrick* had been torpedoed and sunk in the Atlantic. We had apparently been incredibly lucky during our crossing, as U-boats had followed us all the way to England like a pack of sharks.

When we finally found a boarding-house, Mamma installed us in it and set off on her own to explore other possibilities in various parts of the country. The glorious summer weather went on day after day, with the sun shining in a limpid, cloudless sky. We went to the beach every morning after breakfast. Swimming and lying in the sun, we were suspended in a kind of limbo, gathering our depleted forces to cope with whatever would turn up next. Christine, who had until then woken up every night with fearful screams of terror, was beginning to calm down again.

A few days later, without any warning, Mamma suddenly reappeared, announcing that she had been to see her sister, our Aunt Amelie, who had invited us all to stay with her at her large house in Bedford. In spite of her own five children, and one or two house guests, she could still find room for us all. Her hospitality was boundless. And that included John, who came to join us as well after he finished his exams at his latest cramming establishment at Ilfracombe.

Mamma now told us of her plans for the future. She was leaving for Malaya with the next convoy, and would take us all with her. John and I, horrified by this suggestion, said we couldn't possibly leave the country, as we were quite old enough to take part in the war. To our surprise she made no protest, only demanding that we should be suitably employed before she left. Within a week we were both fixed up.

Mamma sailed in an enormous convoy bound for the Far East, with Anne and Christine, and whatever peace of mind she could muster. Initiative, independence, unlimited courage and endurance had always been her most shining virtues. And she was going to need every one of them in the years to come.

John, who was only sixteen, had enlisted in the Youth Regiment of the Beds & Herts. Before long he was transferred to the Red

Devils, as the 6th Airborne Division soon came to be known. I answered an advertisement in the local paper for the post of Junior Assistant at the County Library, and was summoned for an interview. It came as a surprise to all of us when I heard I had landed the job.

Catering exclusively for the County, the Library was housed in a vast, barnlike building without any heating apart from a couple of fireplaces in the downstairs workrooms. Our job was to keep the outlying villages supplied with books, which had to be changed every few weeks. And for this an enormous van fitted with shelves was packed to the ceiling every Friday, and off we went on our rounds. Geoffrey, the Deputy Chief, drove the van, with Za, the Senior Assistant, sitting beside him, while two or three juniors huddled in the back among the bookshelves. Za and Geoffrey were great individualists, both with strong notions of their own. Because of his lack of confidence in the virtue of cows, Geoffrey always had little screw-top jars filled with goat's milk. Za consumed a couple of minute sausage-rolls every Friday and absolutely nothing else. Their views differing in almost every way, they argued a great deal and we listened, voraciously gobbling our Marmite sandwiches and everything else we could sink our teeth into.

Unloading was a tricky business, specially in winter, when books are fiendish to deal with in such quantities; in cold weather they turn into slabs of ice, freezing the fingers, which soon lose all gripping power. It was a joy, however, on lovely hot summer days, when we had jolly bucolic picnics under haystacks and hedgerows, surrounded by bees, birds and butterflies and all the wild flowers of the fields. It was easy to forget the war, and we were as happy as schoolchildren out on a spree.

Meanwhile, at Headquarters, our Chief resided, worked and often slept in the huge office upstairs. But only in appearance. He actually lived and breathed and had his being in the Middle

Ages. Often, as I passed him on the stairs, he would glance up at the clock, sighing 'Ah, would that we could put it back to *those* days!' And there was no need to ask to which days he was referring . . . A born bachelor, he probably remained one to the end of his days. Meanwhile, his kindness to us girls was unfailing. And that really meant something, considering we were there on sufferance; it was only since the war, and the total disappearance of all male assistants, that the awful decision to employ girls had been taken.

When we were not out in the countryside distributing our books or loading and unloading the van, we worked at Headquarters. I was being trained at the pasting bench, where I reigned with an enormous brush and a gallon pot of glue. A new junior, even younger than myself, soon joined me there. Having just left school with all kinds of glowing honours, Tania was putting in time before starting on her undergraduate career at Cambridge. Together we tore all old labels out of books and pasted in new ones. With her natural bouncing vigour Tania threw herself into the job, finding an endless source of fun in the near (or far) misses with the glue brush. She would dissolve into breathless giggles at the slightest opportunity. Dropping a pile of books on your toes, or splashing glue into somebody's hair, would bring her down flat on the bench in hoots of laughter. An only child and gregarious as a puppy, she adopted us all as her family, and has remained a firm friend ever since.

After a few weeks' training at the paste bench, I was promoted to shelving. The books returning to the library had to be restored to their rightful places on the shelves in the Stack Room, a kind of warehouse full of shelves rising way out of reach. A light, narrow stepladder was provided for soaring to the distant heights, and on this I soon learnt to stalk around as if on stilts, from one bookshelf to another.

Fire-watching, one of Tania's special treats, meant sleeping on the premises, which we took in turns, two at a time. I strongly suspect that when she and I were on duty together, one or two alerts may have passed unnoticed by the time we had laughed ourselves into unconscious exhaustion over our efforts at cooking supper over a gas-ring, one holding the pan while the other stirred the coagulated rubbery lumps reeking of sulphur which we concocted out of powdered egg and water. Fortunately the great bombing fleets which roared overhead most nights on their way to the Midlands and the industrial North ignored our unimportant town, except when chased away with some of their load still on board, which they then dropped here and there on the way home. The only time a few incendiary bombs landed through the roof of the Stack Room, Mr Box, our incomparable caretaker who was on duty that night, dealt with the trouble single-handed without disturbing anybody.

The 'senior junior', Maisie, was altogether reliable and conscientious beyond her years. Soon after I arrived she went down to run the Branch at Dunstable, and we lost an invaluable member of staff at HQ. It wasn't long before she had so improved the service of the Dunstable library and acquired so many new readers that she needed an assistant. I asked if I could join her, and got the job.

Maisie found me digs in a little road nestling at the foot of the Downs, with identical houses all in a row and neat little pinafore gardens in front. My landlady was a spruce Beatrix Potter character with a pussy-cat face. Her best friend who lived next door, who looked like her twin sister, was so houseproud that her husband was forbidden to cut his nails in the house. Once a week I used to watch him build a tiny bonfire in his back garden and neatly cut his fingernails into it. That was known as being 'very particler', and was greatly admired.

My landlady's own obsession was electric light. Nobody was

allowed to switch it on until after dark and the blackout drill had
gone into action. Her husband had a coy little trick of turning it
off at the main as soon as I had got into my weekly bath. My
habit of reading in my bedroom was regarded as outrageously
extravagant, so that an extra charge was added to my rent for the
single light bulb and electric fire in my room, stretching my
monthly eleven pounds to its very limit.

I couldn't believe my luck when I was offered lodgings at the
Noah's Ark, the best restaurant in town, which belonged to Za's
friends Gwen and Lear. As the room contained only a gas burner
and a couple of divan beds, I bought a table, three chairs and a
stool for £1 from the local junkshop, all of which was the utmost
luxury.

The library, directly opposite the police station, was a vast vil-
lage-hall type of building, with enormous windows, all of which
had to be blacked out every evening *before* we could switch on
the lights. This, which we dreaded, was always the cause of endless trouble.

A huge stove, which consumed enormous quantities of coke,
was our most precious luxury during the very cold winter I
worked there. Saturday was the busiest day of the week, when all
the housewives in town queued up at our doors to change their
love-stories. Little gangs of school-children trotted in with their
sticky books which, if not glued together with jam, you could be
sure had not been read. I once found a half-chewed kipper in a
Just William story, and another time a grimy comb used as a
book-mark. There was one particular family of scruffy urchins
who always arrived in a pack. One half carried the other, and all
of them had a permanent cold. Maisie took it in her stride when,
on the first very cold day, the leader of the tribe announced,
'We've been sewn in for the winter today, miss.'

'You mean for the *whole* winter?' I asked.

'Oh yes miss, we won't be cut out again until Easter. Me

mother sewed me in and I done them,' she said proudly, pointing at her handiwork on her brothers and sisters.

Around four o'clock every afternoon 'Our Tramp' shuffled in, and settled down comfortably in an armchair in the middle of the room. Grunting and groaning, he took off his boots, then started clawing out the sodden layers of newspaper with which they were lined. As he pushed this into the stove, huge waves of thick smoke puffed out and curled around the room. The boots, which he then stood close to the stove to dry, soon broke out in a powerful, all-pervading stench of their own. People turned and stared unbelievingly as he snored, slumped in his chair, while his filthy bare toes twitched and jerked in time with his dreams.

Maisie's patience was endless. Somebody would come in saying, 'This book's no good, dear. Can't see the print. Now the one you gave me last week was lovely. Can you give me another what's the same, you know, with plenty of love and a happy ending?'

'I should think so,' Maisie would reply. 'Do you remember who it was by?'

'Oh, don't ask me love. Somebody Something or Other, *you* know.'

'Well, what was the book called? Do you remember that?'

'No idea love. Just find me somethink similar, there's a dear, I 'aven't got all day to stand 'ere jawing with you.' And off would go patient Maisie to the love-story shelves, with her customer waddling after her on swollen ankles and tortured feet.

'I think you're a saint,' I would say at the end of one of those days, when all the matrons of the town had come up with the same request. 'They make me want to scream. I can't imagine how you manage to be so patient.'

'They're tired,' Maisie would reply. 'They work all day, get their children off to school, go charring, do part-time jobs in a factory, and though they're worried sick about their men in the Forces, they're always cheerful. Our job is to help them to keep going. Love stories are their only pleasure.' At which I felt thoroughly ashamed of myself, and tried to emulate her tone and manner for the next half-hour, until my own impatient and arrogant self got the better of me again, and crossness and bad temper returned to take over from the bout of unnatural affability. Dear, kind, sweet, infinitely good Maisie. Sometimes, in a spasm of rebelliousness, I would say to her, 'But you encourage them in their ignorance, to stick in their mud forever. They will never get out of their morass.'

'Can you see,' Maisie would ask with a twinkle, 'Mrs Trotter reading Virginia Woolf?' At which of course I collapsed with giggles on the spot. Mrs Trotter was one of our favourite matrons, who brought us treats on her baking days in the shape of little twists of pastry with a cherry on top, or a dollop of her precious jam ration. She had a voluminous bosom which she heaved onto the counter to ease its weight off her short little legs. Her nose was pinched and tinged with blue at the tip, which Maisie said was the sign of a heart condition. Always speaking in whispers and leaning far over the counter, she would confide the latest news of her pride and joy, her only son, whose name was Sonny. We went through his departure for the Air Force, then for Canada where he was going to train for the Fleet Air Arm, and eventually his return to the UK.

'And now,' said Maisie, who was all-wise and all-understanding, and who could see into the future, 'we must prepare for the final tragedy. Sonny will be shot down, and we will have to comfort Mrs Trotter, or at least try to do our best.'

It came even sooner than we feared. One Saturday afternoon Mrs Trotter came up in the book queue, and her pinched nose, apart from the blue tip, was red, and so were her eyes. 'It's happened,' Maisie said in hoarse whisper, 'Sonny's been shot down.'

'I've had a telegram dears,' said Mrs T, her eyes brimming with tears. 'Sonny. Reported missing.' It was utterly heartbreaking. For once I was first to dash out and search for the story with the big print like the last one, with plenty of love and a happy ending. Beside these two human beings, with a flash of insight, I suddenly saw myself as odiously selfish, second-rate and shoddy.

Meanwhile, on the other side of the world, my family were once more fleeing from the invader. This time not from the Panzer Divisions, but from an army on two wheels. Riding their minicycles, Japanese troops had sneaked and wriggled their way along the peninsula, pedalling through the jungle unnoticed all the way down to the Equator. Under round-the-clock bombardment Papa was patrolling the streets of Singapore with the Home Guard, organised by Europeans, wielding any weapons they could lay their hands on.

A troopship in the harbour was taking on women and children for an unknown destination. There was no other way but to split up. With bombs exploding all round, Mamma and the two girls boarded the ship – just in time . . .

Advance parties of Japanese troops were invading Singapore, swarming into the British military hospital, where they slashed the wounded to death in their beds. In the streets the valiant Home Guard were being rounded up and clapped in jail. Papa was locked up in a minute cell with a Chinese murderer and an opium-eater in the last stages of decay.

Transferred to Changi, which had been my great-grandfather's flourishing plantation a hundred years earlier, the prisoners would have to survive for the next three-and-a-half years on a cup of boiled rice a day, with an occasional potato leaf thrown in as a special treat. The crop itself, grown by the captives, was eaten by the guards. From time to time someone was dragged away and beheaded for owning a wireless set, while all the other prisoners had to stand bare-headed and motionless in the blazing equatorial sun from dawn till nightfall. After each one of these ordeals, some of the younger men went off their heads or died of sunstroke.

We only heard of all this much later, after the end of the war. Mamma, who had eventually landed in Australia, was informed by the Red Cross that her husband was still alive, but she heard nothing more until the end of the war. As for me in Dunstable, nobody thought of telling me anything. As far as I knew, they could all have been bombed into pulp, roasted alive in their bungalow, machine-gunned on the lawn, or blown sky-high in an ambush. There was no way for me to find out anything. So that with visions of Oriental torture permanently in my mind, I became even more forgetful and absent-minded than usual.

One evening, when it was my turn to close down the library, I did the unforgivable. Coping alone with the sewn-in children, the love-story-seekers, and throwing out the comatose tramp at closing time, I forgot all about the blackout. As there was no air-raid that night, no harm was done, but the police-station opposite could not possibly close its eyes to all those blazing windows. The next day, a constable presented me with a summons to go before the Magistrate, who fined me £2. Our Chief, at Headquarters, in the kindness of his heart, offered to pay it for me (I was earning £11 a month at the time). Overwhelmed with gratitude though I was, I could not possibly accept his offer.

From time to time, when I managed to save the fare, I jumped onto the London train to pay a visit to the War Artists' Exhibition. My colleagues and I were keeping an eye on the progress of the contributors – Henry Moore we thought would make a name for himself. His 'Shelter Series', with which the walls of the Underground were profusely decorated, was a revelation. The entire exhibition was an endless joy. I spent hours staring at the paintings of Graham Sutherland, John Piper, Paul Nash, Anthony Gross, and many others.

Whenever there was time before the train home, I picked my way through the pathetic rubble of tumbled bedrooms, gaping fireplaces and pulverised furniture after the previous night's bombing. The surviving owners picked their way over their shattered homes and belongings, without much hope of finding any surviving treasures. Sometimes, after a particularly heavy raid, whole streets were blocked off altogether. Many of Graham Sutherland's 'Twisted Girders' – bare, grotesque lift-shafts – rose above the surrounding ruins, standing in an inferno of flames against a blood-red sky. Firemen, like minute insects, swaying at the top of their ladders above the raging furnace, waved long jets of water which instantly fizzled away into clouds of hissing steam. In Piccadilly, sitting in doorways or sprawling at the feet of Eros, lounged hundreds of US soldiers, the famous GIs, forever chewing their gum and watching the world go by.

Sometimes when the nights were racked by constant raids and furious anti-aircraft gunfights, I stayed at a small hotel in Bloomsbury. The bells of fire-engines and ambulances tearing around the streets of London screeched non-stop throughout the night. Under particularly heavy bombing, my bed was sometimes lifted off its feet and I was tossed out on the floor. The other guests were probably enjoying the same experience in their own rooms. Some would have staked a claim in the Underground stations where jolly parties were in progress every night with the squeeze-box and the latest tunes. There mattresses, sleeping-bags and double-bunks stood along the platforms for the duration. Personally, I never even saw the inside of an air-raid shelter. Like most people, I much preferred the idea of being blown up in my bed to being buried alive underground.

chapter twenty-two

Although I knew that my job was a useful part of the war effort I was beginning to feel I was in the wrong place, just not doing enough and not really dealing with the problem. Books were a hobby, and I loved the job, but I wanted to get into the *real* war, and hammer away at the enemy as much as I possibly could. Library work was not what I had in mind when John and I told Mamma that we wanted to play our part in the war. And although I knew that Geoffrey, our Deputy Head, didn't want to lose another assistant, even though a mere female, I began to volunteer for various things.

It was a difficult war to get into. The Wrens wouldn't have me on account of my French grandfather. Only the purest of English blood may run through the royal blue veins of the senior service. When I reminded the Wren who turned me down about '1066 And All That', she said, 'I am not here to listen to your nonsense, my girl.' And that was that.

The ATS, which signed me up for the Intelligence Corps, took so long to draft me that I gave up waiting and tackled the Foreign Office. A spy, I said, was what I wanted to be. The Major who interviewed me looked me up and down. 'You don't look much like a spy to me,' he said.

'What's the use of a spy who looks like one?' I asked. After a while, he said, 'What do you want to do a thing like that for, anyway?'

'To go and rescue my old nanny,' was what I really wanted to howl. It would have been interesting to see his face if I *had* said that.

'Well, I can speak the language, and I know the South of France pretty well,' I told him instead.

'Really? Well my girl, that's all very fine, but I'm afraid it's not enough. Thanks for coming all the same.'

He must have seen my face drop. I was having quite a job not to burst into tears.

'You really want to get into this war, don't you?' he asked more kindly.

'Oh yes, I do,' was all I could manage to say.

'Go to Cambridge then, and see these people.' And he gave me an address which he scribbled on the back of an empty cigarette-carton.

'These people' turned out to be a middle-aged matron who was 'doing her bit for the war'.

'What can you do?' she asked, without looking up. And I delivered my rigmarole once more.

'Oh. I suppose you wouldn't go overseas?'

'Of course,' I said, 'anywhere you like.'

'They're asking for a French-speaking librarian in Algiers. You'd better go and see General Staff Intelligence at the Foreign Office.'

So back to the FO once more, this time armed with a more official-looking document than the empty cigarette-carton. The person who interviewed me that day looked like a don. She stared at me doubtfully.

'You're very young. We don't usually send girls overseas under the age of twenty-four.' What was so magic, I wondered, about twenty-four?

'Why not?' I asked, kicking myself for not lying about my age, as John had done.

'Well, it's, er, pretty rough, you know . . .'

ROUGH! And what was wrong with that? I had visions of pitching tents in the desert, tethering camels, snooping around Arab villages, tailing enemy agents . . .

'However,' resumed the don lady, 'you look steady enough. Not the flighty type.'

'Oh no,' I said regretfully. 'I'm afraid I've got no talent for that.' (How I envied those who had!)

'Don't worry. I wouldn't send you if you had . . .'

And with those words she gave me a staggering number of clothing coupons, for 'sensible hot weather gear'.

The Political Intelligence Department of the Foreign Office controlled all information and propaganda directed to the enemy and occupied countries, through every form of the media available at the time. Secret services, such as the famous SOE and various other operations of the same kind, also flourished under its wing.

PID was lodged on the eighth floor of Bush House, The Strand, locked away behind bars through which we could penetrate only with a special pass. So there, while waiting for a seat on a plane to Algiers, I began to learn my trade. I was to set off with the 'assimilated' rank of captain, to join Allied Forces HQ under General Eisenhower.

One evening, as I was checking out of the 'cage', the corporal on duty told me I was wanted by Major P, the one who had interviewed me the first time and said I didn't look much like a spy. Now he told me I was to leave the next day for Algiers. And would I not breathe a word about it to a living soul. I was to report at five p.m. on the dot to Norfolk House, the London HQ of Psychological Warfare Branch (PWB) at the time.

'Good luck,' he said, as he handed me an envelope. 'Take care of this, and produce it if you're nabbed. It's your certificate of capture. It just says that you're not a spy, and you're not to be shot on sight.' And he added, 'Not that they will pay any attention, mind you, but it's worth a try. Anyway, General Staff Intelligence insist on it.'

And with these comforting words he dismissed me. Within twenty-four hours of my arrival in Algiers this document was nicked out of my handbag, so *somebody* must have thought it worth having.

Norfolk House was the location of the London headquarters of Allied Forces Algiers and the gathering-point for all those on their way there. From the moment you stepped inside, you were cut off from the rest of mankind, forbidden to use the phone or communicate in any other way with the outside world.

A colourful character, who turned out to be a BBC correspondent, half-a-dozen Morse operators and myself were the only civilians on the flight, the rest all being service personnel. We piled into a coach and set off in the dark for an unknown destination. This turned out to be an RAF station at Blackbush airfield, where we were bundled into a waiting Dakota. This, my first flight ever, turned out to be a baptism of fire. We sat in two rows along the fuselage facing one another. On the floor at our feet were mailbags, our various bits of luggage, tin hats and nylon parachutes. The flight to Bristol took a couple of hours, by which time it was dark and very cold. We arrived in the middle of an air-raid, and the sky was ablaze with searchlights, bursts of gunfire, and the heavy black crosses of enemy bombers etched against the flashing lights. Our nimble pilot managed to weave

his way through the falling incendiary bombs and the bright
red streams of racing bullets from ground defences. Great fires
were leaping into the sky over Bristol in the distance. The whole
world seemed to be ablaze in an all-embracing inferno which
filled heaven and earth.

As soon as we touched down, we were hustled into Nissen
huts, while the pilot rushed his 'crate' into a secret hiding-hole.
A warm and cosy canteen welcomed us all as if everything was
perfectly normal, as indeed it was for them, poor souls, since
they were bombed every night in that period of the war.

During a welcome and tasty meal of powdered egg and
dehydrated potatoes, our Nissen hut was almost shaken off its
moorings by bombs exploding all round. We were then told to
line up for embarkation on the next stage of our trip. I was
surprised to hear my name called over the loudspeaker, with
the request that I should go to the head of the queue. When I
got there the corporal in charge said, 'Since you are under-
weight, do you mind taking these kippers on your luggage
allowance?'

Beside me stood a portly brigadier, holding up an enormous
bunch of odoriferous kippers for my inspection. 'I'd be
delighted, but couldn't they be wrapped up a bit?' I asked.

'Don't worry my dear,' said the Brigadier, 'I'll keep them
myself, so long as they can go on your luggage list. I'm a bit
overweight myself, you see, and these kippers just tip the balance.' So I stepped on the scales with my case at my feet, *War and
Peace* and my bear under one arm, and the kippers dangling
from my right hand. 'Thank you my dear, I wish I could invite
you to breakfast, but I'm going to Cairo, and you're dropping off
at Algiers, aren't you?' So the situation was saved, and a happy
brigadier got into the plane behind me.

While we were still climbing, the co-pilot came in to
announce that we had an enemy fighter on our tail. We would

have to go up to 12,000 feet to leave him behind. 'Some of you may be a bit short of wind, but that's nothing to worry about. And it's going to be very cold.' This was before aeroplanes were either heated or pressurised. So for the next five hours we puffed and shivered in stoic silence.

We flew down the coast of Portugal, which was like fairyland. We were used to total blackout, and the glittering lights below came as a delightful surprise, which made us forget our refrigerated state. It was almost daylight by the time we began to drop out of the sky and made straight for the Rock of Gibraltar. How anyone can ever manage to land on that narrow strip of concrete jutting out to sea is a mystery to me. We were soon standing on the tarmac in the warm scented air, dazed by our sleepless night and all the noise and bustle of a Mediterranean port churning about all round us.

I was suddenly grabbed from behind and pitched into a taxi, with my companions tumbling in on top of me. The driver charged straight into the crowd, banging on the door with his fist, as hooting was forbidden in Gibraltar at the time. Frantic at not being able to get through the throng, he yelled and thumped away at the door until it fell off its hinges and crashed to the ground. 'Never mind,' he shouted. 'Now we go.'

Screeching its way round the hairpin bends up the hill, the taxi finally dropped us off at the Rock Hotel. There we gobbled a delicious English breakfast and were told we could sleep for the rest of the morning, as our plane for Algiers wasn't leaving till three p.m. But who wanted to sleep! We set off in search of the famous apes and explored the Rock. After the strain and discomfort of our English winter in wartime, we seemed to have touched down in paradise.

When we finally arrived at Maison Blanche outside Algiers, the airfield had obviously been badly bombed. Our aircraft could only *just* find enough space on which to land. As we stumbled across the pitted ground towards the RAF station, the service personnel from our flight were met and driven away in orderly fashion. The odd ones, the Morse operators, the BBC man and myself, in other words the PWB contingent, were left to their own devices. No one was interested in or had even heard of our obscure unit. So I set off to explore – were there any taxis, coaches or trams going into Algiers? Ha ha, they said, where did I think I was? Piccadilly Circus? Well, was there a phone I could use? . . . No, no, nothing like that, unless the Station Commander would let me use his. Well, he said, it was most irregular, but just for once . . .

It took half-an-hour to get through to PWB HQ. Never having used field telephones before, I didn't realise how lucky I was to make it in under half a day. Major T, the Chief PWB Admin Officer, eventually came on the line. *Who* had arrived? And *what* had we come for? *Who* had sent us? Oh well, since we were there, we might as well get into Algiers and come up and see him. Meanwhile he would try to sort things out and discover what it was all about. No, he hadn't been told we were coming. And he certainly didn't need us. There was no job for any of us. He couldn't think why . . . And how were we to get into Algiers? Well, he'd better send a car to collect us. Yes, we must just wait until he could find one. No, he had no idea how long it would take. We must just wait.

When we finally arrived at his office, Major T said he couldn't make head or tail of all this nonsense. What on earth did London think they were up to? . . . Sending out whole gangs of people like that without any warning! My patience was ebbing. I grabbed the phone on his desk and said, 'Don't worry. I'll ring up PID and say there's been a muddle and we'll be back on the next plane.'

Snatching the receiver out of my hand he growled, 'You'll do no such thing. If anybody rings up London, *I* do.'

I sat down and stared at him. There was a long silence. Finally he said, 'You will report to Basic News in the morning. They are always screaming for bodies there. Perhaps they can make use of you.'

At this point his secretary, who had been winking at me for some time, piped up: 'I'll take you to the Mess now and get you signed on. Follow me.'

The Semiramis Hotel, on the hill, had been requisitioned by the military authorities for the use of British and US officers and civilian personnel. It was run by our American Allies, on their rations and by their rules.

Major T's secretary, whose name was Maria, came up to my room with me. 'You may not think so now, but you'll love it here,' she said. 'Yes,' I agreed, 'I know I will. But will I be able to do what they expect? I thought I was coming here as a librarian.' Maria laughed. 'My dear, there is no library in PWB. Just put that out of your head!'

'That's what I'm worried about. It's all I can do. Books and library work.'

'Well, lucky you,' she laughed. 'You will be quite unique. There will be no competition.' And she left me to go and change for dinner.

The bedroom, which was quite small, had a double bed, a wardrobe and two tiny bedside tables; there was a bathroom and a small balcony which looked down to the street five floors below. What more could anybody want? Maria said the cleaning was done by Italian prisoners of war . . .

Making a big effort, I went down at six-thirty, official dinner-time for the US Army. The dining-room was already full of people, all a good deal older than myself. Feeling like a snail without a shell, I sat down on a bench next to a gentle-looking blond-haired girl. 'You're new here, aren't you?' she asked. It was just like being back at school!

'Arrived from England today,' I answered.

'You'll soon get used to it. Don't drink the tap water, and don't walk about barefoot or you'll get worms under your toe-nails!'

'What's the food like?' I asked.

'Well, we don't get bread here. Only dog-biscuits. Okay if you have good teeth. And they're said to be stuffed with vitamins. Who are you sharing with?'

'Sharing what?'

'Your bed, of course.'

'My bed! I didn't know I would be sharing it! . . .'

'Oh yes, you must be. We're all two to a bed here.'

And she was quite right. When I climbed into the double bed that night I was on my own. But when I woke up in the morning, there was another head on the pillow beside me. While it was still fast asleep, I crept out onto the balcony to watch the sun rise over the warships in the bay below.

Captain B, Major T's Adjutant, looked after the administration of PWB in Algiers. Calm and cheerful, he was never ruffled, and made up with his friendly helpfulness for his superior officer's funny little ways.

'Come and see me in my office,' he said to me when I went down to breakfast that first morning. 'I'll sort you out and put you in the picture.'

Psychological Warfare Branch was a vast, loosely strung organisation, part-military and part-civilian. In Algiers its innumerable activities included control of the local (French) press, producing leaflets for dropping into enemy territory, and setting up information centres known as Prop Shops (the full word 'propaganda' was never used) where you could find pamphlets in the local language about the Allies' achievements in the war. 'D Section', the Intelligence Department, included several other groups of cloak-and-dagger activities, about which we knew very little. 'Political' or 'psychological warfare' were the terms to be used in connection with our work. It was some time before I realised I was in White as opposed to Black propaganda.

I don't think many of us really knew what the Blacks were up to. From time to time a neighbour at the dinner-table or at a party would hiss in your ear, 'He's in Black, you know', as someone walked past. And immediately a glowing aura would spread around him. These individuals greatly enjoyed their prestige, and lived in a world of their own. There was one handsome, swashbuckling colonel, who was to be my Commanding Officer later on in Italy, who had to get himself sorted out in a special hospital after the war before he could cope with everyday life again.

PWB was made up of British and US military personnel as well as civilian linguists, press and advertising writers, art designers, and film and radio experts; also ex-soldiers from the front-lines with special knowledge of occupied territories, and what was known as 'extended awareness'. People came and went, from London, Washington, New York and back again, from and to Cairo, Tunis and various other places along the North African coast, and secret missions behind the lines. All this Captain B patiently explained to me. I was to work in the News Department, where I would be the youngest, the only female and the only Limey, as the Americans called their British allies.

Basic News, in the News and Information Section, was known as the 'nerve centre of the Mediterranean Forces'. We worked in a vast bustling room, with a long central table heaped with untidy piles of newsprint which came straight out of the teleprinters lined up against the walls. Into this huge pile of red-hot war news we all plunged and rooted around for the best story, often with two or three writers fighting over the same item.

The Editor usually stood in the middle of the floor, half-buried in mountains of paper, reading through the bulletins from the news agencies and the war correspondents on the various fronts. He was supposed to decide which stories would be used and who would write what – in theory, anyway. Whenever something caught his attention, he would toss it over to the writer of his choice. 'Here's a bulletin for you Jo. No, make it a flash.' These news items were constantly being cancelled, contradicted, added to, then finally 'killed'. Sometimes one would be torn up and rewritten half-a-dozen times. And occasionally, as it was being read over the air, you had to persuade the newsman to take back everything he'd just said – 'Ladies and gentlemen, in the light of new events that have just occurred . . .' And then you scrammed, because his wrath by then was fearful to behold.

To begin with, as a junior I got all the small, politically insignificant stories, more features than news. When they had to be done in French for the local press, this was my job as well. What I really liked best was to cover some local incident, as it gave me a chance to go and nose around all kinds of corners. One assignment I shall never forget was exploring the Kasbah just before the great annual washdown took place. All the fire hoses were turned on at the top and left to run down the streets, till a whole year's filth was washed away into the sea. A French officer who heard about my plans offered to come with me. No woman, he said, could venture into that den of thieves, smugglers, cut-throats and white-slavers without protection. So off we set together early next day.

Squatting on doorsteps, all along the narrow streets, everybody was selling something – rusty old nails, empty cartridge-cases, cigarette ends, filthy old boots. And in one place, lined up on the pavement, was a row of skinned, bleeding camels' heads with staring bulging eyes, sprawling on the cobbles of the street. We picked our way through mounds of rotting

refuse piled outside every doorway. Down the centre of the
streets ran the drain into which all household slops were flung
out of doors and windows. The stench, which was overwhelming, didn't seemed to worry anyone.

This was just before the plague broke out in Algiers.

My head never stopped spinning during those first few weeks in
Basic News. The noise and the bustle, the incessant coming and
going, all the phones ringing together, the shouting and cursing
of the newsmen, the smell, the heat and the non-stop ticking of
the teleprinters, were unbearably distracting. Added to all this
was the nostalgic crooning of the Italian prisoners, singing 'O
sole mio' as they swept enormous mountains of newsprint backwards and forwards across the floor.

After a few weeks I was put in charge of the daily news bulletin to Averell Harriman, the US Ambassador to Moscow. From
the innumerable wire trays lying around the table I had to pick
what seemed the right information for this great man and weave
it all up into a newsworthy bulletin. My elders, who set the
schedule, landed me, the youngest member of the unit, with
the night-shift throughout most of the week, which left them
with nice long evenings to enjoy whatever social life was available. And so there I was in sole charge of half-a-dozen GIs and
their teleprinters, a couple of Arab typists called Dandelion and
Sweet Pea, and the news network covering the entire European
theatre of war.

The bulletins coming over the printers had to be adapted
from cablese into English, or rather American, and sent off
immediately to AFHQ to our Supreme Commander and his
political advisers, Harold Macmillan and Robert Murphy. Also
champing for the latest information were the war correspondents and the leaflet-writers, whose work, based on the news we
gave them, was dropped behind enemy lines, to seduce the

Italians away from the Axis alliance and to persuade German soldiers to desert their own lines. The briefest of all the leaflets I
ever saw simply stated, in capital letters, 'EI SÖRRENDER'. Waving
these at arm's length, the enemy came streaming over no-man's
land to give themselves up when they finally realised they had
lost the war.

As outgoing news editor, I had to make sure that none of the
units in Basic News, each in its own eyes more important than
all the others, was left out. So I never enjoyed being dumped on
my own for very long, even in the middle of the night, when the
war usually simmered down on all fronts.

By midnight on one such evening, the Editor, who was obviously enjoying his dinner, had not yet returned. He was once
more taking a chance with that 'damblast Limey, no dam good at
anything', as he always described me. Which meant that packing
up for the night was left to me yet again. Nothing more was
coming over the printers, except for a drunken message from
Tunis, 'The bugs are biting, buddy, and baby, how they bite!' To
which I scribbled back, 'He who lies down with dogs must
expect to catch their fleas.' And when the GI had punched this
out on his keyboard with a chortle, I said, 'Come on boys, let's
pack it up for the night.'

We locked the newsroom's doors and windows and crowded
into the lift. As we got out on the ground floor, a couple of war
correspondents bustled along to check on the late news. 'We've
closed down for the night,' I told them. 'Nothing going on at all.
Dead as mutton.'

And to the GIs, but without much hope, 'Will someone give
me a ride home?'

'Not tonight honey, we're going to the PX for doughnuts and
coffee. Stick to the middle of the steps and you'll be okay.'

'So long baby, mind the bugs don't bite,' said another.

Crossing the road, I got my hatpin out of my handbag.

Unobtrusive and effective, this was my only means of self-defence against the drunks, murderers and rapists of the night. When one of these sneaked out of the shadows and made a grab, I plunged the hatpin into his soft parts and took to my heels as fast as I could, leaping up the town steps like an antelope.

Algiers, built on the side of a hill, is made up of parallel streets, one above the other, with enormous flights of stone steps linking the different levels. The PWB offices and Basic News were lodged in the Ministry of Agriculture, at sea-level. The Semiramis Hotel, our mess, was five streets up the hill, so that our lives ding-donged between these two buildings.

Lovely, gleaming-white Algiers, la Ville Blanche, was at that time a witches' cauldron seething with the scum of Europe, an enormous abscess festering on the ultimate fringe of the tidal wave of war. The political situation was unbelievably confused. Admiral Darlan, Marshal Pétain's heir apparent, who had been visiting his son in Algiers, was taken prisoner by the Americans when they landed in North Africa. The Germans, infuriated by this move, counteracted by occupying the whole of France. At which point Darlan decided to join the Allies, on condition that they named him head of the French regime in North Africa. Outraged by this *volte-face*, PID in London didn't know which way to turn. Up till then, their instructions to Richard Crossman, in charge of the British Section of PWB Algiers, had been to shoot down Darlan with all the psychological ammunition he could muster. How could he now wheel round and reverse his policy? De Gaulle, who was already in a rage at not having been given prior knowledge of the landings, attacked Churchill, and one more of those famous explosions between the English Bulldog and the Cross of Lorraine took place.

Then suddenly the situation resolved itself when a young man marched up to Darlan's office, and shot him dead on the spot. The assassin was promptly dealt with by a French firing squad, and the matter was dropped with great relief by all concerned. But in a place like Algiers, a scandal of this kind was not going to be forgotten in a hurry. The story went round that the young man had been hired by the brother of a French general secretly sent to Algiers by de Gaulle to find out what was going on.

At this point the Duc de Guise, heir to the French throne, arrived to take Darlan's place. There were endless plots and counter-plots, which for us in Basic News meant there was always plenty to write about.

One burning problem was the state of the political prisoners, all 10,000 of them, rotting away in unspeakable conditions in concentration camps dotted around the desert. Interned by the Germans, they had at least been allowed to survive instead of going to the gas ovens, as in Germany. We had an ongoing campaign running on their behalf, but it was some time before they were released. When they were, it was up to us to find homes and work for them in Algiers, Tunis and elsewhere along the North African coast.

Although not quite as lethal as the Kasbah, the rest of the town was pretty chaotic as well. The Communists and local French Fascists were conducting their own private warfare. Black marketeers of every nationality did a roaring trade in stolen army equipment. The local landowners made a fortune selling wine, olive oil and farm produce to German agents, who got the loot home through Spain. In the streets at night, Arabs knifed Jews and Jews shot Arabs. The Berber militiamen, the Goums, who walked about hand-in-hand in their ankle-length army skirts in search of a smoke, clubbed anybody who came along for a packet of cigarettes.

So on the whole, lingering in the streets at night was inadvisable, and my main wish after an evening at the office was to get back to the mess as quickly as possible. Not that even that could be relied on as a haven of peace. After toiling up the five floors to my shared bedroom, I would not infrequently find additional company in the shape of one of the young stallions who regularly followed my moonstruck room-mate, Miriam, around the mess, laid out snoring thunderously on the double-bed, or sometimes on the floor. An ejection job had to be done before I could settle down to sleep.

chapter twenty-three

After my visit to the Kasbah, I wasn't in the least surprised when Major T announced one morning at breakfast that nobody would be allowed out of the mess until further notice. Bubonic plague had broken out in Algiers. To my amazement, this was greeted with thundering cheers from the whole company. It was like the unexpected announcement of a picnic at a primary school. But unlike such an event, it started a drinking bout, which went on for several hours. The dice came out, and the poker games were soon in progress.

Collecting my painting gear, I climbed up to the roof terrace of the mess, from which the view all round was staggering. The whole bay of Algiers was full of warships, dotted about on the deep purple of the sea. With my legs hanging over the edge, I peered ten floors down into the street below, where tiny shrouded figures fluttered about like ghosts, spreading clouds of Bubonic bugs all round.

While my colleagues were boozing or squabbling over their

cards in the steaming heat of the dining-room below, I spent those plague-ridden days snoozing and painting in glorious solitude on the roof, while serenely breathing in the poisoned air. As far as I remember, the disease did not rage for very long, and no member of our forces caught it. Nobody knew how many poor Arabs were carried away to the Moslem cemetery on the hill, but the Allies took prompt action, and the epidemic never approached medieval proportions.

By the time we all got back to work, some of us were a little the worse for wear, and relationships in the newsroom were somewhat strained to start with. We were all used to this, as it happened from time to time, after a particularly late night. 'Where would you goddam Limeys be if it weren't for our Aid?' I was asked by one of our pressmen, who wanted to annex my typewriter.

'And where would you be if we hadn't held out for a whole year on our own?' I answered. And the exchange would go on in this vein, until hangovers lifted and it was time for another drink. But our allies were tough cookies with marshmallow hearts. When their copy wasn't straight news, it often dripped with sobstuff.

Chantecleer Leclerc (he had a French grandfather) sometimes joined me at breakfast as I gobbled my powdered-egg pancake and maple syrup (plus a slice of bacon when a convoy had come in) with one eye on the Basic News sheet, counting the printing errors.

'How you can swallow that stuff beats me' was his usual greeting. Poor Chant's head was throbbing visibly with the power of his hangover. A waitress dumped a pancake under his nose. 'Take that goddam stuff away,' he roared, 'and bring me some corfee.' The waitress scuttled away with the plate. 'How you doin', honey?' he asked.

'I'm doing fine thanks Chant.'

'You doin' fine? Gee, that's swell, how am *I* doin' kid?'

'You doin' just fine Chant,' I mumbled through the pancake.

'That's right honey, you doin' fine and I'm doin' fine. I'll tear anyone apart who denies it.'

'Don't worry Chant, everyone knows you're a regular guy.'

'Say!' He thumped the table. 'Did you really mean that, Kid?' As he stared at me, a great belch rumbled from his belly. His elbow, slipping off the table, knocked the cup of scalding coffee into his lap.

'Dam your eyes,' he panted, mopping up the mess. 'Sure you don't think I'm stewed?'

'No Chant, you're just soaked.' And I beetled down the stairs, rather ashamed of my feeble pun.

It was some time before he came shambling into the newsroom, having had to change his trousers.

'Holy mackerel,' he wheezed, as he tottered in. 'Why is everybody so goddam tight-assed this morning?'

'Sit down Chant,' said the Editor. 'I got sumpen special for you today.'

'That's swell Merc. How you doin' Merc?'

'Fine Chant. Here's your copy Chant. I kept it special for you. Do it real good Chant. I'm countin' on you.'

'Sure boss. Just as you say. I'll make it a knock-out,' he wheezed, peering at the paper upside-down. He sat down at the table, laid his head on the typewriter in front of him, and snored the morning away undisturbed.

One day in Basic News, in the midst of our usual chaotic confusion, a great honour was conferred on us. Surrounded by a bevy of high-ranking officers, Marlene Dietrich suddenly appeared among us. Dressed in the dark-green uniform of the US Women's Army, she willowed into the room on those dazzling million-dollar legs of hers, a green chiffon scarf wrapped round her head and dangling down her back like gossamer seaweed. She floated slowly round the room, asking about our stinking, overheated, unreliable teleprinters and Morse-code equipment. The newsmen, silenced for once, followed her round with a bemused look on their faces.

In a flash she was gone. But to my surprise, her presence, however brief, had given us all an unexpected boost. This must be the effect, I thought, that all those great film stars' constant tours of the war-fronts must have on the troops they visited . . . And about which I had felt pretty cynical until then. Psychological warfare indeed . . . I too was caught up in the meshes of our famous net!

But peace and calm never lasted very long in the office. That evening, getting on for midnight, the war seemed to have simmered down on its various fronts, and very little news was coming over the air. Having finished their bulletins and their letters home, the pressmen were leaving. The Morse operators, crouching behind their machines, were having a celebration of their own with a bottle of Scotch. The Editor, in the middle of the floor, was struggling with yards of telex twined all round him like the arms of an octopus. From time to time he croaked, 'Bulletin – flash – bulletin ...' and tearing off a section, flung it at me across the table. My copy for the midnight communiqué was nearly finished. Surely he must stop soon.

'I'm taking my stuff over to the studio,' I said. 'Furze must have a few minutes to read it before he goes on the air. You know the state he gets into otherwise.'

'Sure kid, you do that.'

Ripping the sheet out of my typewriter, I gathered up the other pages and tore down the corridor to the studios.

'What the hell are you doing with that script? Why haven't I had it yet? Look at the time, girl! Here, gimme that.' And Furze grabbed it out of my hand.

The door burst open and the Arab office-boy poked his head in, waving a sheet of paper. 'Flash zur, queek,' he said.

'Dam your bloody eyes,' roared Furze, snatching up the flash. 'It isn't even typed! How the hell does he expect me to read cablese over the air?'

The Night Editor came trotting down the corridor. 'Say Butch, you got that flash? Make it a lead for the midnight communiqué.'

'Dam and blast your eyes,' fumed Furze. 'I'm on the air in three minutes flat and I haven't even read the bloody script. Go to hell.'

'Take it easy kid, you're on the air now,' remarked the Editor, pointing at the light. Furze simmered down at once, and his voice became suave. '*Ici la radio des Forces Alliées à Alger* . . .' His French was faultless, without a trace of accent. The Editor and I stepped quietly out of the cork-lined studio and closed the door.

Back in the newsroom, the Arab boy was standing by the desk, with a fat grin on his face and a yellow sheet of paper in his hand. 'Flash zur,' he said.

'What!' barked the Editor. 'Dam dam dam' (and much worse!). 'Kill that flash,' he shouted, hurling the paper at me.

'But it's on the air,' I said. 'It's too late.'

'KILL THAT FLASH,' he roared. 'Send out a kill.'

Almost weeping for Furze, I banged out a kill on the typewriter and raced back to the studio with it.

'How did he take it?' asked the Editor when I got back.

'Dropped down dead,' I said.

'Boloney. Tell him it was only put out by AP to spite Reuters for having gotten in first on the landings.'

I said I was going round to Home's office to listen to the show on his set. 'Sure kid, go right ahead. I'm going back to the mess. Close the place down, won't you?'

'Okay boss. Goodnight.'

'So long baby, I'm playing poker with the Colonel. Come and join us when you get back.'

'Grrr . . . thanks awfully,' I said, and bustled off to Home's office, which was a cosy little kitchen. Home (short for Homer) was perched on the draining-board, fiddling with the knobs of a radio set lodged in the sink and padded round with newspaper. The floor was knee-deep in reams of yellow despatches, the last three days' news, which he kept round for reference. After that he would poke about among the litter, pick out the essentials, and stuff them into the little oven for safe keeping. The rest would be borne away by the Italian prisoners of war who cleaned out the office.

'Come in and listen to the show,' said Home hospitably. I jumped up on the draining-board beside him.

'Furze is upset,' I said.

'Is that so? What's gotten into him?'

'Usual stuff. Late script. Flash at the last minute. Then a kill.'

'Too bad. Swell guy Furze, but he worries too much. He'll have ulcers before he's twenty-five. Wait and see.'

Home lit a couple of Camels and handed one to me. We were great buddies. As a mature man in his early thirties he was high up in the hierarchy, even senior to the Night Editor. From time to time he strolled into Basic News, where he would settle down to a typewriter next to me and pass irreverent remarks, just loud enough to be heard, about our colleagues, and specially the Editor, all of which reduced me to fits of giggles.

Home Park, dear Home, said I looked like his wife, which I found very flattering until I saw her photograph. I realised then that it was just amiable waffle, to oil the works and help towards cordial relations between the Allies. Mrs Home Parks was a regular Hollywood dame with large gleaming domino teeth, toothpick eyelashes, dramatic hollow cheeks, and beautiful smooth black hair, silky as a Labrador's coat.

As I was so often on the night-shift, Home would send round little gifts by despatch-rider. And one of these, all booted and spurred, would come clattering into Basic News, bearing an orchid snitched from some scented Arabian garden. Or a saucer of Turkish Delight swiped off a dinner-party table somewhere in Algiers. 'With the compliments of Mr Parks mam,' he would boom across the room. 'And he hopes to come by later if he gets through his conference in time.'

Once in a while Home would turn up himself, to take me out to dinner around seven o'clock. The Editor always bristled with indignation. 'See here buddy, I know you're a big shot, but she's got to do the midnight communiqué and she's not going out to no dam dinner with you nor anybody else.'

'Sure she is, and you'll just have to do that communiqué yourself, and your dame will have to wait tonight. Come along sugar, my jeep's outside. Let's get going.'

'You can't disrupt my joint like that, you son-of-a-bitch,' growled my boss, as we dived into the lift. I knew retribution would come later, but for the time being it was well worth it. We would have a delicious dinner at some expensive black market restaurant in a little paved courtyard, with a splashing fountain and a few stately date-palms all a-twitter with exotic birds.

On other occasions Home would collect me after the midnight communiqué and we would stroll off to a small public garden on the side of the hill and perch there on the town steps in the full light of the moon, well away from the furtive shadows heaving with murderous thoughts in their heads. From where we sat we could see the fishermen's boats swaying gently on the harbour waters, and further out, the big destroyers gleaming softly in the moonlight. Fiery shooting-stars criss-crossed over our heads in the dark-blue sky while the palm-trees in the square creaked and rustled in their rat-infested sleep.

Home would tell me about his leisurely life in the Deep South, where the 'cake-walk' originated. This, he explained, started with the slaves' imitation of their masters' way of walking, which they found excruciatingly funny. Meanwhile, the victims of their derision, ignorant of its cause, encouraged the slaves in their mimics and antics, always rewarding a good performance with a slice of cake.

He would tell me about the Queen of the United States, his raving beauty of a wife, and how much he missed her, until I dropped off to sleep, and he would clap his hands, saying it was time for me to go to bed. We parted in the hall of the mess, as we all pretended that he lived there like the rest of us. In fact, everybody knew that he shared a flat somewhere in town, with one of his 'conferences'.

When it was eventually my turn to be posted to Italy, he said, 'That's just grand baby, I sure wish I could be around to keep an eye on you. But you'll be okay, little Limey. Just keep going your own way, and don't let nobody nark you.'

'But I don't want to go. I love it here,' I said.

'When you begin to feel like that about a place, it's time to move on, honey. Soldiers don't grow roots.'

I really did love Algiers, in all its dazzling whiteness, under the shimmering lapis-lazuli sky, with its gentle, rustling breezes, its filthy streets and sinister Kasbah, the ferocity of its night-life. I admired the proud insolence of its inhabitants, in no way impressed by the thundering armed forces invading their land. And above all I loved the dazzling white glare of the moon, my constant companion during my endless spells of night-duty.

chapter twenty-four

The great advantage of being on the night-shift was that you had most of the next day for yourself to do as you pleased. In the scorching heat of the African summer, a 'weapons-carrier', nick-named the 'Madrague Mail', on loan from the British Army, was laid on for the benefit of the night staff, which included the news-writers, the printers and the Morse operators.

Since their liberation from the desert camps, we now also had some immensely intellectual Jews, who joined us on our daily run. Many of them had been absorbed into the beargarden of PWB, where they helped in the German news and leaflet sections. There was one jovial little doctor-of-law, who looked just like Toad of Toad Hall. And most of the others were university professors of one kind or another.

A gloomy-looking Hungarian sergeant was in charge of our party. Among its youngest members was a captain from the Jewish Brigade named David, who was as bright and clever as you could wish. After the war he was to play a leading part in the return of the Jews to Israel. David loved England, the British and their laid-back, easy-going ways, and would have loved to live in Britain, but his conscience drove him to settle in Israel and take an active part in its government.

Driven army-style by an other-rank and his mate, we would set off bumping and swaying along the coast-road to Madrague. We would pass Arab families on the march in army formation. In case of mines, the wives came first, then the children, and last of all the lord and master, regally enthroned on the family donkey.

It usually took about an hour to reach our destination. This was a small sandy cove, with machine-gun posts all along the dunes, every one of which was occupied by several families. Soon after we arrived, they would creep out to goggle at us and our lunatic ways – lying half-naked in the noonday sun, when all sensible beings were wrapped in heavy rugs and cloaks to keep out the heat. A larger, stone-built coastal defence-post served as a kind of officers' mess, where other ranks, in shorts and heavy army boots, clattered around waiting on us at lunch, handing out bully-beef, raw onions, tinned peaches and sour Algerian wine.

These were glorious, lazy days. In Algiers we lived with the war round the clock. It was the subject of every conversation, and the bulletins and news-sheets were our only reading matter. At Madrague, the war was light-years away. We nattered on for hours – or rather, the others conversed in French, English or German, whichever came most readily, and I listened. They were earnest, cultured, serious-minded men. They discussed books, literary magazines, the techniques of all the great European conductors. The culture of pre-war Central Europe was a subject of never-ending fascination for me. Only when, sooner or later, they embarked on politics, did my pea-brain snap shut with an audible click. And I would run down to the sea and flop into the warm, weed-laden water.

Finally, stunned with sun and wine and itching all over with the heavy salt of the sea, we would climb back into the truck and trundle off to Algiers for one more hot night of work.

On Sunday I often went to the races with the war correspondents. Rupert Downing, who had gone through the great débâcle in France in 1940 and written a very good book about it, regarded himself as an expert in horse-flesh. Before placing our bets, we trooped round to the stable to inspect the local talent, which Rupert pinched and prodded on the hocks. After which he peered at their yellowing teeth with a worried frown. Never for a moment doubting his judgement, I still preferred to follow the example of his colleagues, Godfrey Talbot, Eric Linklater, and all the others, who swapped cigarettes with the Arab grooms for accurate information about the winner of the next race. Which meant I always came away a few hundred francs better off at the end of the day.

Apart from a film unit, we also had an officers' club, which catered for all the services in Algiers. This operated in a hot, steaming cellar which had been requisitioned for the purpose. And there we danced to a first-class band.

On one of my very few evenings off-duty, I went there with Maria and her boyfriend Andrew. Soon after we arrived, an army major, who sometimes bumped into me in the office hall and glared when I apologised, strolled up to our table. He introduced himself to Maria, who agreed that she knew him by sight and invited him to join us. But he asked me to dance instead. 'I know all about you,' he said, as we started to shuffle around the floor. 'You're the tiddler from Basic News. And a proper greenhorn at that.'

'What on earth is that?' I asked.

'I bet you've never been kissed,' he added.

'Oh yes I have. At least once.'

He roared with laughter, and shoved me roughly round the dancing couples. I didn't like his tone, and I didn't much care for his manners either.

'You're lucky to have met me,' he said next. 'You'll know a thing or two by the time I've finished with you.'

'What sort of thing?' I asked nervously.

'Wait and see. It's time you grew up.' He didn't sound like my sort of chap at all. And I said I wanted to go back to join Maria and Andrew.

'We will go back when *I* decide,' he said. 'And I'll pick you up at your mess tomorrow for lunch. One o'clock sharp, and don't be late, or I'll come up and dig you out.'

By then Maria had become my room-mate, a wonderful change after sharing with Miriam and all her boozed-up young men, who often had to be dragged out of the room by the feet. When we climbed into our double-bed that night, I told Maria that I didn't care for that major at all and wished she hadn't asked him to join us.

'He's a man of the world, and perfectly all right. Don't worry.' She was obviously impressed by his high-handed manner. 'He thinks you're too withdrawn and need bringing out,' she added.

'Ho. And what does Andrew think of him?'

'That he's a very good soldier, and his men would go through fire for him.'

'That may well be, but I'm not one of his men, and he's not going to push *me* around as he pleases.' And privately I reflected that if *I* needed bringing on, *he* could certainly do with a little putting down. Tiddler indeed!

Next day, terrified he should come up to my room, I was in the hall when he marched in to pick me up. An Arab chauffeur drove us out to lunch, mostly on two wheels, so that I was constantly hurled against the major, who ignored my apologies. He never said a word either during the drive or throughout the meal.

'Come on my girl,' he said at last. 'Drink up your coffee. We must be off.'

At two o'clock sharp the car dropped us off at the office. He bundled me into the lift, and we got out on the second floor.

'Where on earth are we going?' I asked.

'You'll soon see. Your education is about to begin.' My insides lurched at the sound of this. 'I want to go back to the mess,' I said.

He stopped outside an office door and glued his eye to the keyhole. Then, with a satisfied grunt, he stepped back. Pushing my head down, he hissed, 'Take a look at that and tell me what you think.'

Intrigued, I put my head to the keyhole and peered through, staring at the scene before me. Unable to make any sense of it, I switched over to the other eye for a second opinion. Suddenly, light crashed in with a loud bang. 'Good Heavens!' I gasped, staggering away from the door. 'It's . . . It's what the dogs do in the street, isn't it?'

'Shut up, you goose, they'll hear you,' he said, clapping his hand over my mouth and pushing me towards the lift.

'Why did you make me watch them?' I wailed. 'You're absolutely beastly . . . Perfectly horrible . . .'

'Don't be such an ass. People love it. You'll love it too, once you get used to it.'

By then we were back in the car. 'I want to go back to the mess. Take me back at once,' I said.

'Don't be such a ruddy little fool. You've got to grow up sooner or later. Can't you see how they're all shielding you? As long as you stick around with your crowd you'll never learn a thing.'

'I know as much as I want to,' I said with all the dignity I could muster. 'Take me back to the hotel at once.'

'You are coming to my mess with *me*. From now on I am

taking you in hand. In no time you will be thanking me for my time and trouble.'

'I'll jump out of the car if you don't take me back . . .'

The one who was loving it all was the driver, whose head was screwed round watching us, with a great big grin like a slice of melon on his face.

'You're not due back till six o'clock. There's plenty of time. You're coming with me.'

'No,' I shouted, and opened the car door.

'Sit down,' he ordered, dragging me back. 'I'll hit you if you don't keep still.'

I kicked him on the shin as hard as I could. He slapped me on the face, catching me in the eye with his signet ring. I collapsed in a flood of tears.

'You bloody little bitch. All right, go back to your kennel, you'll never be any good. And mind you don't cross my path again.' And he told the driver to return to the PWB mess.

As I didn't feel up to coping with the eccentricities of the lift, I struggled up the five flights of stairs to my room and dropped on the bed choking with tears. Filled with the afternoon sun, the little room was like a furnace. Throbbing with shock and misery, I lay on the burning sheets, with my head threatening to split asunder and my left eyeball slowly swelling out of its socket. By six o'clock I felt so ill that no power on earth could have dragged me to the newsroom.

When Maria came back from the office she said I must have got sunstroke, and had better get into bed and stay there. All night I tossed from side to side, aching in every limb, shivering like a jelly, and hardly able to bear the pain in my head. In the morning Maria took my temperature and then said I must go to the hospital at once. 'Oh no!' I groaned. 'Not hospital! If you get me some aspirin, I'll be fine by this evening.'

'I'll speak to the Major,' she said, as she tripped off to breakfast on her elegant high-heeled sandals.

An hour later she rang up to say that a car was at the door of the mess, and would I please pack my bag and be off to hospital at once. It would, I suddenly realised, be a relief to get out of the tiny, steaming, overheated bedroom. I packed my night-things and *War and Peace*, then set off at a wobble down the stairs. The smells coming up from the kitchen – fried spam, rancid oil and cigarette smoke, made my innards heave. But I managed to reach the car in good order.

The driver, a French colonial who was hiring out his car to the Allied Forces, was kind and full of sympathy. 'It's too bad, a young girl like you, away from home, having to go to a terrible hospital full of rough soldiers,' he said, as we screeched round the first bend. Touched by his concern, and aching all over though I was, I could not really feel sorry for myself. PWB and the Army, working hand-in-hand, weren't doing a bad job . . . To have a private car sent round to your doorstep to take you to hospital, on active service, in the middle of a vast and complicated world war, wasn't a bad effort.

'Well,' I said, to pacify him, '*C'est la guerre*, you know!'

But he stuck to his point. 'I wouldn't let *my* daughter go off on her own to a military hospital like that. If there's anything I can do for you, let me know. You're a brave girl.'

Brave was the last thing I felt. More like past caring. With an eye sticking out like a plum, and shivering with ague, I was grateful for his sympathy all the same. 'Ring me up when you're better, and I'll come and pick you up. Good luck *mademoiselle*.'

The sister who signed me on and took my temperature said, 'We'll have to put you in isolation in case you're infectious.' This suited me fine, and the bare cell they gave me, with its iron bedstead and army blanket for sole furniture, was all I wanted. 'Thank you sister, this is perfect,' I said gratefully. She gave me a sharp look, as if I was pulling her leg. 'Get into bed as soon as you can. The MO will come and see you later. Watch out for the mosquito net.' As she said these words, it came crashing down on top of me. 'Just pull the string and it will go up again. You'll get used to it.'

I sank into a coma, and didn't come round again until an orderly, in shorts and army boots, clattered in with a cup of cocoa. As he handed it to me the net came tumbling down again, knocking the cup out of my hand.

'Is this some kind of joke?' I asked. 'No miss, it just happens,' he answered, as he went down on his knees to retrieve the mug.

'You mean *every* time?'

'Yes, miss, every time.'

'Couldn't we move the bed?'

'Then you wouldn't have the net when you need it, and the mosquitoes would get at you.'

'I'm not sure I wouldn't rather have them,' I muttered. 'And please don't bother to bring me another cup.'

'Oh, I never do, miss. One is the ration.' And he scrunched out of the room on his enormous, high-shine army boots.

Later that evening the Medical Officer paid me a visit. As he sat beside me on the bed, the net came down and wrapped him in its folds. 'I see they've put you in the flytrap,' he said as he struggled out of the netting. 'We'll get you out of here as soon as we can. But first we have to see what the blood tests have to say.'

The blood sample, when duly stewed and curdled, proclaimed I had malaria. The MO seemed surprised.

'I expect you feel like a good dose of strychnine and be done with it, don't you?' he asked sympathetically. 'And I bet you've been giving the mepacrine a miss, haven't you?' The little yellow tablets stood about in saucers on all the dining tables in the mess. Those who took a daily dose developed custard-coloured eyeballs, streaked with a fine network of red veins. Yes, I had been giving the mepacrine a miss.

My black eye got me very little sympathy. 'Been fighting with your boyfriend, have you? Well, serves you right.'

And with that he was gone.

Although the hospital rations were no worse than our mess food, I had lost weight, and looked hideously scraggy when I got back to the hotel. Captain B, catching sight of me on my return, kindly suggested I should have a few days' leave before going back to work. And Maria booked me a room at our station at Bou-Saada way out in the desert. The PWB courier, a three-ton army lorry, drove out there twice a week with supplies, mail and personnel. As there was one leaving next day, I was told to get on it.

A girl from the Admin Office, who had contracted an American baby and suffered the horrors of abortion, was also on board. As her morale was at rock-bottom and mine was soaring, I tried to cheer her up, but without success. In the end I joined in a game of poker with a couple of GIs on top of the mailbags. (On the last trip I'd spent in this way, we'd perched on a sack of hand-grenades, assuming they were army boots.) It took all day to drive the 250 kilometres to Bou-Saada, and as the sun climbed higher, the heat increased to an almost unbearable degree. The game of poker fizzled out, and I swung my legs over the back of the lorry and watched the clouds of sand boiling up from under our wheels.

The convalescent camp seemed to be as spartan as the hospital I had just left. The girl whose room I was to share was called Cherry-Blossom. The great treat was that we each had a bed of our own. But apart from that, there was no other furniture in the room.

We feasted that night on cold bully and lettuce, the usual dog-biscuits, and bunches of dry dates fresh from the trees. Cherry-Blossom, who had become the self-appointed cheerleader of the establishment during the few days she had already been there, had ordered all the officers to take off their shoulder-pips so as to do away with rank. As a result, nobody knew who was what, and the youngest subaltern could chat up an elderly officer who might be anything from a brigadier downwards. All of which made for a much more relaxed atmosphere.

Worn out after the long drive, I crawled upstairs straight after dinner. As I lay on the wire bed which I had dragged out on the balcony, I could hear the growling of jackals, fighting over the scraps and refuse which littered the streets. Downstairs, the assembled company, freed from the tyranny of their pips, were carousing in the bar, lustily singing 'Lily Marlene' under the direction of Cherry-Blossom.

Suddenly the bedroom door was flung open and the light switched on. I sat up in bed on my balcony. The young bombardier in charge of the reception desk was standing in the middle of the room.

'What on earth is the matter?' I asked in alarm.

'You've got an officer in the room miss, and it's against the rules.'

'What on earth are you talking about?' I squealed, outraged. 'Where do you think I could hide anyone in this room? And anyway, how dare you accuse me of breaking the rules? Who is in charge here?'

'The Mess Officer is out miss, and I distinctly saw an officer following you when you left the dining-room.'

'Good heavens, Bombardier, is that all you've got to go by?'

'In this place it usually means one thing miss.'

'Well, search the room. And don't forget to look under the bed,' I said, getting to my feet. 'And then get the hell out of here, or I'll report you to the Mess Officer.'

'Sorry to disturb you miss,' he said, after peering inside and also under the bed – at which I couldn't help laughing. And for the next few days I stopped at his post on my way up to bed every evening.

'Am I to expect another visit from you tonight, Bombardier?' At which he would turn tomato-red and dive behind the reception desk.

During the day we strolled along the narrow streets, which were just dust-lanes between the shamble of huts, shacks and hovels of the local kasbah. We poked about among the carpet stores, the silver stalls and the leather-workers who hammered and tooled their wares and held them up for our inspection. One evening Cherry-Blossom organised a cabaret of belly-dancers, and young girls, no more than twelve years old, put on an exotic show for us in the dining-room. Another time she laid on a 'coach' tour to Biskra, and off we went for a scorching day in the desert, all of us packed into the back of our army truck. When the Allied armies had landed in North Africa, women had lined the roads selling cups of mother's milk to the soldiers. Now, in the desert, we swapped our cigarette rations for what (we hoped) was goat's cheese.

On the last day of my stay, the locusts came up from the South. The first warning we had of their approach was a huge black cloud fanning out into the sky. It was fascinating to watch them advance. The noise they produced was like an approaching bomber squadron. Within an hour they were all round us, churning about with this extraordinary roaring sound. They settled on anything handy, creeping through your hair, dropping to the ground, where they were crunched underfoot until all the streets oozed with a squelchy mush of crushed locust.

At sunset they dropped out of the sky and settled several feet deep all over the town. Locusts travel only by day and feed at night, when you can hear the champing of their jaws for miles around. In the morning the local vegetable plots around the village were cropped down to the roots. And the insects took to the air again at dawn. We all set off together on our way back to

Algiers, and they escorted us all the way to the coast. By the time we arrived at nightfall, they had already moved into the town. At least a thousand of them crept into bed with me when I finally got there. Next day they were swarming again, blocking out the sun, so we had to have breakfast by electric light. Getting to work was another problem, as they lay a foot deep on the town steps. After trying to cope in various ways, we finally had to give up and go back to the mess. In the end Major T had to lay on a fleet of cars and army trucks to get us to our various destinations.

It was a squelchy, crunchy trip, with the wipers working overtime on the liquefied corpses trickling down the windscreen. On every street corner, Arabs had set up little charcoal stoves over which they tossed locusts, selling them to the passing crowd. I didn't try any, but Dr Livingstone said that dipped in honey they tasted far better than shrimps and mayonnaise.

In Basic News the Editor was tearing his hair. Everything on the table was on the move. As soon as you put down a sheet of paper, off it went, carried away on the little shoulders of battalions of insects. The typewriters were gummed up with the creatures, which had spent the night in the works. The minute you hit the keys, thick juicy jets of minced-up locust squirted off in all directions. This went on for three days, after which they were gone, all except for the littered streets and the windowpanes blacked out with their dried juice.

chapter twenty-five

The 6th of June 1944 . . . In Algiers, where we crouched over our typewriters anxiously waiting for news, the sun rose in a mother-of-pearl sky, while on the north-west coast of France Overlord thundered into action. The greatest armada in history was on its way across the English Channel, almost a thousand years after William the Conqueror, going the opposite way, had landed on the beaches of Southern England. Over 5,000 ships of every shape and size, including ancient cargoes, Channel steamers, passenger boats, tankers and hospital ships, were used to transport the troops across the sea. The Americans advanced in 21 stately convoys, while the British and Canadian Task Force numbered 38. These had all sailed in total secrecy, at dead of night, from their meeting-point south of the Isle of Wight. And above them roared 12,000 aircraft with their gigantic load of airborne troops.

The majestic fleet proceeded in orderly, prearranged lanes, with everyone in his allotted place, while hundreds of motor launches buzzed up and down the lanes like agitated sheep-dogs. But the weather was breaking up, and the Channel waters, as if they sensed the menace brooding on their surface, heaved and stirred uneasily. Soon huge waves crashed over the sides of the shallow landing-craft, in which the men, packed like sardines, were soaked to the skin. Cold, stiff with cramp and apprehension, knowing that many of them would never see another sunrise, a great number of them were seasick throughout the night as well. But when they landed, in spite of the misery of the crossing, they fought like demons to establish a foothold. They struggled through the barbed-wire, the underwater obstacles, the sea defences, the mines, and continuous vicious firing from the land.

Between Vierville and Colville, the stretch which the Americans called Omaha Beach, the German sea defences were covered by guns tucked away among the dunes. To avoid these fireworks, the Americans had decided to transfer their troops into landing-craft several miles away from the shore. As the sea was now running high, a great number of these small boats sank hopelessly to the bottom. Many of the soldiers, dragged down by their heavy equipment, were drowned or swept away from their objective. Covering fire from US warships was either aimed too high or exploded on the beach, creating havoc among their own men.

The appalling confusion of the landings and the pitiful number of casualties led the Germans to believe they had won the day on this stretch of coast. At noon they announced victory. But they were counting without the determination and heroic courage of US troops once they were launched. As so often happened, the men on the spot made up for the bungling of their leaders. Veterans from Sicily and Salerno, whose shining spirit was armour-plated against human fear, waded stolidly through minefields, pushed inland, and by nightfall there were over 34,000 men firmly established on shore.

Compared to this particular beachhead, the other landings were smooth and harmonious exercises. The British and Canadian Divisions, accurately covered by faultless firing from the Royal Navy, followed in the tracks of the steadily advancing Sherman tanks. Cunningly adapted, these bristled with protective extensions, such as flailing arms, to set off mines <u>away</u> from the tanks. Racing inland, they had reached the outskirts of Bayeux by the evening.

But before these landings could take place, a great deal of softening up had been carried out inland the previous night by the airborne divisions. US volunteer parachutists came down soon after midnight to mark dropping zones for the 12,000 paratroops who were to follow an hour later. These 'Pathfinders', running into heavy firing, had been scattered in all directions. But in spite of this, they had managed to capture their own objective of Sainte Mère Eglise and Pouppeville. These heroic young men, plus sixty volunteers from our 6th Airborne Division dropped near Caen, were said by Cornelius Ryan in his book *The Longest Day* to have had 'one of the toughest of the D-Day jobs'.

Landing in total darkness in unknown territory, the Red Devil Volunteers, as the 6th Airborne were known, had exactly half-an-hour to find their bearings, locate the appointed zones, and mark them up with flares and radar to guide the main British troops to their landing-stage. This territory, which lay in a 20-mile radius, formed a triangle between the villages of Varaville, Ranville and Touffreville.

The first batch, who were exceptionally lucky, floated down almost on top of their target. The Ranville unit was met with heavy ack-ack fire, which scattered them over a wide area. The Touffreville party, jumping into strong, unexpected wind, lost six of their men, swept away to the flooded Dives River Valley; tangled in their chutes and dragged down by their heavy equipment, they were drowned in three feet of water. In the first Pathfinder plane of the Touffreville crew, my brother John, huddled together with other volunteers, waited impatiently for his turn to jump. The first man to go, stuck in the drophole with his folding minibike, struggled for a long time to get free. When he finally got through, the aircraft was several miles away from the drop zone. So when the rest of the crew finally landed, they had to double back on their minibikes in complete darkness to find their objective.

In Basic News the Editor, who was flicking through a pile of press photographs, tossed one across the table. 'Say baby, is that guy anything to do with you? Same name.'

'Yes,' I said. 'It's my brother.' There before my eyes stood John, with one arm in a sling, in a ploughed-up street in a devastated village, surrounded by a group of paratroopers. The caption said: 'Sergeant Fesq, of Field Security, 6th Airborne Division, was mentioned in despatches for outstanding gallantry in action.'

Although we had been up all the previous night in the newsroom, the noise and bustle, and the non-stop stream of flashes and bulletins pouring in through our machines, kept us hopping with excitement. But for several hours it was impossible to form any clear idea of the situation on the various beachheads. All we could do was to churn out the frenzied information as it reached us over the air.

By the evening a pattern began to emerge. US General Pratt had been killed in the disastrous landings of the gliders of the 101st Unit, most of which were totally wrecked. The 82nd, brought in by inexperienced pilots, crashed into hedgerows and buildings and sank in rivers and marshes, with eighteen pilots killed on landing. Of the 69 British gliders in the Caen area, 49 touched down on the correct strip; although many of them broke up on landing, there were few casualties. The bridges over the River Orme, which were their objective, were stormed and captured within fifteen minutes while the drowsy German guards were still struggling into their boots. By evening, all positions were firmly held.

It was a great triumph, and it was obvious to a jubilant world that the end was now in sight. Monty was once more in his element, cleverly exploiting the national characteristics of the troops under his command to get the best out of them. When, in Caen, he pinned down a large German force with fourteen British divisions, he provided a breakthrough for US troops, who stormed on to overrun Brittany.

After the German counterattack on Avranches, on the 7th of August, the 5th Panzer Division and the 7th Army found themselves trapped, with 50,000 men taken prisoner and 10,000 killed. But Hitler, still holding out, was convinced that the Allies would scrap among themselves and give up the fight, even though so close to victory. Still following his unlucky stars' advice, and launching great battles at their bidding, he simply could not see the facts as they were. Blinded by astrology, day after day he blundered deeper into disaster.

Meanwhile in Basic News, the pace was slowing down on the night-shift as we gradually got used to the progress of the Allied armies. The Editor, leaving me once more in charge of the night-shift, resumed his interrupted social life. I was able to join my friends on the Madrague run again most mornings. In the officers' mess on the beach, the 'old men's' conversation lost some of its appeal for me when young David from the Jewish Brigade and his friend Elliott joined our group.

Active and restless, they could hardly wait to finish their last mouthful of lunch and be up and away, walking briskly along the shore with me trotting after them like a dog at their heels. I found their particular brand of nonsense completely irresistible.

They would rattle on in a rapid give-and-take of perpetual non-sequiturs. Anything was grist to their mill. A couple of decrepit old Arabs crouching on the beach, with a scraggy hen on the end of a piece of string, would set them off on a lunatic imaginary conversation between the men and their old hen. Or a wild-eyed seagull, with a tuft of yellow straw sticking out of its beak, caught their fancy, and away they went. Trying not to miss a word of their dotty gabbling, I would plod after them, laughing until my ribs ached.

But it wasn't only on the beach that they indulged in their favourite pastime. When the devil got into them, they would put on a show in the bar of the Aletti Hotel in Algiers, next to a table of high-ranking officers from AFHQ, who bristled and glared in outraged disapproval. At which I became so hysterical that I had to stagger off to the *Dames* to recover.

PWB HQ was to move to Italy in three weeks' time. After Maria left with Major T and his circus to set up PWB in Naples, I had the bed to myself. This unexpected luxury didn't last for very long. The next day I found a pile of elegant white calf-skin suit-cases stacked on the bed. And within a few hours, I was delighted with my new bed-mate. Jan, about my age, had just arrived from Boston.

She was the daughter of a physician. Her clothes, even every-day blouses and skirts, were all expensive models, in marked contrast to my own curious assortment of garments. She looked like a Giotto angel, with pale butter-coloured hair fluffed out around a perfect oval face, dark-brown eyes and jet-black eye-brows and lashes. The Cats' Club of the unit, with their sharp and bitter tongues, lost little time in proclaiming it all to be arti-ficial, which I indignantly refuted. Jan was a sweet-natured, serious-minded girl, entirely devoid of guile, and there was absolutely nothing artificial about her.

The next day I bounced into the MO's hideout. 'Thank you, dear Loot' (Lootenant) 'for my nice new room-mate,' I said gratefully.

'I thought the two of you would make a good pair,' he answered. Dear man, I could have hugged him when I thought of all the wild Miriams at large in our unit . . . That same day I whisked Jan off to lunch with David and Elliott, as I was longing to show her off to them. David fell in love with her on the spot, a possibility I hadn't even considered. This would complicate everything . . . But he immediately adopted the role of the comic lover, sending himself up, so that we were always laughing with him instead of at him. Elliott took up his cue and the crazy dialogue continued to bounce back and forth between them.

Those last three weeks in Algiers were magical. As a 'real' captain (Jan and I being 'assimilated' ones), David could always produce a jeep when needed. We sometimes drove inland, as far as the foothills of the Atlas Mountains, where the tombs of prophets and holy men lay under ancient cedars and unfriendly tribes glared, daring us to go nearer. On the whole the coast was our favourite run, and we poked about among Roman remains, devastated villages, and tiny fishing ports tucked away among the rocks.

Once we drove to the ancient harbour site of Tipasa, 70 miles west of Algiers. This had been larger and more important than Carthage, even at the height of its fame. Its position on the map made it an ideal spot for overland and maritime trade, which all greedy invaders hanker after, and so it was conquered by the Romans, overrun by the Vandals, captured by the Byzantines, and liberated by the Muslims. All had left their mark in the shape of tomb, necropolis, basilica, forum and amphitheatre, the whole overgrown with asphodel, wild thyme, lentisk, carob-trees and here and there the odd gnarled olive, dignified palm and turpentine pine.

There had been no rain for five months, and under the raging inferno of the sun, the ground crackled underfoot like burnt toast. Snakes basked on the broken seats of the amphitheatre, and enormous lizards glared at us, their throats gulping and throbbing with indignation at our intrusion. The crumbs we threw them were pounced on by huge glistening black ants with claws like forceps and great muscular thighs, and giant furry hornets dived at our faces, crashing on their bellies and backpedalling in confusion. The asphodels, now past their prime and fermenting on the stalk, gave out a pungent intoxicating odour competing sharply with the acrid smell oozing from the pine-trees. And above everything else droned the syncopated chorus of cicadas, like an all-embracing heartbeat pounding up out of the earth.

The brain inside my skull, scrambled to a pulp by the heat of the sun, was spinning out a succession of scenes and images like a technicolor film. I could see motley crowds milling about the harbour. Swarthy little men with black curly beards bustled around. Sailors jumped on and off their boats, flinging ropes at one another. Equally vivid were the crowds in the forum, and groups of dignified-looking men in togas and Roman haircuts. The boom of Gregorian chant came from the basilica, mingling with the agonised screams of men whose tongues and hands were cut off by the hordes of Huneric. In the harbour the water boiled and bubbled with the blood of the martyrs, refusing to simmer down until the bodies were scooped out and given a Christian burial.

Overcome by my visions and the heat, I crept down and slid into the tepid, glass-clear water. A feeling of peace and plenitude pervaded the area. No digs had ever taken place at Tipasa, and untold archaeological treasures lay under a few inches of sand. As I swam close to the bottom of the harbour, I could see the shapes of broken urns, huge chains encrusted with barnacles, and old anchors all lying under a film of silt and weed. Jan and the boys followed me in, and we chased and splashed one another until quite exhausted, and it was time to think of getting back for another night's work in Basic News.

chapter twenty-six

In the hurly-burly of the mess, a withdrawn, sober-looking young US captain went about his business with a calm, relaxed composure, very different from the usual noisy and disorderly behaviour of the rest of our colleagues. Sometimes, while I was gobbling up my supper before rushing back to the night-shift, he came and sat beside me, crumbling dog-biscuits all over the table-cloth. And then, as I was hurtling down the stairs, he would start playing the piano in a most tantalising way. Strains of Schubert or some irresistible Mozart sonata would come tinkling after me. And I couldn't help feeling that, if we had the chance, we might become friends. In the end it was his colonel who set it up. 'C'mon you two,' he said one evening when I was off-duty, 'I'm going to the Officers' Club, and you're both coming along with me.' And we all piled into his station-wagon.

The August night being hot and sticky, we sat in the paved garden, drinking iced lime-juice. (They had rum in theirs.) As they were thirsty, the drinks came and went at an increasing rate. The Colonel was soon past all speech, and my Captain was beginning to open up at last – to tell me about his wonderful mother. I listened with one ear, while aiming the other at the witticisms of the cabaret on the dance-floor just in front of us. Suddenly I realised that my would-be chum was edging up and panting down my neck.

'You're a nice girl,' he hiccuped. 'I always thought so, and now I know.' Whatever made him think so, I wondered, and who on earth would want to be a dreary thing like that anyway? 'My mother would like you, you know,' he added. I nearly groaned aloud.

'Tell me about your job,' I suggested.

'Well, what do you know?' he exclaimed. 'She wants to know about my job! . . .'

'So why don't you tell me?'

'If I told you I would get shot, that's why.'

'For heaven's sake,' I said, thoroughly alarmed. 'Don't tell me then.' But warmed up by the rum, he was not to be held back, now that he was launched.

'Just to show how much I trust you, I will tell you, whether you like it or not.' And moving up closer still, he breathed damply into my ear, 'I am working on Operation Dragoon.'

'Whatever's that?'

'It's what used to be called Anvil, until the Germans got wise to it – the invasion of the South of France.'

My heart gave a great lurch. I clutched his arm. 'Oh, you can't mean it,' I gulped, choking with excitement. 'When?'

'Fifteenth of August is D-Day. And now I'll get shot for telling you,' he repeated, with a slight touch of conscience.

'No you won't, because I'll never tell. But I am so, *so* glad to hear about it.'

'I thought you would be. I shouldn't have told you, though I know you won't rat on me.'

But after a few moments of rapture, I realised the folly of his confidence. If ever I was nabbed, I knew I would spill the beans at the first turn of the screw. And from that moment right up to D-Day, I lived in perpetual dread of being kidnapped, a possibility that had never worried me before, even though my certificate of capture had been stolen on my first day in Algiers.

The 15th of August came round at last, and that night, in Basic News, nobody went to bed at all. Many of our friends were in the show, and as it was taking place on the opposite shore, we felt personally involved. As for me, of course, it meant the liberation of my childhood home. Impatiently waiting for the first trickle of news, their nerves on edge, the pressmen swore and cursed at each other non-stop. I kept well out of their way. At eleven p.m. the Editor sent a couple of GIs to the PX for sustenance. They came back with two buckets of coffee, masses of paper cups, and a quantity of doughnuts.

Only the dullest news was coming over the machines. General Alexander pushing up north of Rome, the Germans retreating from Argentan on the Western Front, all good, steady day-to-day stuff which we had now got used to, with our armies moving forward on every front. But still nothing of Dragoon.

It was steaming hot, with small individual heatwaves coming out of each machine, and great torrid blasts puffing in through the windows from the furnace of the street below. The entire insect population of the town came cruising into this inviting atmosphere. Around two in the morning, as I could keep awake no longer, I made myself a nest in the middle of a huge pile of wood-shavings on the floor and quietly crept into it. In spite of the noise, the smells, the swearing and the heat, I was fast asleep within a few minutes. It seemed only a moment later when a thundering clamour brought me back to life.

'They've landed! They've made it,' came from all sides.

Everybody was shouting, waving their arms and jumping about. I dashed to the teleprinters, trailing wood-shavings all over the floor.

The beaches between Cap Nègre and Agay were covered with landing troops. General Patch's three divisions were wading ashore at Cavalaire, Pampelone, Sainte-Maxime, Fréjus and Le Drammont. During the night parachutists had landed behind the Maure Mountains. French Partisans had paralysed enemy batteries on the heights, creeping up on them from behind with blackened faces, bits of thyme in their tin hats, and a knife between their teeth in true commando style. As there was practically no resistance, there was very little news. Half a million men, 230 warships, and 15,000 aircraft, slightly disconcerted by the unexpectedly easy operation, went through it all like butter.

Expecting a non-stop stream of flashes and bulletins of engagements, advance and retreat, as had poured out of the Western Front on the day of the Normandy Landings, we were standing at double strength in Basic News. After the great build-up it was all falling rather flat. But we were determined to make the most of it and extract every ounce of drama from the situation. The newsmen, bleary-eyed with whisky and lack of sleep, banged about, shouting and swearing and doing their best to work up an atmosphere. After all, this was a great significant moment. We were writing living history. The Editor, still rooted to the middle of the floor, was buried up to the hocks in mountains of yellow teleprinter dispatches. We were all banging away merrily at our typewriters, but it was mostly the same story coming over the air from AP, UP, Reuters, OWI, MOI, and so on. I was doing the straight stuff for radio, and the boys were putting in the sobs for their audience in the States.

Suddenly a couple of freshly laundered GIs came in bearing between them a pail of coffee, followed by Dandelion and Sweet

Pea laden with sandwiches and doughnuts. It was a welcome sight. Falling upon this manna, I helped the girls to distribute breakfast, then settled down to it myself. Everything looked up after that, the lack of gory battles and the disappointingly easy victory began to fall into perspective and I realised the wonder and the mercy of the whole bloodless operation. It had taken five days and nights to assemble the enormous task force of Operation Dragoon, all of it in total secrecy, so that the enemy had absolutely no idea of what was going on. We could at least make the most of that.

For the next four days we were pretty solidly on duty round the clock. Rivers of Scotch and gin helped with rejoicing at the complete rout of the enemy, who scrabbled inland as fast as they could go, while those who couldn't make it were mopped up in the liberation of Marseilles, where General de Lattre de Tassigny popped a cool 35,000 prisoners into the bag. General Eisenhower declared this to be 'the most decisive contribution to the complete defeat of the enemy'.

Originally, this thrust into the 'soft underbelly of Europe' had been meant to coincide with the Normandy Landings in order to draw German troops away from the Western Front. In the end, Operation Dragoon, which had caused such bitter wrangling among the Allied generals, achieved very little, except to keep the war going in Italy for another year. General Alexander, who was desperately struggling against heavy odds in appalling weather conditions, protested vehemently against his troops being taken away in such vast numbers to swell the ranks of Dragoon. But Churchill was overruled by Eisenhower, who in turn was being bulldozed by President Roosevelt. In the end, it was all a question of politics.

When the war in Africa was over, there was nothing left for us to do. AFHQ moved to the Palace of Caserta near Naples, and PWB

Algiers drifted over the sea in groups to set up Basic News in Italy. But before anyone left, the Editor decided to give us a closing-down party in our old office. It was, as usual, a terribly hot night. The insect population was making itself at home, zooming and buzzing around the room in clouds. We felt depressed, superfluous, dispossessed, and at a time like this, nobody was going to stay sober long. In fact, it was a point of honour to arrive already 'in the party mood'.

Scotch, presented by the British members of the mess, flowed steadily down all those thirsty gullets. Dandelion, Sweet Pea and I were kept busy filling glasses. And the noise was increasing in the general pathos of the situation. All round the room, wherever you looked, tears stood in the little pink screwed-up eyes. From time to time a choking voice croaked, 'Gee Spike (or Hank, or Bud), I guess we had some pretty good times here, didn't we?'

'C'mon you guys,' said someone on a sudden inspiration, 'Let's give 'em a tickertape reception down there.' And with these words he grabbed an armful of typing paper and hurled it over the balcony. Nobody needed much encouragement after that. Every available scrap was flung out, and when no paper was left, empty whisky bottles followed suit. I peered over the edge to count the casualties, but dimly lit though it was, the street appeared to be empty. Nobody in their senses would hang about while Basic News was having a party. Everything detachable went overboard. When the telephones were wrenched out of the walls and tipped over the balcony, I felt the time had come for me to go home.

None of the pressmen appeared at breakfast next day. Basic News was a scene of total devastation. I went over to the Admin Office to see Captain B, who was packing files into crates with the help of a corporal and a couple of privates.

'Take a few days off,' he suggested. 'Then get yourself to Naples. Report to Major T when you arrive.'

'But how will I get there? I need travel orders . . .'

'So you do. Come round tomorrow morning, and I'll have them ready for you. And now get out of my hair, there's a good girl.'

When I got back to the mess, the Madrague Mail was standing outside, with the German-Jewish party already on board. The Hungarian sergeant turned a mournful eye on me. 'You might as well come with us to the beach. There's nothing else to do.' So for the next few days we set off every morning for Madrague. But it was no longer the same. We felt restless, unsettled. I could understand the way swallows must feel when the time for emigrating comes round.

One morning, when I realised that this stage had caught up with me, I picked up my kitbag, paid my mess bill, and hitched a lift to Maison Blanche airport. The heat coming off the tarmac of the air-strip took my breath away. It was like trying to walk around in a sizzling frying-pan. Dragging my kitbag, I panted over to an empty hangar. An RAF corporal was inside, reading a comic.

'Anything going over to Naples today?' I asked.

'Not that I know of love. You want to go there?'

'I have to. Do you know when anyone's going?'

'Not a clue sweetheart, better ask the Station Commander.'

This officer's stooge, when I finally tracked him down, said yes, he thought there was a Dakota going over the next morning. 'Do you think they would give me a lift?'

'Nothing to do with me miss, better ask the pilot.'

The third Dakota on whose door I knocked turned out to be the right one.

'Why not? Hop in,' said the pilot. 'I was going to take the old crate over tomorrow to pick up a load of wounded, but I'll fly you over now if you're in a hurry. It'll be cooler up there.'

The heat in the cabin nearly knocked me out.

'Come along up front. Got a movement order, I take it?'

'Yes, do you want to see it?'

'No thanks, come and sit here.' And I squeezed between him and the co-pilot, with the bear on my knee.

It was almost as hot up in the clear, cool-looking heights of the sky. The temperature was still in the eighties.

chapter twenty~seven

A dirtier, gloomier place than the Singer building, which Captain B had chosen as PWB HQ in Naples, I had never seen before in my life. When Maria, who was already working there when I arrived, poor soul, told me that Basic News had now settled in Rome, my spirits rose at once.

'You'll have to find your way there,' she said, 'but stay here for a few days and I'll show you round.'

She produced a car to whisk me up to our mess up on the Vomero, behind Naples, overlooking the Bay. The famous view lived up to its reputation, and it was reassuring to see the Royal Navy on duty out there in strength.

The Villa Amphora, which was the PWB mess, had obviously been subjected to experienced looters. The room I was given was furnished with six iron bedsteads, without a single mattress between them. There was nothing else, not even a pillow in sight. Accommodation was never one of PWB's strong points. A quick visit to the other bedrooms produced a couple of army blankets, which I spread over the bed nearest the window. And in spite of the squeaks and the creaks of the cruel wire mesh, I slept like a dormouse all the time I was at the Villa Amphora.

Downstairs in the dining-room, we feasted on Compo rations instead of the usual American fare. Margarine took the place of butter, and we had tea instead of coffee.

Andrew, by now Maria's fiancé, whose Second Echelon was lodged at AFHQ in Caserta, came over to Naples for dinner, with a jaunty Scottish major who swung his kilt with great panache. He was full of chat, gossip and high spirits, a good dancer. Andrew warned me not to ask him any questions, as he was working in some obscure, top-secret operation connected with the Balkans. I met him again later in Rome. And then suddenly, mysteriously, he was dead: the kind of fate often in store for soldiers in the less regular forms of duty.

I was beginning to feel restless, and told Maria that I wanted to get back to work. She laughed, and said there was plenty of time for that. 'You haven't seen Amalfi or Sorrento. You may never get the chance again . . .'

I did manage to climb Vesuvius, and peered down the crater at smoke oozing out of cracks in the rock hundreds of feet below. It seemed incredible that this quiet, empty cavity could ever belch out millions of tons of liquid, red-hot rock into the sky.

Two or three times a week, the PWB courier left Naples at noon. A war-battered old truck, it was loaded with mail, supplies and sometimes a few passengers and their gear, aiming to reach Rome by six p.m., the GI driver's suppertime. Arriving late meant he'd miss his meal. Maria warned me that it was a dangerous trip, although several people had managed to survive it so far.

Highway Seven, which followed the coast, was used by the courier as a race-track, leaping over crags and craters, sometimes landing in the ditch, or slap into a pile of bombed-out tanks. The driver, his mouth full of gum, was chewing the cud, swinging his jaws from side to side like an angry camel. He sprang and leaped about in his seat, rotating the wheel of the old weapons-carrier from one side to the other. The rumour was that there were more casualties on the courier run than on the Gothic Line. And the PWB mess in Rome was crawling with limping, walking wounded. Cases with broken necks and bashed-in rib-cages were swept away to the military hospital and often didn't reappear for weeks.

The countryside through which we drove was ripped apart by war, the villages along the road reduced to heaps of dust and rubble. South of Terracina, the flooding Pontine Marshes had covered everything in sight, and malaria mosquitoes were spreading over the land. All remaining space had been taken over by the army camps, and there were miles of parking lots for trucks, armoured cars, Bren-carriers, tanks, and great guns brooding under their canvas hoods. And all round lay the wreck-age of burnt-out aircraft, blown-up tanks and other war engines, twisted and tortured out of all recognition.

At Capua we crossed the Volturno over a Bailey bridge, at a point where Hannibal had fooled the Romans who surrounded him in AD 215. To make it look as if his troops had fled in panic, he sent 2,000 head of cattle stampeding up the hill with flaming faggots between their horns.

Before the war Terracina, on the sea-shore at the foot of the mountains, undiscovered by the outside world and living entirely on the fishermen's catch, must have been idyllic. Now the little town lay crumpled and in ruins.

The fighting in the South, unremitting and incessant, took place in appalling weather, pouring rain and flowing mud. In the mountains behind Highways Six and Seven, Monte Maggiore bristled with enemy machine-guns, controlling the road to

Rome. Our soldiers had to crawl up the slippery rock-face on hands and knees, in fog, rain and sub-zero temperatures. Not even pack mules could manage the climb. Iron rations ran out. It took a whole day to bring down the wounded, who often died on the way, under non-stop firing from above. Behind every rock, machine-guns and their crews were kept going with supplies brought up the easier northern slopes.

The fortitude of Mark Clark's 5th Army and our own intrepid 8th almost passes understanding. The enemy had to be picked out and dislodged one by one, in hand-to-hand fighting, and it was one of them or one of ours who tumbled over the edge each time. Some of the troops had been in battle since the landings at Salerno, but hungry, cold and weary though they were, they never lost their cheer. I once met a shy nineteen-year-old who had been promoted from 2nd lieutenant to major in one day, as his superior officers were killed around him one after another.

The Allied bombing of Montecassino Monastery has always raised bitter controversy. Standing where it did, it would inevitably have been used as a key observation post over Highway Six. When it came to a choice between men and stones, General Alexander always spared the men.

When the Allies broke through the Winter Line, it became obvious that they were making steady progress up the Leg of Italy. The Romans set up resistance under the heroic General Montezemola, and from then on information began to trickle through to the Allies. But a trap was set for the General, and he was cruelly tortured at the infamous Chamber of Horrors in Via Tasso. In spite of his unspeakable sufferings, however, he never gave his plans away or breathed the name of a single one of his colleagues.

Next the Communists joined the Resistance. Their first contribution was to bomb a squad of SS marching past, accounting for 32 of them. In the reprisals at the Ardeatini caves near Rome,

General Montezemola was among the 300 Italians who were machine-gunned, shovelled into the caves and walled up inside. When the Allies arrived in Rome, the mass grave was opened up and Sandy McKendrick, Head of the Film Production Unit of PWB, made a documentary of the event, through most of which I had to keep my hands over my eyes.

The Lugado Hotel, requisitioned as the PWB mess in Rome, was a dark and dingy dungeon. The musty little hall was the lair of a sour-faced porter, who had no illusions left after occupation first by the SS, then by the Allies. And he took no trouble to disguise his contempt for humanity.

'Come with me signorina,' he ordered when I arrived. And letting me drag my kitbag along the corridor, he dumped me in the mess office. A swarthy American sergeant looked up as I came in. Then, ignoring me, he went on chatting with his mate. Preparing for a long wait, I fished out *War and Peace*, climbed on top of my kitbag, and began to read.

'Whatyawan sis?' he asked eventually.

'I've been told to report here to work in Basic News. Can you give me a room please?'

'Ha. A room. Ya hear that? The dame wants a room. Be lucky if you gedda bed.'

Thinking I would be even luckier if I got a bed to myself, I said, 'A bed will do, I'm not fussy, as long as there are no bugs.'

'Ya find that out for yaself sis, not my department. Go up to the second floor. Room 76.'

On the landing of the second floor I had to go through ill-fitting glass doors to a small dark lobby leading to a bedroom, with a grimy bathroom and really filthy loo. Suddenly, as I was peering down the hole, the chain, pulled by an invisible hand, flushed out the bowl. The bedroom had the unexpected luxury of twin beds, a *really* special treat! As the room seemed unoccupied, I chose the bed nearest the window. Two floors below, the street was teeming with Italians shouting at one another and assorted soldiery, coming and going. GIs sprawled on the pavement as usual, smoking, chewing gum, hailing the signorinas, and generally passing the time.

That first evening there was a power cut. Looking around the dim twilight of the dining-room, I couldn't see a face I knew. Ah well, we start again from scratch, I thought, and opened *War and Peace* on the table beside me. After dinner we all trooped off to the bar.

It turned out that our Black Propaganda section, which usually lodged in select, exclusive quarters of its own, were now roosting with us in our rough and dowdy mess. This was expected to liven things up for us, and the heroes present were surrounded by an admiring crowd, avid for stories of their exploits. There was one particularly flamboyant colonel who kept us all spellbound with tales of his adventures behind the lines. One of his turns was taking potshots at the fig-leaves of the statues in the little piazzas with his revolver, to demonstrate the infallible accuracy of his firing at long range with small arms.

Opposite the hotel were steps leading down to the Via Veneto, where the PWB offices were lodged in a building previously occupied by the SS, which had done itself proud – behind every major office were marble-floor bedrooms and luxurious bathrooms. Major T, in charge of Admin as usual, was now installed there with his staff. He told me to find my way to Basic News, which had come to roost in the Via Moreno, about a mile away from the mess.

When I asked the Editor about transport, especially on night-duty, he said he was not interested in my private life. It was up to me to sort out my own affairs. And he promptly put me down for the night-shift, since I was as usual the only Limey in this almost entirely American operation, the youngest, and the sole female on the newsdesk.

Eventually the question of transport resolved itself in two ways, which I laid on in turn. The only other non-US pressman in Basic News was a tough little South African terrier of a man, with square yellow teeth (fake, as I was soon to find out), a really filthy temper, and a bottle of Scotch permanently at his elbow on the desk. The greatest phobia of his life was the military police. Sometimes, when I couldn't face the long walk back to the mess alone, among the footpads, the murderers and the rapists, I grabbed South African Teddy by the arm and steered him off in the direction of the mess.

Even plastered though he was, it was a comfort to have him with me, especially when he could stand up. But the fresh air often knocked him out, so I had to half carry, half drag him all the way up the Via Veneto to the mess. From time to time, whenever we passed a US requisitioned hotel or a PX on the way, with a military policeman on guard duty, up staggered my friend and punched the astonished MP on the nose. Reaction was swift and deadly. A huge fist would flash out, and smash my friend's face (and teeth) into next week.

'You'd better get your boyfriend home quick, mam, unless you want to spend the night in the cooler with him,' said the Arm of the Law.

'I am terribly sorry sergeant, but he's not quite himself tonight,' I would say miserably, grovelling about in the gutter for his teeth.

After a couple of nights of these antics, I usually preferred to face the perils of the night on my own. People out on the prowl at that hour were inevitably up to no good. Apart from the usual run of professional criminals, there was a terrifying gang of juvenile brigands armed to the teeth with stolen bayonets, who knifed you in the back first, then searched you afterwards for cash and valuables. You weren't even safe on a bicycle, as they would charge like a pack of wild dogs, dispatch the rider and make off with the bike. Whenever I had to set off on my own, I walked in the middle of the road, with hatpin at the ready, plunging it as hard as I could into anyone who made a grab at me. As they staggered back, howling with agony, I took to my heels and fled as fast as I could.

That first liberated summer in Rome was very hot. As usual, night-duty meant long daylight hours to myself, which I couldn't bear to waste in sleep. All this glorious free time was spent climbing about the Colosseum, entirely overgrown with vegetation and littered with broken statues and buried treasures. The Forum opposite, another nature reserve, was crawling with snakes, caterpillars, and all kinds of exotic bugs and beetles. I sat for hours among the ruins, sketching, painting and staring, watching the busy life around me. And beyond this peaceful, self-engrossed little world roared the life of the Eternal City. Apart from military convoys, three-wheeled taxis chugged around, the only kind of transport available to local citizens.

On other occasions I explored the surrounding countryside, along the Via Appia Antica and past the chapel where Jesus met St Peter and asked him: '*Quo vadis?*' Sometimes we drove out to the Villa d'Este at Tivoli, where it was a joy to wander through the gardens. There wild life had completely taken over, and the loud droning of bees, beetles and cicadas proclaimed victory over their old enemies the gardeners. On off-duty nights in Rome I loved walking in the Borghese and Pincio Gardens, whenever I could find a bodyguard. The mulberry-trees were covered with silkworms hanging on their threads, which they wound round our heads in living, wriggling hairnets.

St Peter's came into its own at Christmas, when the Pope celebrated Midnight Mass for thousands of people packed almost to extinction in the cathedral. There were about as many Allied soldiers as honest Roman citizens. At the end of the service, the Pope was carried around the church on his throne on the powerful shoulders of the Swiss Guard. And afterwards we walked all the way back to the mess in the snow under the hard cold stars of the sixth and last Christmas of the war.

In spite of all my painting and sketching out of doors, I still felt I was getting nowhere. So one day I walked into one of the galleries in the Via Veneto and asked the owner if he knew anyone who might give me a few lessons.

Apart from crime, one thing that never flagged in Rome was art. New exhibitions were constantly being put on in the numerous galleries. The artists went on painting on a near-starvation diet, all living cheek-by-jowl in the delightful little Via Margutta, which looked like an up-market London mews. Their studios were a revelation of artistic design, a mixture of antique and ultra-modern. And everywhere the most riotous combinations of colour reigned. Here the essence of the Italian soul, generous and optimistic if given half a chance, had kept itself going, untainted by all the disappointments, bitterness and corruption of defeat. The spontaneous, creative mood of this little community was an oasis of well-being and sanity in the heart of the violent, crime-infested city. It was a privilege to be introduced to it.

Giuseppe Capogrossi, who became my teacher, had a studio in another part of town, stifling hot in summer and a vast refrigerator in winter. I felt dreadfully sorry for the poor purple-skinned model, aptly named Violetta, who always posed in the nude, whatever the temperature.

'*Il faut toujours chercher la ligne,*' Signor Capogrossi would repeat, in his all-purpose international style. Tolerant and forbearing, he encouraged my fumbling efforts, finding more virtue in some hopeless mess than in what I thought was a more worthy effort.

By the end of August, the Allied Commander, General Alexander, was ready to attack the Gothic Line, the last stronghold in Italy which frustrated our breakthrough into the Po Valley. Stretching from Spezia in the west, it bristled with anti-tank traps and concrete pillboxes, and every inch of the ground was stuffed with landmines.

General Alexander, who had recently lost seven of his divisions to the South of France landings, was now to have the French Expeditionary Force snatched away from him as well. He wrote in desperation to Churchill: ' "If the trumpet give an uncertain sound, who shall prepare himself for battle?"' But Churchill, unusually brutal with his favourite general, and no doubt still under heavy pressure from Roosevelt, ordered Alexander to wipe out the enemy immediately, with whatever forces he had, so as to bring the war in Italy to an end as soon as possible.

The original plan for attacking the Gothic Line had to be changed. General Oliver Leese, in charge of the operation since Monty had taken over the Western Front, preferred to attack on the Adriatic side. Kesselring, the German general, who had been expecting our attack in the West, bundled his troops over to the other side with all possible speed. As soon as Alexander realised this, he ordered General Mark Clark to bring his 5th Army to the West and carry out the original plan after all. If only the Allied armies had been at full strength on the spot, victory would have been instant and final. As it was, our split-up forces suffered heavy casualties. The winter rains, starting early, came down in torrents, and for the second year running our troops had to cope with the now familiar swilling mud of another Italian winter.

Unbelievably, Alexander was to lose five more divisions to

the Western Front before his own offensive the following spring. When Churchill told him to carry out his orders with whatever forces he had left, he meekly replied, 'You already know that my only wish is to serve where I am most useful. And feeling that way, I am well content.' This is the only time I ever felt impatient with my hero. In the face of the enemy, he was a superman. Why did he have to be a mouse to Churchill, who would go on bullying until he met resistance? And this he would never get from Alexander, who would let himself be trampled on without protest. It made my blood boil.

The last battle, which would finish off the enemy in Italy, was launched on the 9th of April 1945, and was 'as hard fought as the first', in Alexander's own words. It was the result of hugely competent and minutely synchronised bombing and artillery fire, and a cunning use of double-bluff. It was made as obvious as possible that we were going to attack in the West, so that the enemy would assume this to be a trick and rush off to the Venetian coast. Which they obligingly did. While after all our offensive *did* come from the West.

chapter twenty-eight

The Basic News Editor in Rome, who was a New Yorker of Irish extraction, never let me forget that I was the only Limey on the team, and that he didn't want one at all! He disliked the Brits, and did his best to run them down, by word and in print, whenever he got the chance. I kept out of his way as much as I could, but we were often at loggerheads, particularly when he censored Churchill's speeches and ignored my protests at his cutting out all the crucial parts. He kept me permanently on night-duty and handed me only the most boring stories.

After a few months of this punishing treatment, I went to see the Big Boss and asked for a transfer to Greece. He was perfectly charming, and promised to remember me if and when a vacancy cropped up. But at that time Athens was going through a civil war (as if *that* would put anyone off!) and no women were allowed into the country at all. So for the time being I had to stick it out.

*

The evenings in the mess, which had been so pleasant and peaceful until then, were suddenly wrecked overnight. A couple of officers, one British and the other American, who arrived from Cairo, were the cause of the trouble. In the bar after dinner and several bottles of wine, they would get on shouting terms. And by the time they went up to bed, they would be hurling insults, army boots and empty bottles at each other. Unfortunately, they shared the room just above mine on the next floor. Soon the ceiling over my head was rattling and shaking, with plaster flakes snowing down over me as I lay in bed, clutching my bear for comfort. From time to time, on their way to bed, they got the wrong floor, and tried to force their way into my room. As there was no lock, in they would crash, and end up on my bed. Delighted with their mistake, they had no wish to leave and go up to their own quarters. I had to push, carry and drag them out, then drop them at the foot of their stairs, where they passed out. And then came a wonderful surprise.

One evening when I went up to bed, I found Joy Packer settling in as my new room-mate. From that moment life cheered up no end. Through the magic of her wit, the bouncing boots on our ceiling, the self-flushing loo and the constant freezing cold of that winter became a source of fun and jokes. But she never let on that she was an established writer, and the wife of the Naval C-in-C's Chief of Staff at Caserta. This all trickled out bit by bit.

One day a book arrived from her publishers, and then she had to come clean. As the story of her life following her naval husband around the world, it was a fascinating tale. Though a working journalist, I never guessed at the time that she was busy writing us all up for her next book.

One night, as she and I were lying in bed in the dark chatting, we heard the dreaded pair approaching the lobby doors. 'Coo-ee girls, here we come,' warbled one of them in drunken tones. Leaping out of bed, I hissed through my teeth, 'I'll deal with them.' Joy, awaiting developments and storing it all up for her next instalment, lay there in her bed without a word.

Outside our window, hanging on an enormous iron hook, was a huge barometer, five foot high. I hauled it up into the room, dragged it across the floor, and propped it up under the lobby's door-handle. If anything could keep them out, *that* should do it! At this point, they both fell forward so heavily that the glass door burst open, sending the barometer spinning across the lobby to explode like a blockbuster on the opposite wall. Glass splinters flew in all directions, spewing rivers of mercury all over the floor.

After that exploit one of them was sent to a drying-out establishment, but the remaining one became more assiduous than ever. To avoid him downstairs in the bar, I would snoop up to bed early and settle down with *War and Peace* and my bear. But he was soon there, perched on the end of my bed, with Joy, student of human nature, watching and listening.

'Why do you hate me so much?' he asked.

'Don't be an ass. I just hate people getting drunk.'

'It's not only that. You don't care. And not just for me. You don't care for anyone. You've just got a bloody great stone for a heart.'

'Don't be so stupid. D'you think I would hang around bored to death at your ghastly parties, and bring you home plastered to the eyebrows, just to save you from the Military Police, if I didn't care?'

'That's just bloody governess kind of care!'

'Well, it's the only kind you're going to get. And to begin with, you can get off my feet.' And I gave him a whacking great kick under the bedclothes.

*

That winter I was to have very little luck with the chaps. One evening, when a nice young subaltern on leave from the front had taken me out to dinner at the Officers' Club, a large bulky figure suddenly loomed over me. My arm was grabbed and I was roughly hoisted out of my chair.

Speechless with horror, I found myself face to face with the major from Algiers.

'Don't look so pleased to see me,' he said sourly. 'And don't just stand there like a tombstone. Go on, get moving.'

And he shoved me onto the dance-floor.

'You've improved,' he said presently. 'Your eyes have narrowed. But don't take that as a compliment. It just means that you're growing up. You'll do for me now.'

Too agitated to speak, I tried to wriggle away. But he squashed me up against his chest in a vice-like grip. 'None of your tricks this time, my girl,' he snapped. 'You're not getting away. So don't try anything on, or you'll be sorry.'

And he squashed his mouth onto mine, and his tongue squeezed through my teeth like a huge, slimy slug. Choking with panic, I brought my teeth together with all the strength of my jaw muscles and scrunched them into the revolting lump in my mouth. He staggered back with a roar of pain, and I punched him hard in the windpipe for good measure. At the table, my young officer was watching the show with some surprise.

'Let's get out of here,' I hissed, handing him his hat.

'Whatever for? It's only nine o'clock.'

'Come on, for goodness sake, I've bitten the major.'

'You've *what*?!'

'His mouth is full of blood. He'll kill me . . .' And ducking between the dancers, I scuttled away to the door as fast as I could.

'He won't come after you now, don't worry,' panted the lieutenant, trying to catch up as I raced along Via Veneto as fast as I could go.

'You don't know him. You just don't know him,' I said with a shudder.

'What *you* don't know, my girl, is that you could get him court-martialled for this. And *he* knows it. Don't worry. He won't bother you any more.' And he was right. Never did I hear from that major again. But I couldn't help saying, 'He got off lightly. I could have used my hatpin.'

There just hadn't been time for that . . .

Norman, already established as a poet in London before the war, had, with many other writers and linguists, joined the German Leaflet Section of PWB. The prose produced by this organisation was dropped on the German troops by the light bombers of Tactical Airforce together with leaflets written by the Advance PWB Units, attached to the 5th and 8th Armies.

Captain Beauclerk, who was in charge of PWB 8th Army, had his own prickly bunch of writers, whose task it was to deal with the enemy front lines immediately ahead. The keystone of this operation was 'Front Post', a weekly newssheet giving the German soldiers the latest news of Allied raids over their home-land, as well as details of all the more spectacular Allied victories on the Western and Eastern Fronts. 'Don't get yourselves killed so far away from home, when you will be needed to rebuild your own country before long,' was one of the encouraging mes-sages of this little newspaper. Tucked up inside smokeshells, it was shot over the lines by our artillery at the front – the 'Tactical' section, operating on the spot. The 'Strategic' leaflets, produced by another group based in Bari on the Adriatic, were entrusted to the big long-range bombers, which went much further afield, right into the heart of Austria. The rivalry between the two leaflet sections, Tactical and Strategic, never let up, each wanting to swallow up the other, seeing no need for more than one oper-ation.

From time to time 'Tactical Norman', as we called him, would grab me by the hand as he passed, saying, 'Come on, let's go out to dinner.' And off we'd go to the Nirvanetta, the Officers' Club, on the Via Veneto. Half-way through the meal, after two or three bottles of Chianti, he would scramble to his feet, muttering, ' 'fraid I'm a bit drunk. Must go and sleep it off. You stay here. I'll be back.' And I would finish dinner, order a Strega with my coffee, and watch the cabaret performing under the stars. By that time most of us got on tolerably well in Italian, and could understand the singing and the jokes. All of us, that is, except for older officers from the First War, who simply stuck an 'o' onto the ends of English words and roared at the 'Wops' when they couldn't understand. Two or three hours later Norman would reappear, and we would resume our shuffling around the dance-floor until closing time.

On other occasions he took me to visit a friend of his, an Italian opera-singer, who had a warm and cosy flat at the top of the Spanish Steps. 'A sensible woman,' was how Norman described her. 'She was nice to the Germans, and now she's nice to us, so she is always comfortable, with plenty of fuel and all the food she needs.' This shocked me at first. I didn't understand how Norman could admire such treachery.

'Don't be so *bourgeois*,' he would say. 'She is sophisticated enough to understand that war has nothing to do with women.' All very well, I thought, but it seemed to have quite a bit to do with me, what with brother John leaping out of aeroplanes on the various Normandy Fronts, my father a prisoner of the Japanese in their infamous Singapore camp, and the rest of my family striving to survive as refugees in Australia . . . However, the opera-singer was a great friend of Norman's, and even made me welcome as well. Her cynical cheerfulness sparkled all round her. Picking up her guitar decorated with gaily-coloured ribbons, she would start to sing as soon as Norman poured out the bottle he had brought along with him. But however much I enjoyed the visits, the thought of German officers sprawling in our seats just a few months earlier made me feel uncomfortable and nagged away at my tight, *bourgeois* little mind.

More often than not, when I got back to the mess from my various activities in the evening, the place, due to another power-cut, was in darkness. One candle would be flickering in the hall and another standing on the counter in the bar. The new Mess Officer, my old friend from Algiers, often appeared with Norman, bearing one more candle and a chessboard. It was always a treat to watch them play. There was something secure and comforting in the sight of an ordinary game of chess, by candlelight, in such surroundings. There we were, in the heart of war-time Rome, in the gloom of a power-cut, ringed round by every kind of crime, vice, murder and treachery rampaging about the streets. And a few miles to the north, young men were staggering in the swilling mud of the Italian winter, leading their patrols through the trip-wires and booby-traps of no-man's land. Knowing all this, Norman and the Loot could still manage to detach themselves enough to enjoy their game. For me, this generated a kind of serenity which was very soothing to the spirit. So I always lurked around, slumped in a chair out of sight or crouching under the grand piano, as happy as the flies on the walls.

That winter we were all very cold, and our rations were dismally dull – spam, waffles and maple syrup for almost every meal. We were used to the general monotony of life, but when food became scarce as well and we went on 'iron rations', people complained vociferously. The reason for it was, as I knew from writing up the copy, that almost an entire convoy bringing supplies to the Med had been torpedoed and sunk. But there was no point in trying to explain all that, unless you wanted to be put down as a creeping do-gooder, and worse, much worse.

Rome doesn't often see snow, but that winter there were some heavy falls over Christmas and the New Year. For several days the fountains in the piazzas were frozen into fantastic shapes. We went up to the Apennines with skis and toboggans, and spent a week-end rattling down the slopes where only a year before the Allies had so desperately fought for every inch of the ground.

General Eisenhower had been transferred to the Western Front, while General Sir Henry Maitland Wilson ('General Jumbo' to the troops) became Supreme Commander in the Med. Poor Alexander, still desperately worried about all his lost divisions, went down with jaundice. I met him only once, towards the end of the war, by which time he was Field Marshal and Supreme Commander. I was overwhelmed by the famous charm, and totally lost for speech. What could a tiddler from Basic News possibly have to say to a Field Marshal? He smiled, shook my hand, uttered a few words, and walked away.

Among our US civilians in the mess was a young man named Kurt, a professor of philosophy at one of the major American universities when not engaged in his war-time activities. He had protruding pink-rimmed eyes, and an enormous Adam's apple which was continually running up and down his long thin neck. Fascinated by this curious feature, I couldn't help staring whenever I sat opposite him in the dining-room. One day he asked me to go to a concert with him. As I could never find anyone else to accompany me, I accepted at once, and off we went to Radio Roma together.

This was the beginning of a new life of culture for me. We went to the opera, which was first-class, and to the ballet, which was not. After which we repaired to his digs for a supper of nuts and honey. Sometimes he took me to see the artist Leonor Fini in her luxurious studio, which she shared with a very grand marchese, who had given up his career in the 'Diplomatic' to follow his muse on her advice. Together they gave fascinating parties, at which everybody was clever and sophisticated in a way that I could only dimly sense. A curious smell of incense (or was it pot?) pervaded the air, and they all talked in innuendoes. I knew I was on the edge of a world I could not possibly penetrate, although I longed to do so. When I asked what they were talking about, they laughed and changed the subject.

At about this time, to my joy, Jan arrived from Naples. I quickly made up a camp-bed for her in the lobby, so that we could keep her with us for at least a few days. I was longing to introduce her to Joy, who was horrified at my home-made accommodation. She went straight off to see the Mess Officer, who immediately gave her a very nice room on our floor. The poor girl was currently being hotly pursued by a handsome young officer, recently arrived, who was determined to marry her there and then, war or no war.

'He's got absolutely everything going for him. He even knows my family in Boston, and they think he's wonderful,' she would say miserably, unable to make up her mind.

'Isn't there anything he's a bit short of?' I asked hopefully.

'Well, he's not wildly exciting . . .'

'You mean he's deadly dull, and let's face it, you're not in love with him.'

Looking even more downcast, she heaved a great sigh.

'I ought to be. He's really too good for me.'

'When in doubt, do nothing. Remember that when you're married he'll be around quite a bit. Could you bear that?' At which poor Jan looked more miserable than ever.

But she must have sent him packing, as she soon joined us again in our various festivities, and came on her own with us to a very jolly New Year's lunch at the Officers' Club.

*

Gradually the weather began to improve, and spring seemed to be just round the corner. The South Africans, together with the New Zealanders and the Guards Brigade, took Florence, which the Germans had declared an open city. In spite of fierce street-by-street fighting, destruction was limited to the blowing-up of all the bridges by the enemy except for the Ponte Vecchio. Apart from this there was little damage, and so the advance units of PWB were able to move in immediately. Joy and her colleagues, with their photos and pamphlets, were urgently needed to follow up the successes of the Allied armies. So off they went, all packed together in the back of a three-tonner.

Joy's departure left a gloomy gap, and the bedroom suddenly looked much more drab than ever before. Once more on my own, I was quite glad to have a little point-two-two revolver, which an English army major brought me back from Cairo. With this tucked up under my pillow, and hugging my bear, I felt perfectly safe. But in the streets on the way home at night, I still preferred my hatpin. It was quiet, unexpected and effective.

On the 23rd of April the British and South African armies, having broken through the Gothic Line at last, joined up behind the German Front at a small town aptly named Finale, on the River Po. The enemy troops were trapped in a circle of Allied fire and steel. Realising the end had come, they laid down their arms at six p.m. on the 2nd of May 1945 – and the war in Italy was over. There was a great party in the mess, and I enjoyed it all a little too much, only getting to bed at four a.m.

When I woke up my precious little revolver was gone, snatched away from under my pillow while I had been fast asleep on Victory Night . . .

chapter twenty-nine

The Psychological branch in Rome was folding up, as all its numerous objectives were now completed. This time, when I went round to the Admin Department to ask where I was to go next, I was told to find my way to Venice and report for duty as soon as I got there. No name, no address was provided.

This was normal procedure, and I was used by now to finding my way around war-battered, newly-liberated towns. The first thing to do was to find the Town Major and make friends with him. He could usually fit you in somewhere for the night and fix you up with a tin of bully-beef, and he invariably knew where and when the next convoy was leaving from. There was always room for another body on a convoy.

In Florence I was lucky, and was able to spend the night in the new PWB mess. Apart from the crumpled banks of the River Arno, there was little damage to be seen. Before dinner I had time for an hour's canoeing down the main stream of the Arno, while children scampered about on the sandbanks between the rivulets, into which the ruins of the Ponte Trinità had collapsed into heaps of rubble. In the light of the setting sun I walked through the city, where sniper and machine-gun bullets had pock-marked the severe countenances of the noble Renaissance palaces, standing otherwise undamaged in their solemn piazzas and narrow fifteenth-century streets.

Early next morning I climbed into the courier to Bologna. The GI driver would not allow my kitbag on board with me, as this had to go on another 'gear-truck', supposed to follow on behind. US Army soldiers, often of Italian origin, once in charge of their own transport, often took to the hills to rejoin their ancestral homes and were seen no more. This is what the driver in charge of my kitbag decided to do that day. So no one on that particular run to Bologna ever saw his or her luggage again. Fortunately I had my bear and *War and Peace* with me, so that the loss of all my possessions didn't worry me unduly at the time.

For the next eight hours we bounced and leaped and sprang about the craggy shoulders of the Apennines along war-ravaged Highway 65. Our truck swung from one pothole to another, swaying wildly on its creaking springs, while in the back my companions and I were hurled about in the usual manner. It was a wonder we didn't disintegrate into a pile of nuts and bolts at the bottom of a mine crater. We reached Bologna in the evening. A visit to the Town Major rewarded me with a sandwich and a bed in an annexe, and a corner in the back of a PU driving to Ferrara next day.

By then the countryside had flattened out, and we bowled along easily, bypassing the craters in our small vehicle. On both sides of the road gutted tanks and burnt-out aircraft lay upside-down in the fields, with the wreck of blown-out trucks strewn among them. And sprouting all round through the twisted steel bloomed thousands of poppies, jauntily nodding on their stalks in splashes of bright scarlet.

The villages through which we now drove were less badly damaged than in the South, where the fighting for each house, each street, had been savage and bitter. On this particular stretch of open road the enemy had been retreating headlong towards the North, only taking time to blow up bridges in his wake. Every time we came to one of the numerous streams and canals in the area, we trundled over an army Bailey bridge, resting on its pontoons in the river. At Ferrara the Town Major knew of an army convoy from Milan, which was having its tea-break just outside the town on the road to the North. It was all fitting in like a jigsaw puzzle.

At the entrance to Venice, a military checkpoint wanted to know my business. When I said I was looking for PWB they told me to find my way down to the Grand Canal as far as the Morosini Palace, which was known to have something to do with our 'queer unit'. And with this information I was handed a sheet of paper printed with the standard rates for gondola fares. Anything in excess of these prices would be exorbitant racket-eering and was not to be permitted. So, armed with my bear and *War and Peace*, now all the luggage I had left, I jumped into a gondola. My gondolier, dressed entirely in black, plied his single oar from the stern, and we made slow and dignified progress.

The sweep of the Grand Canal, with its great mansions on either side, was more extravagantly spectacular than I had ever imagined possible. What struck me most was the blessed silence of the place. No traffic, hooting or shouting, just the gentle lapping of the water as gondolas glided past in a creamy froth churned up by their oars.

At the Morosini, a valet in a black and yellow striped waist-coat, who hauled me out of my gondola, said the Capitano was in his office. We set off up an enormous marble staircase with stat-ues on every step. A huge room, with painted ceiling and frescoes, opened up in front of me. A small kitchen table stood in the centre, and against the wall was a camp-bed covered with an army blanket, from beneath which a couple of faces peered out.

'Come in, come in,' said one of the faces in welcoming tones. The Captain, who was tucked up in bed with his secretary, hopped out, fully dressed in shirt and shorts.

'We felt a bit chilly, so we got under the blanket to warm up,' he explained. *Chilly?* At the beginning of June! Ah well, the checkpoint *had* described us as a 'queer unit' . . .

I told him I was reporting for duty in the News Section.

'Ah, that's old Jeff Petersen. He certainly does need help. He's on his own. You'd better go and see him right away. You'll find him at the printing works, just off San Marco.'

'Fine,' I said, 'and where shall I live? Where is the PWB mess?'

'Nothing like that here, I'm afraid. Haven't you got any friends you can kip down with?'

'I don't know who's here. Anyway, I would *much* rather be on my own. I don't mind how uncomfortably.'

'If you really mean that, you can stay here for the time being. Bags of room. Serafino will find you a corner.'

So I ended up in a sumptuous reception room on the first floor, with massive crystal chandeliers, painted ceiling, marble walls and not a stick of furniture in sight.

'*Ecco, signorina,*' said Serafino proudly.

'*Bellissimo.* But do I sleep on the floor?'

'I will ask the Capitano for a bed for you.'

A few minutes later he was back with a camp-bed, a pillow and an army blanket. I never saw any other furniture all the time I was at the Morosini, but Serafino appeared every morning with a cup of tea, and whisked my scruffy sandals away for a spit and polish. Twice a week, while I was fast asleep, my khaki shirt and skirt were spirited away, to be returned, washed and ironed, with the morning tea. Serafino, an old family servant left behind to keep an eye on his master's property, was a pearl beyond compare.

Portly Lieutenant Peterson, my new boss, though only in his early thirties, was grey-haired and mature-looking. He was so tall that normal human beings, unable to see the pips on his shoulders, assumed him to be of much higher rank. A major he once met constantly addressed him as 'Colonel', so that poor elderly-looking Jeff was unable to sit down until the major had gone on his way . . .

Jeff was extremely friendly when I arrived. All he wanted to do was to sit in his office with the blinds down and control the output of the printing press, which thundered away on the floor below, shaking the whole building to its muddy roots. But the press, in order to keep busy throughout the night, had to be fed a constant diet of stories for the local papers. And trundling around the countryside in search of copy was not Jeff's idea of a good life. So that was where I came in useful, and explained his warm welcome.

When he finished telling me about the situation in Venice, and the attitude of the Partisans, all of them dissatisfied and trigger-happy, he added that I would have to find my own transport. As usual, there was nothing available for me in that line. I realised this would mean having to make as many friends as possible – right away!

The military checkpoint at the entrance to Venice proved the best meeting-place of all. Here you could pick up lifts to all the military centres in Northern Italy. What was often more difficult was to persuade the driver to divert his vehicle into the wilds of outlying villages. It was usually in such places that events – country balls, concerts and riots – took place. And more often than not, the Partisans would make their presence felt. Heads of 'collaborators' would be shaved. Brawls and tumult would break out, shots would be fired, and you could always be sure of coming back with plenty of good stories for Jeff's printing press.

*

After the 56th Division had liberated Venice, the newly-installed military government was hard put to persuade the Partisans to hand over the authority they had assumed after defeat of the enemy. They had so much enjoyed their power during the war that going back to normal life now seemed unbearably dull. So Partisan 'justice' continued to be applied behind the scenes, and corpses were often seen floating down the small narrow canals, with hands tied behind their backs. Girls who had 'befriended' German soldiers could always be spotted by their shaven heads. Further out, in distant villages, far worse punishment was often dealt out, when they had their breasts sliced off with butchers' knives.

To begin with, I was quite nervous of these Partisans myself, until I realised that I was perfectly safe, with my own weapons. Armed with notebook and pencil, I had nothing to fear. They loved publicity, and were instantly cooperative as soon as they heard they would be making tomorrow's news. They had endless tales of bold deeds, daring victories in peril of their lives, and sabotage of enemy equipment. They wanted me to stress that the Allies could never have won the war without them.

Living like outlaws in the mountains, often working with our own cloak-and-dagger boys behind enemy lines, they had set up underground routes for escaped prisoners to rejoin their own units. After a time I even came to enjoy walking down the streets of war-wrecked villages with a troop of these ferocious brigands, in their red neck-scarves and Tyrolean hats. Round each waist dangled hand-grenades and butchers' knives, and a sub-machine gun was tucked up under one arm. But when they insisted on showing me their special 'criminals', in the shape of starved, hollow-eyed wretches tied together with rope and staked to the ground in the blazing sun, I knew quite well that most of these men's worst crimes had been rivalry over a woman, or some private feud, and nothing whatever to do with the war.

Sometimes these trips lasted two or three days and I had to stay in the local taverna, sharing my hosts' ewe-cheese and black bread as well as their fleas, their hens and their geese, since we all had to doss down together in the only room. Finally, if no army truck happened to pass through, someone would give me a lift in a mule-cart to the next crossroads. And in the end I would get back to Jeff's office bitten through to the bone by the fiercest bugs I had ever come across and badly needing a bath. But my notebook would be bursting with eyewitness stories for his ever-hungry printing press.

After a few weeks of country work, my boss sent me to the local prison to find out what was going on there. It was a shock I have never forgotten. Tucked away behind the Doge's Palace, connected to it by the Bridge of Sighs, the prison contained medieval cells which were actually *below* water-level. And there the prisoners dabbled up to their knees in foul-smelling, stagnant sewage, where they had been since arrested by the Partisans under collaboration charges.

My report after this first visit was so vehement that Jeff tackled me about it.

'Look here old girl, that story of yours about the prison . . .'

'Yes? What about it?'

'Well, it can't possibly go through as it is, you know . . .'

'Why ever not?'

'You'll have to tone it down. All that stuff about swollen, spongy knees, and the men paddling in sewage, fighting off the rats . . .'

'It's the truth. You don't expect me to write lies, do you?'

'All right, all right, keep your hair on. It's just got to be watered down a bit. You know the Partisans. We can't have trouble with them now . . .'

Infiltrated as they were by active Communists, we knew that the Partisans were always on the lookout for slights and criticisms. They were involved in political problems well beyond my understanding.

'Anyway,' Jeff concluded, 'this question of prisoners must be dealt with by Italian justice.'

'Italian *justice*!' I said bitterly.

Two or three times a week, early in the morning, Serafino called a gondola to take me over to the Law Courts on the other side of the Grand Canal. The first time I watched one of these trials, I could hardly refrain from shouting at the judge.

As I arrived, people were streaming in, packing into the court room, squatting all over the floor and standing three-deep on the benches. The prisoner was wheeled in, crouching on a stool inside a cage just large enough to hold him. Old shoes and insults were hurled at him as he passed, and a couple of bottles burst like bombs against the bars of the cage.

Counsel for the Prosecution, a self-important character in a Doge's hat, opened the proceedings. He addressed the court on the subject of his own virtue and rectitude throughout the German occupation. His speech, which went on for an hour, had nothing whatever to do with the case, but the judge let him ramble on as long as he pleased. During the second hour he charged the prisoner with every crime he could think of. There were no specific accusations, no witnesses, and no Defence. The accused in the cage was nothing more than a scapegoat, to be loaded with the common guilt from which every Italian suffered to some extent at the time. Slumped forward on his stool, he was the picture of hopelessness and despair. He knew as well as we all did that he hadn't got a chance. The trial was a travesty, the outcome a foregone conclusion. Boiling with indignation, I hissed to the journalist next to me, 'They aren't giving him a chance. This is not a fair trial.'

'He's a bad man *signorina*, he deserves to die.'

'But he can't even defend himself!'

'There is no forgiveness for his crimes.'

'Why is he in a cage?'

'For his own protection. He would be torn to pieces otherwise.' Remembering what had happened to Mussolini and his mistress in Milan, I could well believe it.

'What will happen to him?' I asked, although I already knew the answer.

'He will be condemned to death,' said the journalist smugly. And of course he was, to the insane cheers of the entire audience in the court, who then bustled off triumphantly to a fat lunch of pasta and vino rosso. My report of that trial took a lot of toning down before Jeff would let it go through his press.

But lovely Venice was not all hard work and harrowing experiences. After I turned in my copy at the end of the day, my favourite pastime was sitting on the terrace of Florian's Café on the Piazza San Marco, watching the pigeons wheeling overhead and the crowds wandering round what has been described as 'the salon of Europe'. It was now more like 'the world', with servicemen from all continents mixed with the local people. There were South Africans and New Zealanders, Americans and Brazilians, Poles, Frenchmen, Indians and Rhodesians, to say nothing of the British Empire.

Then came the day when the great Cathedral was uncovered, and the boards protecting the face of San Marco were ripped away, while the famous lions and horses were restored to their columns, ledges and plinths. The whole town gathered in the Piazza, a military band played all the national anthems, and the RAF staged an impressive fly-past. After that it felt well and truly like the end of the war and the beginning of a new life.

Compared with Rome, much as I loved her, Venice was an extraordinarily restrained and law-abiding city. Once the

Partisans had gone back to their mountains there was very little crime, and although I was often out late at night, I never once had to use my hatpin. There was a wonderfully serene atmosphere, with people out in their gondolas or strolling around the Lagoon, singing, laughing and shouting all through the night. And even in August, a refreshing breeze rustled along the edge of the canals.

One evening there was a party on the Island of the Giudecca across the Lagoon. My boss, various colleagues and I, who had been invited, all set off together in the press launch. After sweeping over the water in a giddy loop, raising a hideous backwash which infuriated the gondoliers, we were approaching the landing stage when suddenly a blinding flash burst out of the engine. There was a deafening explosion, and off we all flew in different directions, with fragments of the launch.

After a few minutes floundering through the wreckage and a heavy layer of stinking black oil we took a roll-call, and realised how lucky we had been. There were no casualties. Paddling ashore, we pulled one another out and, covered with engine oil, approached our host.

'Children . . .' he exclaimed. 'Oh never mind. Come on, quick, the girls this way, the men over there.'

And we were all bundled off in different directions. I spent the rest of the evening in an elegant Egyptian caftan, far more exotic than my eternal khaki-drill uniform.

Dinner parties on the Giudecca were always elegant and stylish, with a well-laid table and *placement*. The menu was thought out by an inspired cook, and the rations certainly didn't come from the Quartermaster. Anyone who drank too much was blacklisted and never invited again. Sometimes, when we had talked late into the night, Hamish, our host, would say to me, 'Why don't you stay? You've got all you need, your book and your face, haven't you?' To which I always said yes, although in those days I didn't bother much with my face. It had to get by with sunburn and tap-water, which made life much easier to deal with.

In the morning the batman would bring me a cup of tea, draw the curtains and run the bath. The dining-room smelt of toast and bacon, and breakfast was kept hot on the sideboard. You could have been in a well-run country-house in England.

Hamish was man of infinite resourcefulness. The story of his escape from a prisoner-of-war camp would fill a book. One of my favourite incidents occurred when he was just about to rejoin our lines. He had to cross a bridge on which a German soldier was stamping up and down with a rifle and fixed bayonet. Hamish, who was unarmed, knew he wouldn't stand a chance in hand-to-hand combat. So as he came up to the bridge, he let the man catch sight of him, then quickly dropped his trousers and squatted on the ground. The soldier, intrigued, peered down at him. Blushing and confused, he stood back, muttering '*Verzeihung*', then turned and walked away. At this point Hamish leaped forward, hurtled into the man's legs and brought him down. What followed was swift, efficient war work. And that is how Hamish crossed the last bridge to freedom and got back to his regiment.

An American captain who had recently joined our unit approached me one day in the bar at the Luna Hotel where we had our meals. Although we hardly knew each other, he said out of the blue, 'What do you say we go to Milan for the weekend?'

'What a good idea!' was my instant reaction. I knew that Joy Packer was there, and it would be wonderful to see her again. And then a thought struck me. 'What's the snag?' I asked.

'I want someone to drive the car. There's a party on tonight, and I won't feel up to all that driving tomorrow.'

'But I can't drive,' I said sadly.

'Don't worry. You'll know how to by the time we get there.'

So, bright and early next day, we were at the military check-point, where the captain's car was parked. It was a captured German vehicle, an Opel Kapitän, which the captain swore was as 'safe as hell'. Just made for mountain roads, it was in fact in perfect condition. Which was just as well, considering the terrible battering it was about to take. The captain then confused me hopelessly over the gears, the clutch and the brakes, after which he fell asleep beside me.

It took a few false starts, with various combinations of the controls, to get the engine going, and we were off. After several more tries, not all of them successful, I finally got into third gear and decided to stick there. Apart from an army convoy a mile long, there was mercifully no traffic on the road. We chugged through Vicenza, Verona, Padua and a lot of empty countryside in the wide-open spaces of the Po Valley.

In Milan the PWB mess was next to the Cathedral, and we had the most wonderful view of all its magnificent sculptures and buttresses. Birds flew in and out of the stone lacework, eminently suitable, with all its intricate patterns, for training their young.

When I went in to lunch, there was Joy Packer, cool and twinkling, at a table by herself. I joined her, and for the next hour we prattled on, exchanging news and gossip. It was just like an ordinary girls' lunch in a London restaurant – except for the table-cloth, which was stained with wine, OK sauce and tomato soup. And the rough, off-hand waiters . . .

As the coffee was slopped into our cups, my US captain came over to our table. I introduced him and Joy asked him to sit down.

'I want to go to Como tomorrow,' he said. 'Will you drive me there?'

'Of course,' I said, delighted, 'if you know the way.'

'I didn't know you could drive,' said Joy, surprised.

'I learnt today on the way from Venice,' I said proudly.

Next morning my captain produced a friend.

'This is Buck Sepp,' he said. 'He's coming to Como with us.'

I managed to get the car going after only a few minutes this time, and we were off. To my relief, both my passengers fell asleep at once.

Como was a revelation. The Swiss mountains, grey-blue and misty, came right down to the edge of the lake on the other side.

'Get us a boat honey,' said Buck. 'We wanna go for a row on the ocean.' And he waved his bottle of Scotch over the water.

They somehow managed to crawl into the boat, while I took the oars and started to paddle along. Why, oh why, I asked myself, did I always manage to get landed with drunks? Still waving his bottle, Buck fell on his knees, and the boat lurched sideways. 'Sit down, both of you,' I ordered. 'You're upsetting the boat.' 'C'mon honeybunch, come and cuddle up to your li'l ol' Fatso,' burbled Buck as he began to crawl towards me. I gave him a great shove in the chest with an oar, and the little craft began to dance merrily on the lake. After a few minutes it was going round in circles. Standing up to try and restore the balance, I shouted at the boat boy, '*Aiuto! Venite! Sùbito!*'

Leaping into another boat, he was beside us in seconds.

'Back to the shore,' I panted; '*Prestissimo, per favore*,' rattling off my emergency repertoire.

And he hooked us back to safety.

'And now,' I announced, 'I am driving back to Milan. You can either stay behind or come with me, as you wish.'

My captain unfortunately had enough sense left to want to come back. Getting his friend packed into the car took some doing. Loose limbs kept flopping out every time he tried to close the door. We were hardly out of town when it suddenly swung open, with Buck trying to get out of the car.

'Pull him back,' I shrieked in a panic, as I had forgotten once more how to stop the engine.

'I wanna throw up,' wailed Buck.

'Stop the car,' bawled the captain.

I stamped on the brake, and Buck rolled into the ditch. The temptation to drive off and leave him there was overwhelming. Somehow I managed to resist it.

That night, as I finally got to bed and dropped my throbbing, splitting head onto the pillow, I couldn't help wondering if it had all *really* been worth it . . .

chapter thirty

Very sadly, the day finally came when our job in Venice was done. As my friend in Algiers had said, 'Soldiers don't grow roots', and we had no choice but to move on.

I would gladly have spent another year in beautiful, seductive Venice. Just to *be* there was a constant, fulfilling joy. The cost that had to be paid, in the long treks out into the wilds in and out of feuding, crumbling villages, plodding for miles on foot, hoping for lifts in mule-carts, was all well worth it, if only to get back eventually to the canals and their gondolas. I loved the long warm evenings, with people laughing and singing all round to the twanging of guitars, and the moon coming up over Santa Maria della Salute across the Lagoon. As there are no gardens in Venice, every house is crowned with a wooden plat-form, on which families relax in the evening, with their squeeze-box and mouth organs. Sitting up there among the roof-tops, with all those musical instruments playing away, you could dream yourself back into the days of Marco Polo with no effort at all.

Marshal Tito had moved his forces into Trieste before any Allies had arrived in the town. When British armoured units, the New Zealand Division and an Indian brigade arrived, they found it very difficult to persuade Tito to retreat to his own stamping ground. The idea was to shunt him and his troops further east, behind an agreed frontier known as the Morgan Line. Even when he did finally agree to move there, his men were constantly trickling back to stir up trouble and make sure that no peace could reign in the town. The inhabitants of Trieste spoke neither Italian, Croat nor Slovene, but some obscure dialect known as Triestini. Fed up with always being bossed by their neighbours, they now insisted on their independence and refused to come under anybody's control, including the Allies who had liberated them.

When the PWB contingent arrived, the British Officers' Mess, which had been occupied by troops from beyond the frontier, was in an unbelievable state of filth. The lifts and the baths had been used as loos, and the waiters told us that the soldiers had washed and shaved in the lavatory pans. It took over a week for the whole place to be cleaned up and thoroughly disinfected by the Army.

PWB was now known as 'Allied Information Services'. Our new Editor was a battered Fleet Street man with a heavily lived-in face. Kindly and easy-going, he left me to decide on the stories he needed, which suited me very well.

Trieste at the time was in such a state of confusion that not even the Allies could control it. Shooting in the streets never stopped, and nobody knew who the victims or the aggressors were. Every group, almost every man, lived according to his own law. Whenever peace reigned for a day or two, troublemakers quickly stirred things up and then vanished to the mountains behind the town, where you couldn't possibly find them and winkle them out. The people in the countryside were harsh and violent, and far more aggressive than the kindly peasants around Venice.

One day, as I was returning from the Austrian border with an army captain who had given me a lift, we decided to stop by the roadside to eat our sandwiches. As we were crossing a field looking for shade, the captain suddenly froze to the spot.

'Stay where you are. DON'T MOVE!' he said, staring straight ahead of him.

'Why? What on earth is the matter?' I asked.

He looked stiff and unnatural, and said again, 'Whatever you do, don't move. We're in a minefield.'

'A minefield? How on earth do you know?'

'Can't you seen the notice over there – MINEN?'

'For goodness sake, why don't they mark it up properly?'

'The peasants pull up the signs for firewood. *They* know where the mines are. And they don't care about anybody else.'

Turning round, we slowly walked back to the road, earnestly hoping to step into our former footfalls. The distance, which was only about thirty yards, felt like a mile. It was a huge relief to get back to the road.

'Remind me to report it to the engineers when we get back. Somebody could get blown up,' said the captain, as we climbed back into the car.

Another time I was wandering about Southern Austria with a British officer stationed in Klagenfurt, and he took me round a DP camp, where Displaced Persons had been herded together while waiting to be sent 'home' in due course. These wretched people, who had been carted around Europe by the enemy as slave labour, came mostly from Poland, the Baltic States, the Balkans, and various other occupied countries. The Allies had rounded them up into camps which at least provided food and shelter.

As we were leaving, we drove past a depot of captured equipment left behind by retreating armies.

'We don't know what to do with this lot,' said my companion. 'Let's see if we can pick out a nice pair of skis for you. They will come in useful next winter.'

And so I went back to Trieste at the height of summer with a pair of Cossack skis on my shoulder.

The 56th Division, known as the 'Black Cats' (on account of their arm badge), who had landed at Salerno, captured Naples and seen bitter fighting all the way up Italy, were now comfortably settled under canvas in the hills behind Trieste. Oliver, their colonel, and his officers, had inherited a stable of 'race-horses' left behind by the Yugoslav Army. You really had to *know* they were racers. To me they looked more like medieval chargers. Anyway, whatever they were, they had to be exercised every morning at dawn.

Oliver came to collect me in his jeep before daybreak, and we set off in the dark, rattling through the streets to the stables up in the hills. It was a romantic scene, with officers saddling their horses by the light of storm-lanterns hanging in the trees. The great beasts neighed and snorted and pawed the ground, while powerful odours oozed out of their stalls in the dark. The colonel leapt onto a huge, dark-brown animal called Tito, and I was given the smallest they could find, a tough, mustard-coloured little brute named Baby. As he set off on three legs, it was more like riding a racing camel, rocking from side to side in agonising discomfort.

With Tito in the lead, followed by Baby and me, we climbed a rocky mountain path in the dark. By the time we reached the top, the sky was milky white. We were in a wild part of the mountains, with huge rocky boulders on one side and stunted pines on the other. At that point the sun came out, catching us straight in the eye. As we rode on blindly, a shot rang out, followed by two more. Soon the whole plateau was echoing with sound like rolling thunder.

Tito stopped, and Baby began to dance on the spot.

'Keep still,' ordered Oliver. 'They're shooting at us.' And to me he added sternly, 'Hold onto that horse. Whatever happens, don't let it rip.'

After a few minutes we set off again, only to bring on another burst of gunfire.

'Get under the trees,' said the Colonel. 'We'll cross the wood and come out on the other side.'

Riding through the wild copse, with low branches and thick undergrowth, was no easy matter. But emerging on the other side onto a high plateau, we were met by a glorious sight. Endless fields of stone stretched off in all directions, with low walls for easy jumps, and the sea sparkling and glittering in the distance. It was all as inviting as could be. Tito galloped away in ecstasy, and Baby, throwing his rump in the air, cantered off sideways like a crab. But I was ready for it, and hung on like a leech. It was not till our third ride that he managed to throw me off, head-first into a pile of stones.

Sometimes we set off in the afternoon, with the sun behind us, providing good targets for the Jugs, our pet name for the mountain braves who were shooting at us. But we were lucky. They missed every time.

Joy Packer, who had left Milan and come to join us, introduced me to the Royal Navy, now based in Trieste harbour. The captain invited us to drinks in his cabin, and we often had dinner on board, sometimes watching a film on deck with the officers afterwards. At other times we went sailing with the cruiser's senior officers, or else the lieutenants borrowed the admiral's launch and we did some water-skiing. These young men were a bois-terous lot. Their chief aim was always to throw us off our skis. Joy and I returned their hospitality by taking them to our Officers' Club, where we danced on the terrace under the stars to the sound of the waves breaking on the rocks below.

The Commander-in-Chief of the Royal Navy in the Mediterranean frequently dropped in on his ships in Trieste. One evening, as we were having drinks in the captain's cabin, I asked the admiral if I could join one of his minesweeping oper-ations one day, as it would make a good story for the local press. 'A girl on a minesweeper!' exclaimed the C-in-C, in horror, 'Whatever next! I've never heard of such a thing . . .!'

But the following morning, the captain of the minesweeping fleet rang me up before breakfast.

'You know that trip you wanted to go on,' he asked.

'Yes, too bad the C-in-C wouldn't have it.'

'He changed his mind after you left . . .'

'Oh hurray!' I yelled, jumping a foot up in the air. 'The darling man! Give him a hug for me . . .'

'Aye,' said the captain, 'I'll do that. We're off on Monday morn-ing. I'll send a rating round to pick you up at six a.m. Don't be late or you'll miss the boat.'

The minesweeping fleet consisted of fourteen ships following one another in a slanting line, all connected together by a strong cable dragged below the surface of the sea, which cut through the wires attached to the mines. The first and last boat of the fleet were in the most dangerous position, as they were exposed to the mines at the end of their wires. The week before, the leading ship of another minesweeping fleet had been hit and blown into eternity. This time we were hoping for better luck.

Stationed on various parts of the bridge, the captain and his officers were keeping vigilant watch all round. After the sailors had lowered the wire-cutting tackle into the water, they went to the guns, waiting for the mines to spring out of the sea. It wasn't long before a shout of triumph was heard on the bridge: 'Mine to starboard!' And at that moment we saw an enormous cannon-ball, covered all over with spikes, come leaping out of the water as a German K-type mine, severed from its anchor by our cutting wire, flew into the air.

After that they came up thick and fast all round and the gunners went to work, blowing them up as they appeared. On the bridge I was hopping with excitement under the benevolent eye of the captain. His skill in manoeuvring about in the minefield filled me with admiration. Time simply flew as we steamed on with guns firing and exploding mines shooting up huge bubbling fountains all over the sea. As they came up, the captain could tell whether they were of German or Italian origin. When I asked what the difference was, he told the sailors to bring one of each kind right up to the boat for my inspection. 'We can have them both up on board if you like,' he offered obligingly, but I declined the opportunity.

At noon we went down to lunch in the wardroom. The officers, who were all in high spirits, were full of stories about their best friends hitting mines on this kind of operation, and going straight down to feed the fish. After lunch they told me there was another treat in store for us, as we might be going in close to the Dalmatian coast, and the locals would take pot-shots at us to show their gratitude to the Royal Navy for clearing their waters for them.

The Editor was pleased with my story when it appeared in the local press, with splendid photographs of mines exploding all over the sea.

The days were growing shorter, and one more summer was coming to an end. The Bora, which was blowing down from the Alps more and more often, had grown so strong that ropes had been strung along the streets for people to hang onto whenever lifted off their feet by the gale. I was beginning to shiver in my summer drill and open sandals. With all my gear gone, I hadn't even got a pair of stockings or a pullover to wear. So when my boss asked me one day if I would like to go to Vienna instead of him, I agreed at once. He'd had his fill of 'overseas', and was longing to get back to Fleet Street.

Oliver gave me a first-class farewell dinner, and lent me his own 'command car', with a couple of army drivers, to take me up to Austria. It took the whole morning to climb over the long range of the Alps. At midday we stopped for lunch by a stream full of speckled trout, wriggling about among the stones. No self-respecting other rank is ever seen without his teapot and kettle. 'When in doubt, brew up' was a notice seen on the back of a truck in the Desert War. So, faithful to custom, my soldiers brewed up and we sat swallowing scalding mugs of tea beside our trout-filled mountain stream.

At Klagenfurt they dropped me off at the Post Hotel, then departed on the long trek back to Trieste. Klagenfurt on the Wörthersee, an enormous lake surrounded by mountains, was a magical place, but I was bound for Vienna and didn't feel justified in lingering unduly. There was just time all the same to have a quick look at the famous 'Wurm', an enormous stone dragon of great antiquity slumbering in the main square, said to waggle his tail whenever a virgin walks past. According to local legend, the tail hasn't twitched within living memory.

A truck was leaving early in the morning for Graz, the next stopping place on the long road to Vienna, and cluttered up with my unwieldy possessions, now including the Cossack skis, which made some people smile and a good many others audibly swear, I climbed on board.

Graz is a charming little provincial town with a clocktower perched on a rock in the central square, and narrow picturesque streets lined with houses painted all over with gay colourful frescoes. Our mess there, under the control of young Major Greaves, was a haven of peace and order, or so it appeared to me after the various bear-gardens in which I had lived so far.

Although I arrived well after lunch was over, nobody kicked me out on the spot, *and* a meal was miraculously produced without any grumbling or swearing. I was beginning to feel I had arrived at the wrong place, until I met the gentle, courteous major in charge. It was obvious from then on that the influence of his personality had soaked right through to the basic foundations (kitchen and staff at least) of the mess. In some mysterious way beyond the reach of corruption, he was one of the few human beings I had yet met whose inner strength and moral rectitude had in no way been affected by the demoralising influences and experiences of war.

chapter thirty-one

From Major Greaves I learnt that a convoy was assembling to confront the hazards of crossing the Russian Zone. At the end of the war, Austria had been divided into four parts, of which the Americans controlled Salzburg and Upper Austria, the French had the Tyrol and Vorarlberg, and the Russians, who were allocated Lower Austria and the Burgenland, clamoured also for the territory surrounding Vienna, so that nobody could enter or leave the capital without their knowledge. The British were responsible for the provinces of Styria and Carinthia in the south-east, which included a tiresome frontier with the truculent Jugoslavs.

We were strictly forbidden to enter the Russian Zone. With a special pass, not by any means granted to everybody, we were allowed to travel through their territory in order to reach our own region. Sometimes, for no reason at all, passes were torn up, vehicles 'confiscated' and travellers sent back on foot through snowed-up mountains. Every day new tales of incidents in the

Russian Zone came to light, and nobody undertook the journey through it lightly. The darlings of Roosevelt and Churchill were proving less cooperative than expected.

The magic grey passes, without which no civilian ever squeezed through the Frontier Post, had been applied for in Vienna, and were expected at any moment. As these had to be brooded over by the Russian authorities at Headquarters, and receive their official stamp, it could take anything up to a week or more to obtain them, and once they came, it was made abundantly clear that stops at any point on the way were strictly *verboten*.

And so we settled down to wait, and meanwhile I made friends with my convoy mates. Sir Alexander Bethune, who had been at the British Embassy in Kuybyshev during the early part of the war, could speak Russian, and would act as interpreter at the frontier in case of trouble. Captain John Cox, an enigmatic and mysterious character who spoke in a soft and feathery voice, was moving to Vienna with a detachment of Austrian young ladies, who naturally became known as Cox's Orange Pippins. (Among them was Gretl, who was to marry Norman Cameron in the following year. She became a lifelong friend.) A sprinkling of blond, handsome young men, who were somehow connected with the Pippins, made up the contingent of the convoy, which consisted of three trucks and a couple of small vehicles. All packed and ready (at least those who had something to pack), we were only waiting for the word go. This finally came through a couple of days later, when a telephone call from Vienna announced that Lieutenant Barry Evans, as official Pass Bearer, would shortly be on his way, and we were to meet him at the frontier.

For extra safety the pretty Pippins, potentially irresistible to the wild and passionate instincts of our Slav Allies, were locked up in the back of the truck, while I, a leathery old campaigner, and in uniform anyway, was considered a lesser risk and allowed to sit in front with the driver.

For such a haphazard arrangement, the operation was remarkably well timed. We hardly had an hour or so to wait before we saw an open jeep roaring up the road towards the barrier. Lieutenant Evans, all smothered in a huge army great-coat and standing up in the vehicle, was waving the passes above his head and shouting, 'Triumph, Eureka, got 'em!' Tense and apprehensive as we were, and dramatic as the situation then seemed to us, it was with exaggerated relief that we saw him materialise.

In the back of the truck the poor Pippins were holding their breath. As the Russians had assumed the right of life and death over Austrian nationals (whether legally recognised or not, this was in fact the case), people were continually being dragged off convoys without rhyme or reason, and were never heard of again. The philosophy of the Russian troops was simple and straightforward. They didn't bother their heads with refinements of humanitarian principles or fair play. If they wanted some-thing, they took it. If resistance was offered, they bashed and grabbed. Marshal Koniev's Divisions, fighting all the way like demons, had managed quite well without supplies, living off the land throughout the campaign, so that his soldiers, in good training and well practised in the art, saw no reason for aban-doning such rewarding methods at this stage. Anyway in their eyes, the enemy who had lost the war deserved no quarter. Knowing all this, the Pippins trembled, and we trembled for them. But this time at least, all was well. No objection was raised, and our convoy rumbled through.

As fighting in Vienna had been heavy, many of the streets were just enormous heaps of dust and rubble. It was difficult to believe that this drab and shabby town had ever been the glit-tering, dancing capital of the Congress of Europe and of the

Hapsburg Emperors. Autumn leaves drifting off the trees whirled about and settled on the pavements and piles of rubble, adding an infinitely melancholy air to the already desolate aspect of the city. People in dark overcoats hurried along with hunched shoulders and blank, shut-down faces. Furtiveness, fear and suspicion were everywhere.

Our convoy stopped outside the Park Hotel, where Alexander Bethune and I got out, while Captain Cox whisked his Pippins away to settle them in civilian flats. Bustling and comfortable, the Park Hotel was warm and welcoming until you reached the bedroom floors. At least I had a room of my own. However, it was ice-cold and uninspiring, furnished in the dismal provincial style and depressing bad taste of the Thirties. With no wish to linger, and after a hasty and abbreviated wash in cold water, I beetled downstairs to the bar to see who was there. You never knew where or when old friends would turn up.

An English girl, recently arrived from London, introduced herself, and we decided to go and explore together. As Olive had even less German or Russian than I, we thought that joining forces would be fun, and could do no harm from the security point of view. So after a quick lunch in the large warm dining-room full of wives and children, with their military lords and masters, down the Underground we went, making a note of our own station of Hietzing for future reference.

The ramshackle little train of the Stadtbahn, which rattled and clanked along on its rusty rails, was packed with surly figures bearing rucksacks upon their backs. As Vienna was a starving city, its inhabitants were continually on the move, collecting or delivering black market food and articles of barter. Once you knew your way around, you got your meat from a pram shop or the barber round the corner, fish from the dentist and sugar from the draper's, in exchange for an army blanket or a tube of toothpaste or a second-hand pair of boots.

Olive and I returned from our first expedition just before dark, dazzled and amazed. Walking from the Stadtpark to the Ring and into the old medieval city, we wandered through the ancient narrow streets, with everywhere the same furtive people slinking around, and none of the nonchalant Latin love of passing the time of day out of doors. The Russian soldiers we scuttled past looked sinister in their jackboots topped with baggy trousers and high-necked tunics, belted round the middle like mouzhiks, each carrying a rifle or tommy-gun. Women soldiers, square-cut and broad-shouldered, equally accoutred apart from a skirt instead of trousers, roamed the streets as well. We saw a couple of them pick up an overturned jeep, set it on its feet and climb back into it, dusting their hands.

That evening Norman appeared in the bar of the hotel. It was a very welcome and unexpected treat to see him there. After dinner, which we had together, we went to the ballroom to indulge in a spot of the special shuffle we had perfected in Rome. The room was crowded. Although a few familiar faces appeared here and there, a great many new people had arrived from the Allied Commission HQ in London. In Austria our name was changed once more. We were now Information Services Branch of the Allied Control Commission. Or just ISB ACA for short.

Norman introduced me to our CO, ex-Captain, now Colonel Beauclerk, in whose tracks I had unknowingly followed all the way from Norfolk House in London.

'What are you doing here?', he asked me, after inviting us to join his table.

'The AIS News Editor in Trieste asked me to come here instead of him. He wanted to go home.'

'How very tiresome. I particularly wanted *him*. There was no need for you to come at all,' rasped my husband-to-be in most unwelcoming tones.

'Oh dear, well, I'd better go back to England. I'm due some leave anyway. It will fit in quite well.'

'You're not due anything at all,' snapped the colonel. 'Leave is a privilege, not a right. Let's go and dance, anyway.'

'So when shall I go back to England?' I persisted.

'I didn't say you could go back,' he answered. 'Do concentrate now.'

The dance-floor was glittering with uniforms. French officers, with revolvers bouncing on their behinds as they did their hopping version of the Viennese waltz; Russians, with all the heavy ironmongery of their medals clanking and jingling upon their breasts; smooth American captains and majors gleaming like mahogany with all their polished leather and impeccable haircuts; and of course, our own aloof, distinguished-looking officers, in their stylish, Savile Row service dress. While I, in the midst of all this elegance, was prancing about in my old KD shirt and skirt and battered sandals.

Suddenly, the music changed to a Paul Jones. As the lights dimmed and the usual reshuffle was taking place among the dancers, it seemed that all was not well in the centre of the ballroom. There was shouting, and suddenly a shot rang out. One of the chandeliers exploded, splattering glass splinters all round. The music stopped, and we all stood rooted to the spot as an apoplectic Russian officer, reholstering his revolver, stamped angrily out of the room. Unfamiliar with the Paul Jones, and not caring for it when explained to him, he just wasn't going to have his partner snatched out of his arms in the middle of a dance.

And that was the end of my first day in Vienna.

*

The weather was daily growing colder, and Norman, who was well over six foot tall, realising my plight, presented me with an enormous pair of his heavy-duty battledress trousers, which I laboriously unstitched and sewed into a skirt. One of his vast khaki pullovers, reaching down to the knee-cap, made a warm cosy tunic, and to complete the ensemble he added a pair of his long knitted stockings, whose ends I chopped off for a snugger fit. These blunt square knitted toes, stitched together with coarse brown cotton poking out of open sandals, did tend to catch the eye on more formal occasions, but beggars can't be choosers, and I was glad to be warm, and immensely grateful to Norman for his generosity.

Since our Roman days his mood had changed. The following Sunday he rang through to my bedroom at seven o'clock in the morning. 'Good heavens,' he exclaimed, 'are you still in bed? Well, get up quick and I'll be round for you in twenty minutes. We're going to church.'

Struggling into my home-made uniform, I went down to the hall, where he was waiting for me, with his curly hair standing on end and his enormous army greatcoat flapping around his ankles. Under the cynical eye of the hall porter, no doubt used to the impeccable turnout of German officers, we set off together into the cold November morning, bent on our Sunday devotions.

Low Mass was in progress in the first church we called at. The faithful, discouraged by the perishing cold and few in numbers, contributed little to the atmosphere of devout sanctity which Norman was probably looking for. After a few minutes he announced in a loud voice, 'I don't think much of this place, let's push off and find something more lively.' So, blowing on our frost-bitten fingers, we proceeded to the next church down the line. There wasn't much to be said for this one either. 'Why are all these prelates so bloody pompous?' complained Norman.

'Come on, we're wasting our time here. I expect you'd like some breakfast?' As that was the first welcome suggestion I had heard that morning, I heartily agreed, and we dived into Sacher's blissfully warm interior, all reeking with the aroma of army sausage and toast.

Hotel Sacher, in the Ring, had been requisitioned for senior British officers, and was at that time giving asylum to the distraught person of Nijinsky, who had suddenly appeared outside Vienna, springing into the centre of a group of Russian soldiers squatting around a bonfire one night soon after their armies had overrun Austria. And until his future could be sorted out, the British Commission, watching over him like a mother, had given him one of the best rooms in the hotel.

Over our pot of tea and substantial well-earned breakfast, Norman's disappointment over his frustrated and fruitless spiritual search evaporated, and he reverted to his usual robust and cheerful self. He was in reminiscent mood. 'Talking of clothes,' he remarked, eyeing the bat sleeves of my oversize khaki pullover, which hung in loose folds around my wrists, 'did I ever tell you about my swim in a German river before the war?'

Replete with sausages and tea, I leant back in my chair ready for a good yarn.

'While I was at Oxford,' he said, 'I went on a walking tour through Bavaria during the long vac. It was terribly hot and dusty, and when I arrived at a river and there seemed to be no one around, I took off my clothes and dived in.' The water, straight from the glaciers, was blissfully refreshing, but he had reckoned without the swiftness of the current. Halfway across, he was carried downstream like a blade of grass. Struggling desperately for the opposite bank, he was relieved to reach a bend, behind which suddenly appeared a totally unexpected village. A small jetty stuck out into the stream, and to this he hitched himself.

'There was nothing else for it,' he concluded. 'I just had to pelt down the village street with my hands over my privates, while all those stupid Krauts hustled their womenfolk into doorways bawling, "Madman! *Polizei! Hilfe!*"' At which point the adjoining tables in the dining-room, much to his surprise, collapsed with laughter. Looking around I could see Lord Schuster, who was in Vienna to de-Nazify the Federal Government and disentangle Austria from the German tentacles in which she had been entwined since 1938, and Fifi Schuster, his daughter, who conducted an agreeable café existence in the Ring with her Austrian friends. A young Count Tolstoy, who was supposed to be on his way to America, sat aloof and alone at a table in the window. Lord Pakenham, on a lightning visit from England, was surrounded by an animated group of ACA officials. Benjamin Britten, firmly buttoned down behind the mask of his noncommittal face, kept his eyes on his plate, discouraging would-be chatterers. Graham Greene, also an inmate of the hotel, usually breakfasted in his room on pink champagne. I was later to meet him at a cocktail party where he had his back to the wall and his look of intense misery effectively kept most people away. I approached him with the object of trying to cheer him up, but within a few minutes *I* was the one to be giggling at his stories, one of them being about John Betjeman who, at a party rather like the present one, was approached by a young lady who asked him if he liked foxhunting. To which he replied, 'I can't even sit on a horse, let alone shoot from one!'

The Allied Commission was divided into several Divisions, of which the Information Branch, as part of the Political Division, was ruled over by our CO, Colonel Charles Beauclerk. This Branch included the usual newsdesk, a German-language newspaper called the *Weltpresse*, on which Pippin Gretl worked as a reporter, and the British *Morning News*, which was issued for the consumption of the English contingent throughout Austria. The usual radio and monitoring stations were farmed out in the Zone.

The newsdesk, on which I found myself once more on the night-shift, was now operating under the direction of Max Wilde, who had discovered in his heart a great love and admiration for the Russians. With a few words of their language at his command, he laudably did his best to chat them up on all occasions, in spite of which they appeared to regard him with as much suspicion as the rest of us. I remember a garden party at the High Commission, where Max, ever conscious of his role of peacemaker, was earnestly addressing a Russian general, who steadily fixed him with a baleful eye while consuming one vodka after another and tossing the empty glasses over his shoulder into the bushes, where lurked a couple of agile batmen who caught them nimbly as they came flying through the air.

We were allowed to roam over most of the city at will, but not of course to enter the Russian Zone. The constant incidents of house-breaking by the soldiers, usually followed by rape, theft and sometimes murder, were indignantly brought up by the Western Allies at the weekly Quadripartite meetings, without getting any change out of the Russians, who gave no reason or explanation for anything that ever happened. Everything always had to be 'referred to Moscow', which was the last you ever heard of the matter. On one occasion, feeling myself being prodded between the shoulder-blades, I turned round to face a bayonet with which a Russian soldier was trying to shift me along. Unknowingly, I had been walking along the pavement *behind* one of their requisitioned hotels in the Ring.

That winter a sinister feeling of menace hung over the city, stalking the streets and pervading the air, so that you didn't even feel secure in your own home. At any time of the day or night, a great battering on the door could bring doom and disaster. People, once kidnapped, were never heard of again, so that you never knew what fate to expect, and the very few who did escape never dared tell.

Although in Rome crime had flourished in all its multifarious aspects, here in Vienna you felt a more determined and purposeful malevolence floating in the very oxygen you breathed. Graham Greene who, on arrival in Vienna, had sniffed and soaked up this atmosphere with the appreciation of a connoisseur, was frustrated for a long time at not being able to discover a theme worthy of it for the filmscript he had come to write. Colonel Beauclerk, bringing his fertile mind to bear on the case, dredged up the Sewer Police and performed the introductions, so that Mr Greene's dilemma was solved, and the plot of *The Third Man* gradually began to take shape.

Since the Park Hotel was a long way from the ISB offices, and ACA transport was as erratic and unreliable as PWB's had been, Gretl managed to find me a flat on the floor below her own, and produced a friend who wanted to share my room, while Olive, who also moved in with us, had a tiny bedroom to herself. The remaining space consisted of a living-room, a bathroom, and the entire flat depended for sole heating on a boiler enthroned in the middle of the kitchen. As no fuel of any kind figured on the official rations, we trekked out like any other citizen, with rucksacks on our backs, to the Vienna Woods to collect sticks for our fire.

By this time I had acquired an Army officer's overcoat which, though the smallest size available, enveloped me from head to foot like a burnous. Huddled inside this garment, crouching in my seat on the Underground, bent on one of my stick-collecting excursions, I suddenly felt myself being seized by the collar and swung into the aisle, while a gruff voice growled down my ear in German 'Out you get, young man, and make room for me.' And a bulky Viennese burgher dumped himself in my place.

Collecting sticks was a rewarding occupation until the snow gradually began to engulf our world. As it fell more heavily and persistently over the desolate city, the hideous heaps of war rubble slowly turned into bizarre, lumpy shapes, and the outlines of jagged ruins were softened, as the whole place deceptively acquired a bogus fairytale quality. Bereft of fuel, our boiler turned stone-cold, and our flat became an ice-box. Town gas came on for early birds, between four and five o'clock every morning, and we, who kept different hours, had to get used to rising at dead of night to brew a hasty pot of porridge, then race back to bed to consume it there and drop off to sleep again until a more reasonable hour. In the evening, the gas was switched on between seven and eight, just giving us time to heat up a tin of soup or a ready-made steak and kidney pudding, which we then gobbled in the living-room with a hot-water bottle in our lap and one candle on the table. Electric light was either kaput or being saved up for industry.

Gretl's adventures as a reporter on our German newspaper were numerous and picturesque. When Malcolm Sargent paid us a visit, it fell to her lot to attend his press conference. Having had a full-scale business lunch, she arrived late through no fault of her own, then promptly fell asleep. Waking up suddenly at question time, and wanting to make her mark and show she was on the ball, she piped up in her best English, 'Tell me, Sargent Malcolm,' but never got any further, the rest of the question being drowned by the hoots of laughter of the other pressmen present. As winter progressed and the weather continued to grow colder, when on night-duty she would change into her nightdress in the office, where a fairly warm temperature was maintained, then, under the nose of the startled night porter, would beetle off into the snow in her nightgear, making for her icy flat as fast as she could and jumping straight into bed when she got there.

The thermometer dropped to thirty degrees below zero. People sometimes dropped dead in the street, frozen to the spot. The snow now rose to the level of the first floor in the streets, and one fine day, to cheer ourselves up, we decided to give a party. Shortly before, we had managed to acquire a couple of electric fires of lethal design, made of painted pinewood and equipped with a bar apiece. If we were lucky, and no one in the building was using a vacuum cleaner or an electric iron when we plugged in our fires, all was well. But more often than not, the entire fuse system of the building would blow up, and the infuriated inmates of the other flats congregated on our doorstep, cursing these bloody Englanders who caused nothing but trouble.

The evening of our party, plugging in fortunately took place without incident, and we were able to raise the temperature in the flat by one or two degrees. I was busy chipping the frozen limejuice out of its bottle with a knitting-needle, in order to melt it down on the gas as soon as this came on, when suddenly a wild demented banging on the front door made me jump out of my skin. Gretl was standing there in a great state of agitation. 'There's a Russian soldier in our flat,' she panted. 'What shall I do? We're all terrified . . .'

'Hold on,' I said, dropping the bottle, 'I'll ring the Military Police.' As these gentlemen assured me they would be round in a jiffy, we galloped upstairs, hoping that the sight of my uniform would act as a deterrent to whatever the Russian was plotting. There he was, standing in the middle of the kitchen, with his tommy-gun on the table, bemused and lost-looking, while all the Pippins were hiding under the beds.

'*Engliski*,' I announced in my best Russian, and pointing at my battledress jacket, 'What do you want?' Whereupon we were treated to a verbal flood of which we didn't catch a single word. There we were, all three standing around helplessly, when the Military Police, good as their word, arrived on the scene.

'Okay, girls, we'll take over,' they said soothingly, as they led the unprotesting youth away. It turned out after all that, suddenly feeling like a cup of cocoa, he had wandered into the building and rapped with the butt-end of his gun on the first door that took his fancy.

After this little excitement was over we realised that time was flying. Gretl and the other Pippins, now coming out of hiding, offered to help with preparations for the party. The gas, having flickered briefly and gone off again, had by now been switched off at the mains. And here was our limejuice, standing up solid as a rock inside its bottle. Ingenious and practical as ever, Gretl tipped one of the fires on its back and upon its single bar placed the saucepan, into which we quickly dropped the icicles chipped off the main iceberg and the situation was saved. Greatly relieved, we were treating our chilblains to a quick warm-through when all of a sudden a loud rap on the door made us jump to our feet.

'Heavens, not the guests already!' I exclaimed, making for the entrance. On the mat stood a couple of soldiers, this time our own, surrounded by crates and boxes of food.

'Good God,' I squeaked, horrified, 'it's the Russians!' Wednesday was Ration Day, when the Quartermaster, using our flat as a distribution centre for all the British officers living in the area, unloaded the stuff on us. Olive, with her Northern accent, pronounced 'rations' as 'Russians', so that all of us with one accord followed her example without even thinking about it, which generally resulted in a certain amount of confusion.

In the living-room, poor Gretl started to tremble all over again, '*Noch einmal!*' (Not again!) I heard her exclaim in alarm.

'It's all right,' I shouted; 'it's only the rations. Please come in,' and I led the way into the kitchen. At this point Olive, returning from the office, erupted into the kitchen. 'Oh my God, it's the Russians tonight! I forgot all about it.' Within a few minutes, and just before the party, our tiny kitchen was overflowing with groceries, great lumps of old Danish cow and New Zealand ram, and tins of jam and golden syrup, frozen solid like amber.

Since I had nothing to wear, Gretl lent me a flame-coloured organza dress, all heaving and bouncing with detached floating panels. Never in my life had I ever had anything so beautiful on my back. And had the party been a total flop, I would still have enjoyed the evening on account of that dress. The Pippins' boyfriends had constructed a false ceiling of wire mesh, nice and low, which they covered with multi-coloured crêpe paper, through which the electric bulb on the ceiling flowed dark-red and lurid, as in a really sleazy dive. I presume it was a good party since nobody went home until morning.

Although I was apparently not due for any leave, the Colonel nevertheless granted me a few days off when I heard that my father was being sent to London from Singapore by the Red Cross. My mother had already returned from Australia with Anne and Christine, and together we went to Victoria Station to meet his train. Looking up and down the rows of stunned, bemused ex-prisoners, we could not spot him anywhere. In the end I asked a policeman who, amazingly, led me straight to him. At the time it never occurred to me to wonder how he could possibly have known my father. In the topsy-turvy world of the last few years anything was possible, and you took what came your way without asking questions.

He looked unfamiliar, diminished, and frighteningly thin. He and his fellow prisoners had only just been rescued in time. For the past few months they had been forced at gunpoint to dig tunnels, into which they were to be herded, doused with petrol and burnt to death if any Allied landings took place in Singapore. The first atom bomb had been dropped on Hiroshima on the 6th of August, and the world was stunned to hear that nearly 100,000 people had been annihilated by one bomb. The resulting outcry of appalled indignation which rocked humanity did it credit, but it should be remembered that these courteous people, who bowed to one another all day long, also tortured their prisoners in an unbelievably atrocious way.

Mama had booked us all into a grim and depressing hotel in South Kensington, and there we gathered in the hideous lounge, making polite conversation.

Anne, who had trained as a nurse in Australia, was informed on arriving in England that she would have to start again from scratch if she wanted to practise in the UK. She told me of their last nightmare days in Singapore under intense Japanese bombardment, with a fearful thunderstorm crashing simultaneously around the sky, so that you couldn't tell a clap of thunder from an exploding bomb. Staying with friends while waiting to join the last refugee boat in the harbour, they had watched an incandescent ball of fire sweep in through the window and roll slowly along the floor between their feet, then continue calmly out to the verandah to rejoin the chaos outside.

On the way back from Australia they had taken three months to zigzag across the Indian Ocean and sail round the Cape, to be finally abandoned half-way by their convoy, which galloped on ahead at twice the speed that their old cargo was able to squeeze out of its antiquated engines. The ships disappearing over the horizon left behind a feeling of utter desolation, which was reinforced the next day when a rowing boat, seemingly empty, came floating towards them. Suspecting a Japanese booby-trap, they scrutinised it cautiously before approaching any closer. But it turned out to be a genuine case of survivors, only just still alive from a boat torpedoed and sunk a couple of weeks earlier. And although, at great danger to itself, the little cargo tarried a couple of days, searching around for other survivors, nobody else remained on the surface of the unfriendly sea.

Christine, who was a lively sixteen-year-old and feeling she ought to be doing something useful, had written off to the Admiralty, saying that she was thinking of becoming captain of a warship and would be happy to have one assigned to her as soon as possible. A courteous reply came from Their Lordships, regretting that, at the moment, there were no vacancies for young ladies in top-ranking appointments in the Royal Navy. But they would keep her in mind and inform her as soon as something suitable turned up.

But in spite of toiling and moiling to renew the old family ties, after so many years of separation we were strangers to one another. The atmosphere, stiff and strained, amazed me. I never imagined that this moment, which I had looked forward to so much and for such a long time, when we would swap tales of our adventures and misfortunes and rejoice together at still being alive after it all, would be such a painful experience. Papa, who had never been exactly intimate with anyone in his life and who had withdrawn still further into himself since his ordeal in the concentration camp, was obviously longing to get away from us all.

After a few days of this disappointing get-together, I felt guiltily relieved to return to Vienna, to the unexacting, problem-free existence to which I had now become addicted. My last day in London was spent in Harrods, buying shoes and heavy winter clothes, and great quantities of glass balls for a really first-class Christmas tree.

Among the commissions and gifts for various friends with which I returned to Vienna was a hefty parcel for a family of young Austrians whose aunt I had met in London. Thinking they would come and collect their loot from my office I rang them up on arrival, but they insisted I should deliver it in person, so that I could see for myself how destitute they truly were. To my surprise I found a jolly, high-spirited, well-dressed crowd of people clustered round an enormous porcelain stove reaching up to the ceiling. The room, a good deal warmer than any of our messes in requisitioned hotels, was in no way to be compared with the deep-freeze conditions in which I lived in my little flat. As I expressed genuine surprise, they exclaimed indignantly, 'But we have lost everything! The Russians have taken everything away, furniture, clothes, pictures, all we had. We are very, very poor.' Having said their piece, and as they paid no more attention to me, I got up to leave. To my surprise, one of the young men sprang up and opened the door for me. 'I'll walk you back to your hotel,' said Bobby gallantly.

'Please don't bother. I'm going to the office anyway.'

'That will do just as well.' And taking me by the arm, he steered me expertly through the frozen ruts of the street.

'How do you come to speak such good English?' I asked, more and more puzzled.

'I had an English nanny.'

'Oh, did you! And where is she now?' I asked, thinking of the horrors of the Bolzano concentration camp.

'Just been liberated. She was interned during the war, poor old dear. But now she is back at our place in Carinthia.'

'I'm so glad. And now, this is my office, thank you for seeing me back.'

'I'll collect you for lunch tomorrow,' he said, and to my surprise, he did.

After that I was often invited to stay at 'our place in Carinthia', a Gothic castle built on top of a perpendicular peak near the

Jugoslav frontier. Like so many Austrian families, although their possessions had been decimated, they appeared to live in great comfort. Their vast estates provided plenty of firewood for the huge porcelain stoves, while roast duck and poultry, venison, capercailzie, trout from their own stream and all sorts of other delicacies appeared at every meal. To one who had been living on army field rations for the past two years, this was like visiting another planet. If it hadn't been for the constant plaints of the older generation, who moaned incessantly that they had lost everything, it would have been hard to remember that there had been a war at all. Another thing that took me time to get used to was having my hand kissed by the maids every time they came into my bedroom.

We spent the weekends skiing with an enormous collection of cousins, and in the evenings we danced in the vast stone-floored hall, the walls of which were lined to the rafters with generations of stuffed chamois heads. Although my school German was beginning to improve, there was little chance to practise it, as everyone spoke excellent English.

The parties with which ACA celebrated Christmas were very different from the year before. The Colonel's driver and I toiled off to the Vienna Woods to seek out the biggest and finest tree we could manage to bring back. Decorated with all my glass balls from Harrods, it was the centre of the festivities and rejoicings that took place in the mess.

When festivities were over, our usual routine was resumed and the normal life of the city gradually began to get under way again. The concerts and operas were a great joy. Elisabeth Schwarzkopf and Ljuba Welitsch sang Mozart. Karajan frequently conducted the Vienna Philharmonic, as well as Kripps and Klemperer, a terrible old goat who pinched all the bottoms within his reach. There was an artist's restaurant, all upholstered in red plush like the old Café Royal, where we met all these characters after the evening's performances. A great treat for late supper was *fogosch*, a delicious fish from Lake Balaton in Hungary, secretly brought into Vienna by the engine-driver of the night train from Budapest. The headwaiter, full of pomp and circumstance, would come up, announcing importantly, '*Der Schmuggler ist da.* Do you wish *fogosch* tonight? And of course, since the smuggler was there with his *fogosch*, we had to have it, however expensive it might be.

One day I was transferred to the British *Morning News* office. On a daily paper there was actually something to show for your work, whereas on the newsdesk your stuff, which you never saw again, just disappeared into limbo, and might for all you knew never be used at all.

John Cox (of the Pippins), the Editor, ruled over a neat and orderly office of half a dozen journalists, whom he kept in a constant state of gloom and despondency. He detested the breed and all they stood for, feared their irreverence and distrusted the cheerful inconsequence of their ways. As a result, all dash and glamour having gone out of their work, they toiled reluctantly in sullen silence under his sway. A news office, he used to say, should be run like a greengrocer's shop. Inscrutable as a Buddha, he sat at his desk, upon which you couldn't even see a paperclip. The copy, as soon as it was rushed in, still warm from the teleprinters, was stored away in his drawers to cool its heels there until all the excitement of a red-hot piece of news had evaporated into thin air. Then, and only then, was it doled out to us. The writer who was summoned by his soft whispery tones had to go to the desk to collect his work, just like trotting up to the teacher at school. If anyone was bold enough to stand up and stretch his legs or hiss a few curses into his neighbour's ear, John would breathe at once, 'What's the matter? Are you stuck? Do you want a dictionary?' These were kept locked up in the filing cabinet behind his desk and handed out on request.

In the morning, Cobby, a real hard-bitten pro from Fleet Street, would totter into the office an hour late, swaying in on her high-heeled rickety sandals, with enormous round holes in her fishnet stockings and bright orange-coloured powder spread in great irregular streaks across her face. 'Good evening, boys and girls,' she would croak before John had time to remark on the lateness of the hour. Then she would pick up the copy on her table and begin to poke about on the keyboard. 'Damn typewriter keeps jumping about. Darling, be a love and give me a cigarette, and for Christ's sake Cox, stop looking at me like that!' And I would fish out a cigarette and light it for her. 'Thanks darling, that's much better. Now let's see what we've got here.' And her professionalism would carry her through the worst part of her hangover until mercifully released by the lunch-hour, when she would clatter round to the mess as fast as she could for a reviving gin and tonic.

Escaping on the dot of one, the others would follow her to the bar to recover from the strain of the morning, and complain bitterly about the unnatural and undignified treatment to which they were subjected. Colonel Beauclerk, who was firm but just and sympathetic, mixing and joking and drinking with everybody, listened to their complaints and explained the reason why things had to be as they were. Quite soon, restored by their favourite tipple and their own witticisms, they had forgotten their troubles, and all resentment evaporated under the influence of the Colonel's infectious optimism. Owing to his personality and talent for knitting together people of different social and intellectual levels, it was a happy mess, with a minimum of intrigue and malicious gossip.

Life was also more predictable now that the Americans were

no longer with us. I must admit that I missed their flamboyant extravagance. Nothing with them was ever impossible. Their working methods, and their picturesque turn of phrase had been a stimulating experience. Now life was more earnest, though only by comparison with an American mess. The view taken at the top was that as long as people did their job, their private life was their own affair, and the usual drinking and fornicating flourished uninterrupted and as happily as ever, without blame or reproof of any kind.

Cobby, who was the life and soul of the journalists' world, held court every evening in Sacher's, where any man around was irresistibly drawn to her table by her husky voice, her infectious chuckling, her vitality, and the boldness and lewdness of her conversation. As drinks came and went, the party grew in size and boisterousness until, around nine o'clock, she would totter to her feet and lead her chaps, tight as ticks, into the dining-room for dinner. Her parties, which often lasted all night, were very popular. I was never invited. One habitué explained to me that she carried on in this way because she had only three months left to live. Ten years later, when I saw her again, she was still as hale and indefatigable as ever, having lost none of her vivacity, her charm or her magnetism.

Bobby, my little Carinthian baron, had invited me to open the New Year's Eve Ball with him in Vienna. This tradition, which has survived the war and continues to this day to be one of the main social functions of the season, gets the New Year off with a bang. The girls, all decked out in virginal white, line up with their escorts round the edge of the enormous ballroom, and at the first note of the Blue Danube, sail off in one huge spinning garland of rustling, flying white. I was much looking forward to this lark.

Idly chatting in Sacher's one evening, and thinking nothing of it, I informed the Colonel of my New Year's Eve plans, adding that Bobby's nanny was kindly sewing me a white dress for the occasion. To my surprise, he was most indignant.

'Certainly not,' he said firmly. 'There is no question of your going to the New Year's Eve Ball with an Austrian. You will join my party in the ISB box. It has all been arranged, and nothing can be changed now.' And the subject was closed.

Bobby, who was furious when I told him, lectured me at great length on the frivolity of my ways and my disgraceful behaviour. Going out with a different man every night could not possibly do my reputation any good. Laughing in his face, I informed him that I didn't give a damn for my 'reputation', that I would go out with whoever I pleased at all times, and that no man would ever boss me around or curtail my freedom. Independence and freedom of action, I informed him haughtily, were what mattered to me most in the world.

Brave words. A year later, matrimony having caught up with me, I willingly surrendered my precious, much-vaunted freedom, and for the first time in my life I began to consider my appearance and to deplore the shortcomings of nature. Scrutinising the features of the girls around me, I began to register envy, a new and uncomfortable kind of feeling I didn't like at all. How was it, I wondered despondently, that I seemed to be the only Plain Jane among them? As the Americans would say, so dumb was I that the possibility of makeup having anything to do with their dazzling looks never even crossed my mind. Still less did it occur to me to experiment with it myself. Since I assumed that nothing could be done to improve the situation, I deliberately and resolutely decided to forget all about it, and set out to make the most of my new existence. Beauty or no beauty, married life, if I had any say in the matter, was going to be fun.

ANTONIA WHITE
A LIFE

Jane Dunn

'One of our best biographers' – *Sunday Times*

'Oh I *did* want to be happy as a woman . . . But I'm a monster and must accept being one. Not all writers are monsters. But my kind is.' .

Antonia White is best known for her masterpiece *Frost In May*, for having come back from 'Bedlam' hospital and madness, and for the public feud between her daughters over the editing of her diaries. This is the first biography to tell the complete story of a life courageously lived against most difficult odds. This is the story of a woman who – two generations too soon – attempted to live the modern female life of single parent and working mother but longed for the artistic and intellectual stage. Antonia White wrestled throughout with the large questions of faith, the attractions and repulsions of Catholicism, the problems of being a woman and an artist. And over it all hovered the threat of madness. This book reveals her as a woman unafraid of extreme experience and honest enough to accept the consequences: self-obsessed, funny, fascinating and tragic – and ultimately heroic.

A WOMAN OF INDEPENDENT MEANS

Elizabeth Forsythe Hailey

'Bess is so remarkable a character that I seem here
to be reviewing not *A Woman of Independent Means*
but the woman herself' – *New York Times*

At the turn of the century, a time when women had few choices,
Bess Steed Garner inherits a legacy – not only of wealth but of
determination and desire, making her truly a woman of
independent means. From the early 1900s through the 1960s,
we accompany Bess as she endures life's trials and triumphs with
unfailing courage and indomitable spirit: the sacrifices love
sometimes requires of the heart, the flaws and rewards of marriage,
the often-tested bond between mother and child, and the will to
defy a society that demands conformity.
Told in letters we follow the remarkable life of Bess Steed Garner
from her childhood in 1899 to her death in 1977.

CHRISTINA ROSSETTI

A Biography

Frances Thomas

'Sensitive and sympathetic . . . Here is a valuable contribution to Rossetti studies' – *Claire Tomalin*

'An exemplary biography' – *Isabel Colegate*

Why is Christina Rossetti so invisible today? This is the central question addressed in this authoritative biography. Rossetti, author of the widely known *Goblin Market, My Heart is Like a Singing Bird* and *In the Deep Midwinter*; has long been overshadowed by her more colourful brother, Dante Gabriel. Now this perceptive study, drawing on many previously untapped sources, pieces together a more complete picture of this passionate, contradictory and enigmatic woman.

REMEMBER, REMEMBER!

Selected Stories of Winifred Holtby

Edited by Marion Shaw and Paul Berry

This selection of Winifred Holtby's short stories is drawn from her two published volumes, *Truth is Not Sober* and *Pavements of Anderby*, which were published posthumously by her two friends, Vera Brittain and Hilda Reid and have been collected here in one volume for the first time.

Brightly written, in an unselfconscious, matter-of-fact style, these stories are irreverent and entertaining, fulfilling what she saw as the short story's purpose in a reader's life:

'nice for chance guests – easy to pick up and more tantalising for one's bedside than a novel'.

Many of these stories are autobiographically based, and feature the Yorkshire farming community in Rudston where she was brought up. This was the setting for her most famous novel, *South Riding*, also published posthumously. Some of the stories relate to the last years of her life when she was contending with the incessant headaches and nausea of Bright's disease.

Now you can order superb titles directly from Virago

☐ Antonia White	Jane Dunn	£9.99
☐ A Woman of Independent Means	Elizabeth Forsythe Hailey	£6.99
☐ Christina Rossetti	Frances Thomas	£8.99
☐ Selected Stories of Winifred Holtby	Ed. Marion Shaw and Paul Berry	£6.99

Please allow for postage and packing: Free UK delivery.
Europe: add 25% of retail price; Rest of World: 45% of retail price.

To order any of the above or any other Virago titles, please call our credit card orderline or fill in this coupon and send/fax it to:

Virago, 250 Western Avenue, London, W3 6XZ, UK.
Fax 020 8324 5678   Telephone 020 8324 5516

☐ I enclose a UK bank cheque made payable to Virago for £
☐ Please charge £ . . . . to my Access, Visa, Delta, Switch Card No.

Expiry Date ☐☐☐☐   Switch Issue No.

NAME (Block letters please) . . . .

ADDRESS . . . .

Postcode . . . . Telephone . . . .

Signature . . . .

Please allow 28 days for delivery within the UK. Offer subject to price and availability.

Please do not send any further mailings from companies carefully selected by Virago ☐